Rough Justice

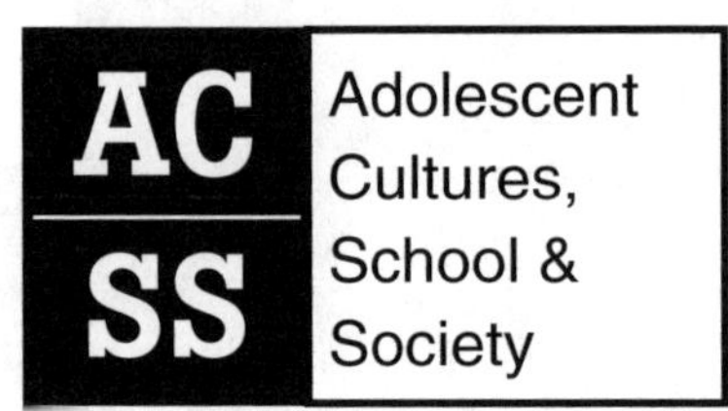

Joseph L. DeVitis & Linda Irwin-DeVitis

GENERAL EDITORS

Vol. 32

PETER LANG
New York • Washington, D.C./Baltimore • Bern
Frankfurt am Main • Berlin • Brussels • Vienna • Oxford

Trevor Gale

Rough Justice

Young People in the Shadows

PETER LANG
New York • Washington, D.C./Baltimore • Bern
Frankfurt am Main • Berlin • Brussels • Vienna • Oxford

Library of Congress Cataloging-in-Publication Data

Gale, Trevor.
Rough justice: young people in the shadows / Trevor Gale.
p. cm. — (Adolescent cultures, school, and society; v. 32)
Includes bibliographical references.
1. Poverty—Australia. 2. Marginality, Social—Australia. 3. Poor—Australia.
4. Poor youth—Australia. 5. Youth with social disabilities—Australia.
6. Social work with youth—Australia. I. Title.
II. Series: Adolescent cultures, school & society; v. 32.
HV473.G34   362.5'0994—dc22   2004020878
ISBN 0-8204-6802-9
ISSN 1091-1464

Bibliographic information published by **Die Deutsche Bibliothek**.
Die Deutsche Bibliothek lists this publication in the "Deutsche
Nationalbibliografie"; detailed bibliographic data is available
on the Internet at http://dnb.ddb.de/.

Cover design by Lisa Barfield

The paper in this book meets the guidelines for permanence and durability
of the Committee on Production Guidelines for Book Longevity
of the Council of Library Resources.

© 2005 Peter Lang Publishing, Inc., New York
275 Seventh Avenue, 28th Floor, New York, NY 10001
www.peterlangusa.com

Printed in the United States of America

To my mom,
who experienced her fair share
of rough justice growing up

TABLE OF CONTENTS

ACKNOWLEDGMENTS

For one reason and another, this book was a long time in the making. I am grateful to the publishers who remained patient with me, particularly in the final stages. I am also grateful to the "characters" represented in this book who granted me access to their thoughts and lives. Many are courageous people with remarkable stories to tell yet they rarely appear in honor rolls or in the society pages of newspapers. The outcome of my engagement with these extraordinary individuals is not just the content that follows but also a better understanding of myself, for which I thank them. My presence is very evident in this book, deliberately so. I am hopeful that my attempts at self-examination will encourage readers, particularly professionals who work with young people in the shadows, to do likewise. Less explicit in the text, though, is Pam's involvement in its construction. Pam handled most of the transcription, referencing, copyediting and typesetting; feats that appear minor when listed but which occupied hours of exacting work. She also endured numerous discussions in which I explored the events and issues of the project, trying to make sense of them and how I might convey that sense to others. I think it is probably fair to say that without Pam, this project may never have started and may never have been completed. My thanks also to those who read and commented on early drafts of the manuscript. This includes some of those who appear within but also family, friends, and colleagues; in particular, Bernie, Kathleen, and Liz. Kathleen, whom I admire greatly for her scholarship and activism and who has become a close friend, also provided the book's conclusion. Finally, partial funding for the project was provided by the Faculty of Education, Monash University, Australia.

Without impunity

The way things are

Some people in western societies live their lives with impunity. Like all of us, they make mistakes—sometimes intentionally, sometimes not—yet, unlike most, they are not faced with the same consequences for their actions or at least not the full weight of these. Others live without impunity. Almost all of their indiscretions—and sometimes the failings of others as well—are credited to them in full. So, when a company finds itself in financial difficulties due to its mismanagement, a common solution is to "downsize" (code for sacking workers, typically semiskilled and unskilled laborers first) and, if the media and/or shareholder fallout is severe enough, a further option is to pay out the contract of the company's CEO (Chief Executive Officer). When this happened a few years ago at one of Australia's largest insurance and investment companies, the departing CEO's "golden handshake" (A\$13.2 million) was greater than the total severance pay received by the company's 3500 workers who were also asked to leave.

In western societies today, such disparities in remuneration (and penalties) are not unusual. For example, the annual income of Bill Gates in 2003 equaled the combined incomes of the lowest 40 percent of the entire population of the United States. More generally:

> Executive Remuneration levels in Australia grew over the decade 1992–2002 from 22 times average weekly earnings to 74 times average weekly earnings…[while] The finance sector emerges as a case study in corporate excess, with CEOs of the four major banks averaging 188 times the pay of their customer service staff…[Yet] The often-stated link between high executive pay and company performance does not exist. Indeed, the evidence is that as an executive's pay increases, the performance of the company deteriorates. (Shields et al, 2003, iii)

Some argue that this increasing "income gap ratio" doesn't matter. They point to rising wage levels for even the lowest paid workers. So, while the top 20 percent of Australian incomes rose by an average A\$220 per week from 1999 to 2003, the bottom 20 percent of Australian incomes also rose over this period by an average A$20 per week (Community Affairs References Committee 2004). Rises in income for all workers has been typical of Organization for Economic Cooperation and Development (OECD) nations over the last decade. However, as the above figures suggest, average incomes have been inflated by greater than average income rises at the upper end of income brackets. Moreover, income rises for the lowest paid workers do not necessarily account for rising living costs, particularly for those whose incomes fall below 50 percent of the median disposable income[1] relative to their domicile country. Using this measure, Forster and Pearson found that "on average across 21 OECD countries, the incomes of the poor are some 28 percent below the poverty threshold of 50 percent of the median" (2002, 10). In the United Kingdom, the figures were slightly better; in the United States they were slightly worse. In 1998, for example, the United States had the highest income gap between rich and poor since its Census Bureau began publishing annual figures in 1947 (see the Conclusion to this book).

It is important to note, though, that these figures relate to the employed not the unemployed. They are concerned with "income poverty"; that is, the working poor. Clearly, for many, employment is not what it used to be. Over the past decade, unemployment rates in most western nations have fallen from their highs of the mid-1990s and, in some cases, to their lowest levels for several decades.

Some point to this creation of jobs as evidence of the success of an invigorated capitalism, given greater freedoms by governments withdrawing from their manipulation of or "interference" in markets.[2] Colloquially, such benefits are indicative of a "trickle-down" effect: the conditions that enable corporations and industries to thrive are said to have a flow on benefit for populations more generally. That is, inequitable financial arrangements for some individuals and organizations are justifiable because the beneficiaries are the same people creating employment opportunities for others. More crudely, to quote Gordon Gecko in the film *Wall Street*, the message is "greed is good."

However, others note that the "trickle" all but dries up by the time it reaches the bottom. A "jobless recovery" from recession, for example, is now a reality for western economies such as the United States, with companies cutting jobs in an effort to increase shareholder profits, replacing workers with new technologies or increasingly outsourcing or "offshoring" their work to a cheaper labor force located in developing countries. Even those who remain in work are increasingly likely to be employed in "low paid, part-time and casual jobs in the service sector, which are largely non-unionized" (Bell 1997, 111). Accounting for unemployment has changed so dramatically that the Australian government now defines employment as anything above two hours of work in any given week. Unemployment rates are not sufficiently revealing of this redefinition of work, deliberately so it would sometimes seem. Falls in the proportion of people in full-time work are so hidden that in Australia and Canada full-time work now represents less than 50 percent of all paid work (Lacharite 2002).

Evidence of rising income gap ratios, of stable if not increasing income poverty, and the rise of casual and part-time employment suggest that, despite the incredible growth in western economies over the latter part of the twentieth century and the early part of the twenty-first century, the benefits of this growth have flowed largely to a privileged few. As noted above, such rewards appear unwarranted given the performances of many of society's elite. Much of this privileging goes unexamined. Instead, it is the poor who are required to prove themselves as deserving in order to receive assistance. Welfare fraud, for example, is estimated to cost the Australian government approximately A$15 million per year; a figure that has been used to justify a vigorous campaign against welfare cheats. Yet, at the same time, the government tolerates tax avoidance of approximately A$700 million per year attributable to family trusts (Peel 2003).

It is an approach to poverty and wealth, sanction and reward, writ large on the world stage. For example, annual global expenditure on developmental aid is currently running at US$50 billion, while US$300 billion is spent on agricultural subsidies and US$1000 billion for military purposes (DAC 2004).

Clearly, poverty is not restricted to wealthy western nations. Many poor countries pay more in interest on past loans than on their education and health programs (DAC 2004). One consequence of this is that almost 3 billion people (half of the world's population) survive on less than US$2 per day; half of these (1.5 billion people) survive on less than US$1 per day. Three billion people also have no access to sanitation while 130 million children do not attend school at all (DAC 2004). For example, in Sierra Leone—one of the poorest nations located on the poorest continent on earth—the average newborn baby currently has:

1. an 18 percent chance of not surviving birth (his/her mother has a 2 percent chance of not surviving the event either),
2. no access to sanitation facilities,
3. a 50 percent chance of not receiving adequate nutrition,
4. a life expectancy of 37 years, and
5. a 60 percent chance of being illiterate (World Bank 2004).

In short, statistics from the United Nations Development Programme suggest that there is increasing poverty, misery and destitution in the world but also "deepening wealth and income gaps [and] permanent eviction from work and social and economic redundancy…[in] ever wider chunks of the population" (Bauman 2001, 114–15). This is hardly surprising when around 17 percent of the world's population (almost exclusively from within western nations) controls 80 percent of the global economy (DAC 2004). In the United States, the wealthiest of western nations, the imbalance is even greater: one percent of US households control more wealth than the bottom 95 percent of the US population (see Conclusion). Bauman (2001, 114–22) describes this as the human effects of globalization, between and within countries. In describing these effects he distinguishes between "world poor" and "country poor," between absolute poverty in the third world and relative poverty in the western world. His point is that the effects of globalization are more severe on people in third world nations, not that real poverty does not exist in the western world. In these terms, most citizens of Sierre Leone are world poor, whereas the poor in the United States are better described as country poor; better off than those in Sierre Leone but poor nonetheless.

Bauman also critiques the views of justice that inform discussions of poverty, which he describes in terms of three value-sets: (1) an economic value-set (involving the distribution of wealth and income and access to paid employment), (2) a pity, compassion and solicitude value-set, which dominates most approaches to poverty, and (3) a social order orientation. He regards these views not as flawed in themselves but nevertheless ignorant of two critical factors: (1) the role of the new poor (as the engine room) in the reproduction and reinforcement of the new global order, and (2) the fear of poverty on which the new global order depends for its self-perpetuation. Bauman argues that this fear of the "poor as other" maintains the insecurity and uncertainty that keeps the globalized order in its place. It is this uncertainty and risk at local levels that has the effect of producing privatized and insecure individuals who mostly cannot act in a concerted way.

The homeless—particularly the "country poor" within western nations—are of this order, representative of the threat to new global arrangements and to what they promise for western societies and economies. Yet, this homelessness is on the rise and becoming increasingly visible, despite our best efforts to "sweep them under the carpet," banishing them from cities (such as Atlanta and Athens) hosting the Olympic Games, for example. And homelessness is not confined to traditional stereotypes. As MacKenzie and Chamberlain explain:

> Primary homelessness includes all people without conventional shelter, such as people living on the streets, sleeping in parks or squatting in derelict buildings. Secondary homelessness includes people who are staying in any form of temporary accommodation (friends, relatives, youth refuges, etc.) with no other secure housing options elsewhere. If young people remain homeless for any significant period of time, they usually move frequently from one form of temporary accommodation to another, some spending occasional nights on the streets. Tertiary homelessness refers to the occupants of single rooms in private boarding houses who live there on a long-term basis (three months or more). (2002, 25)

In 2001, around 100,000 or 0.6 percent of Australian people were estimated in the national census to be homeless, although by its nature it is difficult to determine this with any great certainty, particularly primary homelessness but also secondary and tertiary forms. More rigorous analyses of census data confirm that the homeless population in Australia "has increased over the past 40 years" (Chamberlain and MacKenzie 2003, 8). Also increasing is the number of homeless young people aged 12 to 24 years, currently 36 percent of all homeless people (Community Affairs References Committee 2004, 125). Australia is not an isolated case among western nations. In the United States (see the Conclusion) and Canada (Lacharite 2002), for example, homelessness is also witnessing growth at unprecedented levels. Many welfare organizations also believe the official figures grossly underestimate the real levels of homelessness. They point to demands on their services by the homeless growing exponentially and beyond what they can manage given their current resources (Community Affairs References Committee 2004). For example, in the 2002–2003 financial year, 67,000 requests from Australian children, families, young people, and others for Supported Accommodation Assistance Program (SAAP) services could not be met (Australian Institute of Health and Welfare 2003).

In the face of diminishing resources, some welfare organizations have begun to resort to neoliberal approaches to welfare, as a way of not just meeting demand but curbing it. For example, in 2004, St. Vincent de Paul introduced a "user-pays" system in its food distribution center in Melbourne, Australia, charging A$1 for a sandwich and A$2 for a more substantive meal but only to those who first registered their financial details. This had the effect of reducing demand by 80 percent.

Despite these resource shortages, in December 2004 the Australian Federal Government announced a reduction in funding for the homeless; the same year the country enjoyed one of the highest economic growth rates among western nations and five of its major cities were ranked by the London based Economist Intelligence Unit among the six most livable cities (from a field of 130) in the world (*What's this? Melbourne's best 2004*). The reduced-funding announcement slipped out quietly without detection, partly because of its intentional proximity to Christmas, but also because it was overtaken by subsequent events and a pledge of A$1 billion over five years to Indonesia to aid in addressing the aftermath of the Asian tsunami; an amount lauded by aid agencies not just for its size,[3] but also because it was aid money not already committed elsewhere!

Still, tucked away in an editorial, one of the nation's newspapers revealed that:

The world's most liveable city [Melbourne] has a shadow[y] side. Just ask one of the homeless teenagers who live there. A week before Christmas, the Federal Government announced it planned to cut $30 million in funding for Victorian [state] services to the homeless over five years. Although Treasury expects the budget to be in surplus by a healthy $6.2 billion this financial year—$900 million more than the amount forecast in September—the poorest and most vulnerable among us will have to get by with a little less....For the most part, these children escape public attention. The death of 13-year-old Emma Oates in October was a reminder of the shadow[y] world inhabited by homeless youth. Emma had run away from a residential care unit and had gone to the abandoned Lonsdale Street power station—which has long been a haunt for street kids—before slipping and falling seven metres [to her death]....the [Australian] Council to Homeless Persons gives [a second] example of two sisters aged 12 and 15. The younger sister was taken into care but the older one ended up 'couch [sofa] surfing' (moving between friends' lounge rooms). A 15-year-old is too young to be accepted in the private rental market, while public housing is rarely an option because of its scarcity and the length of waiting lists. Even special accommodation for the homeless may be inaccessible to young teenagers. Some residences do not accept children under 16, and the mix of residents—including drug users and the mentally ill—can be unsuitable for them. But the alternative of living on the streets is worse….the young homeless not only need access to accommodation but to long-term support as they need it. Unfortunately youth homelessness is not a new problem but the Federal Government's decision to make a budget cut to homeless services during boom times is an unexpected—and deplorable—development. (*Down and out on the streets of Melbourne* 2004)

For some time now, many have been concerned about the widening gap between rich and poor in first world countries,[4] particularly since the fall of the Berlin Wall (1989). Among other things, this event symbolized the demise of communism as a legitimate and productive way of organizing national and global economies and positioned capitalism as not just the only viable alternative but also as the savior of previous communist regimes.[5] It is not, of course. Irrespective of the virtues and vices of communism, capitalism is far from savior. There are other ways of organizing economies, even other ways of organizing capitalist markets, which are not primarily concerned with self-interest and individualism. For example, Shosaku Yasui, chairman of the multinational company Teijin, explains the more compressed wage differential in Japan and in other Asian countries (compared with Australia, the United Kingdom, and the United States) in the following manner:

In the West, civilisation is built around a hunting mentality. Japanese society, however, is based on agriculture. Westerners would make a kill and horde [sic] the bounty for themselves, but in Japan harvests were shared equally among all the members of the community. This mentality persists. (*Income Gap a Reflection of Culture* 2004, 29)

Despite this differentiation within capitalism, the capitalist–communist binary and its good–bad connotations remain strong in the psyche of world politics. Western governments have shown incredible belief in the ability of neoclassical economics to deliver prosperity to their countries. However, prosperity for some has come at the expense of others. As previously argued, while a few increase their wealth to extraordinary levels, many others fall far behind. Irrespective of whether they are in employment, increasing numbers of people in western nations are living in poverty.[6] Further, the poor are increasingly seen as personally responsible for their condition (Peel 2003), paralleling how they are viewed in many third world nations. Also on the rise, particularly among our youth, are incidences of drug use, solvent abuse, property crime, suicide, and the disproportionate incarceration of people of color, especially males; a list with strong associations with poverty.

There are other social indicators to which we could also refer and which are equally worrying. Many of these seem attributable to the actions of western governments that are bent on retreating from the regulation of their economies, ceding to the "invisible" hand of the market, and their reluctance to do much about redressing the flow of capital from poor to rich and its associated problems. Indeed, several governments see it as their primary task to make it as attractive as possible for multinational companies to grace their shores with their presence, thereby generating employment for their citizens; a practice justified in terms of marketized (and ill-informed) versions of social justice.[7] In short, governments are retreating, with increasing vigor, from the welfare state secured at the end of the Second World War, reworking welfare within the confines of a "vibrant" economy. On the whole it is not working, at least not for many.

Increasingly, but not exclusively, it is nongovernment, nonprofit welfare organizations that are at the forefront of research that illustrates this. Indeed, research has become an important part of the work they now do. Such agencies have also become de facto arms of government, left to "pick up the pieces" following the withdrawal of government from all but the regulation of the social welfare scene. The problem for these agencies is that there are increasingly more "pieces" and fewer resources available to support their work. Self-interest promoted by capitalist markets has permeated social life to such an extent that philanthropy is difficult to attract, at least in Australia and particularly from corporations.[8] While corporate giving is rising by 10 percent each year and individual giving is rising by 16 percent (Philanthropy Australia), by comparison with the United States, Australian philanthropy is coming off a very low base.

For example, in 1997, 8.6 million Australians donated A$2.8 billion to nonprofit organizations, while in the 2000–2001 financial year, Australia's business sector provided A$1.4 billion to nonprofit organizations as gifts and sponsorship. Listed companies, in particular, can appear unable or unwilling to justify to shareholders why profits should be distributed in these ways. What is donated, then, is more targeted, in line with shareholder interests. Hence, insurance companies commit funds for research on cancer, for example, justified on the basis that it will potentially reduce claims, or they get involved "in helping to reduce crime and accidents with the corporate imperative of helping to reduce insurance costs" (Clark 2004, 18). Indeed, many are willing to admit publicly that "good works may conveniently be good for the bottom line…[but are less willing to openly concede that]…good deedsmanship may also distract public attention away from ballooning CEO salary packages" (Clark 2004, 18).

Despite the lack of funding, the numbers of new nongovernment welfare organizations are on the rise. They tend to be small concerns with low overheads, relying on the goodwill of their voluntary workers. Many are run by churches and parachurch groups; others are secular. What they lack in expertise is compensated to some degree by their commitment and genuine concern for those suffering the effects of others' economic prosperity.

The trouble with the way things are

The above is perhaps a long-winded way of saying that people are not simply rewarded and punished on the basis of their actions. The adage that "people are paid what they are worth" is clearly false. Instead, some are rewarded and punished more than others on the basis of quite similar actions, although not arbitrarily. Reward and punishment can even be assigned despite one's actions. A few, for example, live their lives with impunity. Frequently, they are unfairly rewarded and rarely held to account for their transgressions. As unjust as this may seem, it is not my intention to focus on these few beyond their backgrounding above and their cameo appearances throughout the rest of this book. Some say that the poor will always be with us. Those who live with impunity lay claim to a similar longevity.

Instead, in the following pages I seek to foreground the experiences of those who live their lives without impunity, particularly youth living on the edge of society. These are the young people who are afforded little grace, if any, for their mistakes. Indeed, it sometimes appears as if we—those of us who live somewhere between the extremes of impunity and censure—are waiting for and willing these mistakes to be committed, to justify our assessment of them and of ourselves. To make matters worse, we attribute to them mistakes that are not of their own making. We even invent mistakes for them out of our own explanations of how life should be lived and understood. We construct systems through which smooth passage relies on understandings and circumstances similar to our own, which are then championed and glorified in the process while the understandings and circumstances of others are interpreted as deficient or deviant. Difference is tolerated within narrow bands but even then restricted by social, political, and economic hierarchies. Hence, poverty is not simply about being without money. Increasingly, poverty is seen as a measure of an individual's failure rather than of a failing system.[9]

For me, the central problem with this assessment of the poor and their condition is that it lacks sociological imagination; it attempts to conceive of public issues of poverty as private troubles or, at best, fails to make connections between these. To clarify:

> *Troubles* occur within the character of the individual and within the range of his [sic] immediate relations with others…*Issues* have to do with matters that transcend these local environments of the individual and the range of his inner life…An issue, in fact, often involves a crisis in institutional arrangements, and often too, it involves what Marxists call 'contradictions' or 'antagonisms.' (Mills 1959, 8–9, emphasis in original)

By arguing for a relationship between troubles and issues I do not mean to simply attribute, in a structural way, the private troubles of the young people within this book to their social and cultural circumstances, nor to imply that certain structures will necessarily deliver particular personal troubles. Rather, the structure-agency dialectic—which Anthony Giddens (1984) has referred to as "structuration" and Pierre Bourdieu (Bourdieu and Wacquant 1992) calls "constructivist structuralism" or "structural constructivism"—is at the heart of thinking sociologically. That is, *at the one moment*, one's private troubles can be attributed to both the constructions of individuals *and* to broader social, political, and economic arrangements. Nelson Mandela's speech in London's Trafalgar Square, to launch the "Make Poverty History" campaign, is a good example of this sociological imagination at work, producing quite a different explanation of poverty and inequality. As he argues:

> Massive poverty and obscene inequality are such terrible scourges of our times—times in which the world boasts breathtaking advances in science, technology, industry and wealth accumulation—that they have to rank alongside slavery and apartheid as social evils.…Like slavery and apartheid, poverty is not natural. It is man-made and it can be overcome and eradicated by the actions of human beings. And overcoming poverty is not a gesture of charity. *It is an act of justice.* (2005, emphasis added)

The difficulty in thinking this way about the social world was brought home to me by a group of college students who contributed the following comment to the electronic discussion list in one of my courses. The course was concerned with how society and professionals deal with difference. This particular group of students asserted:

> We believe that every student has the opportunity to excel academically. We stress the word *choice* as today there are academic scholarships, tuition support as well as various other forms of support, which can be easily accessed by students from lower socioeconomic backgrounds who are serious about furthering their education and in some circumstances attending university and breaking the unemployment, poverty, illiteracy and social disharmony cycle. If these students are serious about their learning, they can receive the support to further their education and obtain a creditable job within society.

Reading their comments, it struck me how little they seemed to appreciate the private troubles of poverty and how unprepared they were to connect these understandings with the public issues of the day. "Choice," for example, is not the great equalizer that my students and dominant political rhetoric imagine. Our choices are always constrained (see Gale and Densmore 2003, 13–4) and in ways that tend to favor the wealthy over the poor. For example, wealthy parents are more able to purchase houses in the catchment areas of good government schools. But even if poor students live in these areas, or the geography of one's domicile is not a determiner of entry, the capacity of good schools is also a constraint on choice. That is, "choice by one has effects on others—one child going to a particular school reduces the chance of others going" (Burgess 2005, 9). More broadly, a recent study, *Sorting and Choice in English Secondary Schools,* reveals that "a greater degree of choice is associated with greater sorting by both ability and disadvantage" (Burgess 2005, 10). In short, increased choice of schools works against poor students to locate them in the worst schools, irrespective of where they live, and thereby segregates school communities (see also Gewirtz et al. 1995 and Whitty et al. 1998).

It would seem that some professionals and would-be professionals do not know or do not want to know anything about the experiences of being poor. Others who face up to these realities, even in limited ways, are happy to attribute issues of poverty to individual choices. Yet, when professionals first come face-to-face with the lived experience of their clients' poverty, it has the potential to challenge their values and beliefs in quite significant ways, as the following extended extract illustrates:

I was teaching in an English grammar school where homework was considered to be so important that failing to do it was punished by lunch-hour detention. In one class (13 to 14 year olds) there was one girl called Mandy whose class-work was good, but whose homework was usually poorly done, and sometimes not done at all. I always seemed to be sending her to detention. One evening after school I was sitting in the staff room with some colleagues when the school secretary put her head round the door, and seeing me, asked if, when I went home, I could give a lift to the girl who had missed her bus. In the hallway I met Mandy.

Missed your bus?

Yeah.

That's just typical, isn't it? You not only can't do your homework, but you can't even get sufficiently organized to catch your bus. OK then, what happened?

Went shopping.

You went downtown? You know that it's not only against the rules to go shopping after school, but you should also know that you've not time to get there and back and catch the bus. What'd you go there for anyway?

Had to get some meat.

Why did you have to get the meat? Doesn't your mother do the shopping?

No, Mum's gone away.

Sorry to hear that. But if you knew you had to get the meat, why didn't you get a chit [note] from your tutor and go in the lunch hour?

'Cos you sent me to homework detention.

And as we drove home the story emerged. Mandy's parents had split up when Dad met Joy. Mum had moved to another town with Bill, but the children (Mandy 13, and the twins, 9), had stayed with their father and Joy so that they could all continue in the same school. They spent most weekends and the holidays with Mum and Bill. Mandy liked that, they had a pony there. But Dad was a commercial traveller who was often away for up to three nights a week. Joy had left Dad, and Mandy's Gran, who had lived in the same village, had died a few weeks ago. Not only was Mandy having to cope with the considerable pressure of grammar school work and competition, not only had her family broken up and her grandmother died just as she was entering adolescence, but at 13 she was looking after her younger twin brothers alone for several nights a week. And I had put her in detention for not completing her homework.

The following day in class, Mandy had not done her homework again. I said nothing, but was about to send another student to detention for the same thing when he asked why I was sending him but not Mandy, who's offended two days in a row. I said I'd found out that she had enough problems on her hands, and so I wasn't going to make her do homework for the rest of the term. I asked the class if they thought I was being unfair by making an exception, and discovered not only that they agreed

with my action, but that they already knew of her situation, and they had been helping her by doing her homework for her in other subjects. Unfortunately, the kind of
work I was setting in English meant that she alone could do it, which was why she
had been caught. (Tripp 1993, 103–4)

Not all professionals are moved to reflect on their values and beliefs and change their practices. For example, I recall a similar story, relayed to me in the context of a recent research project, of a young girl who lived in quite desperate conditions: in cramped and dirty housing with alcoholic parents, frequent parties, and younger siblings for whom she also cared. Arriving for class one morning, she was refused entry by her teacher until her homework was completed and her clothing washed and ironed. With no way of immediately remedying the situation, the girl was directed to the principal for disciplining.

Such stories are not restricted to educational contexts. A similar report I encountered in another research project was of a young man, accompanied by his two young children, who approached Centrelink (the Australian government department with responsibility for issuing welfare benefits) about the termination of his payments. At the time, his wife was in hospital recovering from brain surgery. In the course of the conversation in which he explained his financial and emotional difficulties in providing for his family, he said to the person behind the counter, "Can I leave my kids here with you while I visit my wife in hospital? Maybe you can give them something to eat while I'm gone." To which the official replied, "If you do that I'll call the child protection agency to collect them. Then you won't have any problems finding money to feed them."

We could be tempted to regard these stories as simply anecdotal and not indicative of a more general approach by the professions in dealing with people's troubles. However,

The [Victoria, Australia] State Government's Youth Homeless Action Plan, released
in May [2004], found young people could explain their situation to at least 10 different workers or services before they received help. (*Down and out on the streets of
Melbourne* 2004)

Submissions to a recent Australian Senate inquiry into poverty also revealed surprisingly similar accounts. For example,

Grantleigh, 42, had problems dealing with Centrelink forms due to illiteracy. He was too ashamed to tell anyone that he could not read. Normally his wife helped him by reading out the forms but she went to hospital for four weeks for a major operation. In that time he received a letter from Centrelink. He was subsequently breached [financially penalized] for failing to attend an interview [when directed]. He did not realize he had been breached until his payments were reduced. He rang Centrelink to ask why his payments had been reduced and they informed him of the breach. First he claimed that he had not received the letter but he eventually plucked up the courage to tell them that he was illiterate. The breach was nevertheless maintained. (Community Affairs References Committee 2004, 412)

It is easy to demonize the professionals and bureaucrats in these stories and to wonder what happens to people when they occupy positions of authority. However, such individuals are themselves frequently under pressure, working within financial and procedural constraints informed by an anti-welfare mindset that is important, as Bauman (2001) argues, for the maintenance of a new global order. A recent Centrelink internal memo, leaked to the Australian press, illustrates well this pressure placed on the welfare sector to privilege all things economic. Extracts from the memo advised staff that:

It's now time to move to the next phase, from advising customers about volunteer work and support programs to economic participation for all, with few exceptions....The focus now needs to be not why someone should go to a JNM [Job Network Member; that is, a privatised employment agency] and pursue employment, but why not. Don't come up with reasons why someone can't go, and avoid letting customers come up with reasons why they can't go....For parenting customers with children under 13 years, and disability support customers, there's no requirement that they go, so if asked, you'll need to answer the question correctly, but avoid having it as part of your spiel....Remember every working age customer at every opportunity. The Secretary wants a significant increase in JNM referrals by the 24th of September. (Kirk 2004)

Because the self-interest of capitalist markets now so fully permeates social and economic life (see the Conclusion for a discussion of this), it is also difficult for professionals (who often stand to benefit from this way of thinking) to recognize the troubles of young people living on the streets as public issues. As Mills explains:

To formulate issues and troubles, we must ask what values are cherished yet threatened, and what values are cherished and supported, by the characterizing trends of our period. In the case both of threat and of support we must ask what salient contradictions of structure may be involved. When people cherish some set of values and do not feel any threat to them, they experience *well-being*. When they cherish values but *do* feel them to be threatened, they experience a *crisis*—either as a personal trouble or as a public issue. And if all their values seem involved, they feel the total threat of panic. But suppose people are neither aware of any cherished values nor experience any threat? That is the experience of *indifference*, which, if it seems to involve all their values, becomes *apathy*. Suppose, finally, they are unaware of any cherished values, but still are very much aware of a threat? That is the experience of *uneasiness*, of anxiety, which, if it is total enough, becomes a deadly unspecified malaise. Ours is a time of uneasiness and indifference—not yet formulated in such ways as to permit the work of reason and the play of sensibility. Instead of troubles—defined in terms of values and threats—there is often the misery of vague uneasiness; instead of explicit issues there is often merely the beat feeling that all is somehow not right. Neither the values threatened nor whatever threatens them has been stated; in short, they have not been carried to the point of decision. Much less have they been formulated as problems of social science. (1959, 11, emphasis original)

Half a century later, Mills's assessment of our indifference and uneasiness seems even more apt. Many within the middle classes appear indifferent to the private troubles of young people who "sleep rough" and are uneasy when confronted with the growing public issues of youth homelessness, because of the challenges these present to their own value systems. In writing this book, then, I am concerned: (1) to write in such a way that encourages readers to identify their cherished values, to bring these to the surface so they can be considered and examined; and (2) to challenge those values, in part by presenting alternatives but also by representing these as plausible, believable, and ownable by readers.

I am hopeful that readers might at least recognize that if found in the same position, they might well think and act similarly. This is not an attempt to justify the misdemeanors of young people located on the edge of society and it is not intended as a romantic account of poverty. As noted above, that the private troubles of the poor can sometimes be attributed to their mistakes and indiscretions is not in question, although the universality of this truth across groups and classes also needs to be recognized. That is, the poor are not alone in making mistakes. Instead, I invite readers to move beyond this, to connect many of these troubles with public issues, in particular, with the ways in which we now govern our economies and political and social systems.

An invitation to the reader

As a way of drawing attention to such troubling matters, I have written the main body of the book as a narrative and in the first person, bracketed by this Introduction and the Conclusion, which are more argumentative in style. I have chosen to write in this way to engage readers' emotions not just their intellect. However, adopting a narrative style should not be read as meaning the work is any less rigorous than traditional academic texts. The issues remain, perhaps more strongly conveyed in places because of the social and material realities for individuals. There is also more involvement required of and encouragement given to readers to employ a sociological imagination, which is no bad thing. I am hopeful, too, that the narrative will invite a broader readership, but particularly those engaged in the "helping" professions of education, law, social work, nursing, psychology, and medicine. Separating the Introduction and the Conclusion from the body of the book is a deliberate ploy in this regard. I fully expect that some will begin "on the street," moving later to the professional conversations and personal accounts in search of explanation.

In this search, I invite readers to take seriously the lived experiences of the characters portrayed. They are all real people and events although names have been changed and place names altered or eliminated to protect identities. It is enough to reveal that at the time when the research was undertaken they could be found in medium to large western cities. I am indebted to them for sharing their lives and entrusting their stories to me. Their responses to seeing their accounts in print were also encouraging. Typical among these were: "I think it's funny in places but also moving"; "It makes you ask questions"; "It's unsettling, disturbing"; "It made me think and feel, which is an interesting combination." In particular, Joan (see Chapter 18) felt compelled to put pen to paper:

> I found it riveting and compelling, yet emotionally disturbing. The background picture of a van on the edge of a dark silent park is brilliantly tangible. I have a strong feeling that I am a silent onlooker seeing the homeless emerging from the dark shadows into a pool of light around the van. Yet my feelings are confused. I feel: (1) guilt, that I have done nothing to help; (2) helpless, that I can't do something to change the situation; (3) annoyed, because they can't do something for themselves; (4) anger, because even those who try to help can't agree on what to do; and (5) sadness, for the apparent hopelessness. It's like a merry-go-round, going around and around in circles: young people starting with high hopes and dreams of a better life,

accepting the disappointment of rejection but still believing that life could be better
if they could just find another way. It is such a complex problem that it is impossible
to solve, at least if the solution relied on me.

As the narrative progresses from one part to the next, less of my voice
and the voices of authority are evident, although I am aware that I am never
absent from the construction of the text. In *An Invitation to Reflexive Sociology* (Bourdieu and Wacquant 1992), Bourdieu identifies three types of biases
in doing research: (1) the social origins and coordinates, the position and
trajectory of the researcher within the social space (for example, gender,
class, nationality, ethnicity, education, and so on); (2) the position that the
researcher occupies in the academic field; and (3) the contemplative or
scholastic stance the sociologist necessarily assumes in the study of society. I
have admitted freely to the last and invite readers to do likewise, without for-
getting the first or second; that is, our general and specific positionings.

My social origins and coordinates can be described as white, middle
class, middle aged and male, although I have distant working-class origins
evident in the stances I frequently adopt. I am hopeful that being so positioned does not preclude me from understanding the positioning of others.
Indeed, such understandings of our similarities as well as our differences are
important if we are to talk meaningfully with one another. Nancy Fraser
(1993, 22) I think describes such distinctions between "being" and "sensing"
in her explanations of solidarity premised on *shared identity*, encompassing
the circle of those whom we feel to be like ourselves, while excluding those
whom we feel to be different from us; and solidarity premised on *shared responsibility*, encompassing the circle of those upon whom we feel entitled to
make claims for help and those whom we feel obligated to help in turn. In
this book I make claims for young people living on the edge of society,
aware that I might not share their identity but that I (along with you) do share
responsibility for their positioning.

The first part of the book is an ethnography consisting of eleven chapters
focused on a mobile charity and its distribution of free meals to young people
on the streets; a mission that is both extraordinary and mundane. Its ordinari-
ness is related to what has already been eluded: it is one among many. Yet it
is also remarkable, as I trust these pages will reveal, because of the work that
is attempted and also as an example of the groundswell of concern with the
social effects of self-interest within western societies. I endeavor to reveal

the participants "warts and all" for this is the reality of working on the streets. There is no explicit or implicit claim here that the mission's work is beyond critique. Indeed, its volunteers can be found wanting in some areas. But illustrating the best way to go about doing this kind of work is not my primary purpose, even though examples of what others might call "good practice" may be found within these pages. Rather, the intention is to make the connections between the private troubles and public issues of young people on our streets more widely known and to challenge the values of those who represent these young people and/or their "dysfunctional" families as singularly responsible for their own condition.

The second part contains four chapters that draw directly on interviews with individuals from the "helping" professions: a social worker, a welfare worker, a nurse, a magistrate, a community worker, a psychologist, a youth worker, and a teacher. Each chapter focuses on a particular theme: (1) what drives young people to the margins of society and what that life entails; (2) the involvement of the helping professions and how "helping" is conceived; (3) engaging with social systems; and (4) future prospects. Not all of the views expressed in these chapters are ones that I share and there is minimal commentary to direct readers' thoughts. Instead, I have arranged the data under headings and in themes that seem pertinent to my agenda and I have attempted to juxtapose professional comments in ways that highlight their insights as well as their shortcomings. Although all of the interviews were conducted in isolation and in anonymity, there is a sense in which the reader might imagine these chapters as conversations between professionals, collectively reflecting on their experiences of the troubles of marginalized youth.

The third part of the book consists of three stories of troubled adolescents, as told by these individuals themselves. Presented in three chapters, each is crafted from extended interviews and attempts to maintain the author's voice while ensuring a chronology of events and bowing to the conventions of the written word. The three characters—Jordan, Jenni, and Joan—are at different life stages when they tell their stories but each focuses on the period of their youth. Jenni's is probably the exception to this, adding stories of her own children's youth and also her observations as a mature-age student teacher of the ways in which some schools continue to deal with the marginalized. There is much that is remarkable in their stories, not least of which are the similarities that extend over time and place for young people on the edge.

The book ends with a Conclusion, written by Kathleen Densmore.[10] Kathleen's agenda is to address why things are the way they are and to challenge this with alternative ways of viewing the politics of poverty. Together with this Introduction, it seeks to raise the private troubles of marginalized young people in western societies as public issues. In particular, the Conclusion connects these lived experiences with the ideology of neoliberalism and capitalist markets. The Introduction and Conclusion, then, bracket more particular and individual accounts with broader frames, putting these into context and providing them with explanatory power. Some may choose to enter these explanations through the book's narratives, but to move beyond responses of pity, compassion, and solicitude (Bauman 2001) will require, I think, an engagement with these broader matters. I invite you, then, to enter into the discussion. It is an invitation to think differently about what it means to act justly.

NOTES

[1] Measuring "income poverty" is disputed territory. The measure used here is that adopted by the OECD. A similar measure utilizes the average rather than the median income, which can deliver quite different results. Income measurements too can vary depending, for example, on whether they include or exclude housing costs. Disposable income, the measure utilized here, is an adjusted figure after housing costs.

[2] In fact, barriers to trade, such as subsidies and tariffs, are alive and well in capitalist markets, despite the efforts of the World Trade Organization (WTO) to deliver a fairer system for all of its 146 country members. For example, after years of negotiation, it was only in August 2003 that agreement was reached to allow poor countries to import cheaper generic drugs in times of emergency or to fight such things as AIDS.

[3] Many western nations made generous pledges to countries tragically affected by the Asian tsunami, although some think the United States, in particular, was stung into action by Jan Egeland, the United Nation's Under-Secretary-General for Humanitarian Affairs and Emergency Relief Coordinator, who initially characterized wealthy nations as "stingy" in their offers of tsunami relief aid.

[4] This is not to suggest that I am uninterested in or unsympathetic about poverty in other parts of the world; that is, "world poverty." Rather, my comments are directed at defining the boundaries of what this book addresses: "country poverty" or, more accurately, western poverty. Such boundaries are not arbitrary. As Young explains, "because I conceive critical theory as historically and socially situated, I have restricted discussion of social justice in this book to Western welfare capitalist societies" (1990, 257).

[5] When Ronald Regan died, media commentary repeatedly positioned him as the savior of western capitalism who had single-handedly brought down communist Russia and rescued the world from totalitarianism. Their reports frequently quoted his triumphal commentary concerning the Berlin Wall: "Mr Gorbachev bring down this wall." Dissenting media opinion was rare with little discussion about what actually happened to the impoverished people of East Berlin after the wall came down, how they were confronted with the consumerism of West Berlin only then to return to their homes of comparative poverty in the East. The contrast between the social and economic situations of East and West Berlin was very stark but was barely mentioned and the exploitation that resulted when a tide of enthusiastic capitalists raced into the East was not discussed.

[6] In Australia, current estimates range from 10%–20% of the population, depending on the way in which it is measured.

[7] See Gale and Densmore (2000) for a critique of market versions of social justice.

[8] The outpouring of financial generosity in response to the Asian tsunami was an exception to this, particularly the philanthropy of individual citizens.

[9] See Bauman's (2001) account of the new role for the poor above and the examples of how this plays out below.

[10] Kathleen Densmore is Professor of Education, College of Education, San Jose State University, California, USA.

PART ONE

On the street

I've always had this idea of setting up a 24-hour café somewhere where people could come, sit down, and have a quiet chat, somewhere where they can get off the street and just have a cup of coffee or something. (Jordan)

CHAPTER ONE

Fleeting memories

Tonight is my first on the street. I expected to be more anxious. Instead I am somewhat subdued, suffering the effects of hay fever and enduring the medication with its own wearying effects. Even so, the whole event is far more low-key than I imagined. I can't say with any certainty what I anticipated except that I expected it would be more dramatic. It's dark, around six in the evening, and Maggie and Suzanne are already here, at our meeting place, loading up with food.

I have known Maggie for a while now, although it is only in the last couple of months that our relationship has grown from a casual acquaintance. She is in her early 70s and has recently lost her husband. I say "lost" as many people do when they are trying to be polite about death. Before and after the event Maggie has remained an active old lady; hardly old really, at least if her energy and activity are any guide, and certainly a woman of stature. She is respected by all who know her as a gentle soul and genuinely concerned for others. The ideal grannie. It's not surprising, then, that she should be here, getting ready to venture into the shadowy parts of the city. Suzanne, or Suzie, is far younger, in her early to mid-20s. This is the first time I've met her. She seems relaxed, sure of herself, and recently returned from two years' work as a teacher in some remote corner of the world. We pack the food and I travel with her to our destination: a semilit patch of the city's park. Maggie travels in her own car. Apparently, there is safety in having two vehicles.

We're not there long before another car arrives and, along with it, my first pangs of doubt. We're outnumbered, three to three; three naive do-gooders to three streetwise, well-built guys, around "20-something," although the smaller one is probably in his late teens. Suzie takes the initiative: "Hey guys, can you help us with our van? The radiator light was on all the way over here and we can't work out how to lift the front seat to have a look." The larger two take charge, inspecting the seat and adjusting its clasps to reveal the motor. Their interest in solving the problem is reassuring and I drift back into my previous subdued condition.

Attention turns to the food, and Maggie and Suzie spell out the alternatives: roast lamb and vegetables, curried rice, or spaghetti bolognaise. It's somewhat Eurocentric and "homely" and not the range you would find at the takeaway outlets down the road, but I sense that for our guests the choice is as exciting as the prospect of food itself. Nick decides quickly, taking our only serve of spaghetti bolognaise. Luke and Brett's decisions are more considered, weighing up their remaining options. They are goaded continuously by Nick, celebrating his good fortune at having scored the prize selection on the menu. Together we sit on the camp chairs and around our portable folding table; Nick, Luke, and Brett hoeing into the food and Maggie, Suzie, and myself supplying the utensils, condiments, and side orders of buttered bread, flavored water, and eggnog.

The discussion eventually moves on to other things, to a topic of conversation familiar at many dinner parties—work. Nick has a job with a local cleaning firm. He wears the company polo shirt; the small, embroidered logo on his chest looking more like a yachting club emblem, so it takes a while for me to figure out what his duties entail. His disordered patter doesn't help much either and slabs of spaghetti bolognaise are sandwiched between slices of bread as he talks. "I must be a bit dull," I confess. "What kind of work do you do?" Nick points to the insignia on his shirt and trots out the company spiel; Maggie provides the interpretation. He is very animated, almost to excess, but no one else seems to notice.

Brett has recently applied for a similar job with the same company, which has a contract to clean a nearby power station. He has worked at the same site before but for a firm that "collapsed" and left him redundant. I can't help thinking that his work experiences give new meaning to the phrase "being taken to the cleaners"! Maggie consoles him that it isn't his fault he is out of work and that the new company shouldn't hold his dismissal against him. We ask about his chances of securing the new position. Having previously worked there, he has all the required certificates; all the qualifications that allow him to be hung upside down by ropes and pullies, meters in the air, for eight hours at a time to clean the machinery.

Throughout the entire exchange Nick shakes his head and says to all who will listen, but especially to Luke, that you'd have to be mad to do that kind of work. "You wouldn't catch me doing that. I like to have my two feet on the ground." I'm inclined to agree but I ask Brett whether the work attracts any danger money. "Eighteen dollars an hour," he replies. Gauging Brett's demeanor, it is obviously above the award rate and Maggie responds appropriately, commenting approvingly on his potential salary and the value of his qualifications. I reflect on how much more I get paid for keeping my feet under a desk. "Don't you get a headache being upside down for so long?" I ask. "Yeah, but it doesn't last for long and you get used to it." I decide that the office air conditioning might not be so bad after all. Like me, Nick is unconvinced and continues to voice his disdain. Maggie counters that everyone is different, that it might be OK for those who have a head for it.

It's Luke's turn but he doesn't say much. He too has applied for a job as a cleaner and at the same company, but not in the line of work that Brett now contemplates. Revisiting the cleaning industry provides Nick with an opportunity to expand on his dislike of heights. Still, he's flying to the other side of the country soon, to live. His girlfriend has moved there to be with her father. She is pregnant to Nick. A house and a job with the father's security firm are in the offing. Maggie emphasizes the need for him to be responsible now that he is to be a father, to make the most of his new opportunities. Brett and Luke say they are going too. Luke is Nick's cousin. I look for a family resemblance but it goes undetected. "Are you going for a holiday or to live there permanently?" Suzie asks. "For good," they reply. I wonder about Brett's earlier aspirations for employment as a cleaner at the power station, contemplating how sincere he was about his desire to secure the position and how well qualified he was for it. I decide he is serious about both; anything that will improve his circumstances. "It isn't any better over there, you know. Jobs are still hard to find there, just as they are here," Maggie warns. They seem disinterested in her counsel. From their perspective, the grass is greener on the other side of the country.

Suzie asks about the whereabouts of the girlfriend's mother. "I wouldn't be going if she was there," Nick declares. "She's an old bag." He continues for a while with various descriptions of the relative use to society of women of her vintage. Gender equity is not high on his agenda. Maggie is uncomfortable with the turn in the conversation and introduces her own diversion: "You'd better finish your dinner before it gets cold." Indignation is clearly evident in the tone of her voice. They do as she instructs, although without remorse, and then trash their plastic utensils. They depart on good terms and we are left to ourselves.

Some of my earlier expectations have become clearer through the encounter. I was expecting street kids to be younger and certainly not to arrive in cars. Suzie and Maggie inform me that Nick, Brett, and Luke are at the upper age limit of those that drop by and that few others have cars, although there is another regular visitor, Scott, who lives in his car. No one will rent him accommodation while he has two dogs. I still wonder how it is they can afford a car, and even dogs, but not a meal. "They probably could buy their own," says Suzie, reading my mind. "And they probably do most of the time. We only see them here every now and then. But it's hard for them to find work without a car. Public transport doesn't operate at three in the morning when Nick starts his shift."

Across the road from the park are the lights of a fuel station, its signs advertising the latest rise in prices. I think about how an increasing percentage of Nick's wages is going into the coffers of the Organization of the Petroleum Exporting Countries (OPEC) that are manipulating the production and supply of oil, raising prices and profits. For his part, OPEC's secretary-general points the finger at oil excise. We can have cheaper fuel, he says, if we reduce the government tax. I am reminded that the politics of minimal government is not overly concerned with the reduced public services that result for young people like Nick. I also recall a recent item on the news about the wonderful weather people are experiencing this summer on the West Coast of the United States, prompting lots of touring and greater fuel consumption and adding to the scarcity of oil.

Three more figures appear on the horizon, silhouetted by the streetlights. Maggie and Suzie speculate on who they might be. It becomes clearer as they approach that they are female, around 16 years of age. "How are we, girls?" I cringe a little at Suzie's welcome—the voice of authority, identity politics in the hands of professionals. It reminds me of the condescending tones of some nurses who use the first person plural as a way of identifying with their patients (for example, "How are we feeling?") but also, more paternally, as a way of making decisions for them (for example, "It's time to take our medicine."). Unlike the royal "we," it is the disempowered "other" to which the "we" refers. Later it occurs to me that the reference to pathology reveals a lot about how the middle classes generally understand people living on the street—as deficient in some way, in need of remediation, rehabilitation. I am also reminded of Michel Foucault's (1979) account of "the examination" in *Discipline and Punish*. Of course, Suzie means none of this, at least not consciously. She is busy sorting out names and taking orders for food. More kids arrive and I leave Maggie and Suzie to attend to the girls.

The new arrivals are two girls in their mid-teens and a boy around 12 or 13. Young, black, and "deadly." We exchange names but later I can only remember Jackson's, which is ironic; he says very little the entire time and positions his back to most of us. Perhaps my mind is fixated on his tender years; he looks too young and innocent to be on the street. I pass them some food and then sit down with them on the ground. Like Nick and his friends, the girls are willing to talk. One has been to court today, charged with stealing a motor vehicle six months ago.

"Does that worry you," I ask, "having to wait all that time before the case gets to court?"

"Why should it? If you do the crime you do the time."

Her words roll off her tongue in a Texan drawl that wouldn't be out of place in a Hollywood movie. I ponder how easily she adopts (or perhaps parodies) the discourses and the accent of the white middle classes, how accepting she is of her fate and yet how hollow it is as a deterrent.

"But aren't you worried about going to jail? What about all those stories of black deaths in custody? Doesn't that worry you?"

"I don't know why they kill 'emselves. I wouldn't kill myself. I got a little kid to look after."

Her story is truly sad. Her stepfather raped her when she was 13 and her 2-year-old daughter, one of the outcomes of the incident, has been placed in the care of her aunt.

"So, what happened at court? What did the magistrate say?"

"I got a five-month good-behavior bond so if I mess up, I go to jail. And I have to pay $1500."

"That's a lot of money. Where will you get it from?"

"From my father or if he won't give it to me, I'll steal it."

It occurs to me how crazy the legal system is. Presumably, the fine was given to her as a punishment and a deterrent, but if the government is to receive its money it will cost someone else, not the vehicle's illegal driver. The system, ostensibly established to deal with crime in our society, seems to generate more of it and at the expense of the innocent and the guilty. I think all this but I don't have time to sort it out in my mind and I suspect there is much more to the story that I don't know. I engage in conversation with the second girl. She, too, has an appearance at court scheduled for two weeks time, for being in a stolen car. "She's my accomplish," the driver explains. I am amused again by her use of language.

Suzie comes over and the girls inquire whether she has seen their friends here tonight. "No, they were here last Friday and I wasn't very happy with them. They spent the whole night chromin'."

"Crying?" the second girl asks, appearing to try to make sense of Suzie's displeasure but, more pointedly, drawing attention to the disjuncture between Suzie's language and her social position.

"No, chromin'," she replies, pretending to sniff from a plastic bag.

"You mean sniffing paint?" the first girl laughs.

Our attempts at using street talk provide the girls with their own amusment.

"It kills your brain cells, you know. It's not worth it," says Suzie.

"They've got no reason to do it," the first girl agrees. "I do it but I got a good reason."

She tells her story again about her rape and Suzie focuses in on the positives of having a child. I note the contradiction between the girl's earlier reaction concerning black deaths in custody and her solvent abuse, but I let it pass.

Their meals are finished and they depart. The three young girls who arrived before them have also left, along with Scott who dropped in while I was busy elsewhere. We clean up the leftovers, load the van, and make the return journey to our starting place. It's a short trip. We see some of the girls on the way but don't wave. Suzie says it's not appreciated and we don't have room for them in the van. We arrive and unpack, storing in the freezer what can be used again.

I linger for a moment in the darkness, next to the van parked on the street. Two cars pass, heading in the other direction. I hear a thud as they go by and see a black cat writhing in pain in their wake, springing into the air but eventually succumbing to the impact. The comparison between the cat's death and living on the street seems powerfully strong in my mind. Seeing a "road kill" is upsetting but it doesn't take long before it is forgotten. It provides a strong metaphor of the middle classes, who seem momentarily moved with compassion by images on their television screens of people starving or fleeing wars in foreign lands, before they slip back into the comfort of their lounge rooms. The hype of the 1984 famine in Ethiopia, drawn to the world's attention by Bob Geldoff (for which he was later knighted), is a case in point. Twenty years on, more Ethiopians now live on the verge of starvation than ever before. Of all third world countries, Ethiopia now receives the most in relief aid and the least in development aid.

I think all this and decide that, like the plight of the Ethiopians, adolescents on our streets are a momentary thought in the minds of many in western societies. Indeed, recognizing homelessness can be difficult for many, who imagine it to be the exclusive domain of old men with two-day shadows, clothed in grubby overcoats, smelling of cheap alcohol, and with yesterday's newspaper to insulate them from the night air. Such stereotypes mean that we forget the homeless families frequenting soup kitchens and secondhand clothing shops and the youths whose lounge rooms are the local mall and whose bathrooms are the public amenities in parks and bus depots. Aware of my own middle-classness, I realize that I too am not immune to such selective amnesia. I wonder how long it will take me to forget the kids I met tonight, how long till they become just a fleeting memory, how long till they return to the margins of my consciousness.

CHAPTER TWO

Going without

Maggie is not here tonight. She is caring for her grandchildren while her daughter is away. Debbie takes her place. She is 50-something and likes to talk. She heads the work on the van and is out several nights every week. It was Debbie I approached recently about joining the team. I was, she declared at the time, an answer to prayer. "We need more men."

Elizabeth is of similar age and similarly inclined to conversation, perhaps more so. Tonight she takes Debbie's place, warming the food before we leave. We are introduced and I ask her how long she has been working on the van. "For about 12 months. Actually, I did a counseling course first. I didn't know how I would cope. My son's a drug addict and I don't cope well with that so I didn't know whether I'd be able to work on the van, but it's different. Most of the kids on the street don't have much going for them whereas my son has had every opportunity and has no respect for anyone, including himself."

"How old is he?" I ask. I'm conscious that "age" has become an issue for me. It seems increasingly difficult to discern from appearances. It is also a bit like discussing the weather; it fills a void in the conversation. Elizabeth stops, it seems, for my reaction. If I remember anything of value from my meager introduction to Rogerian counseling as a college student, I need to say something without passing judgment. Age seems a safe bet.

"He's 25. He's really my stepson. He lives with his girlfriend and her three kids. She says the youngest is Ben's, but she was pregnant when they met. Anyway, that's their business; I can't live their lives for them. They've got our number. They know where we live. But I'm not taking any of their nonsense. He rings up all the time, abusing me because I won't look after her kids all day, every day. But I don't think I deserve that, being spoken to like that; I haven't done anything wrong. We're willing to help but they have responsibility for those kids, not us. Of course, the trouble is I'm his stepmother. I'm the woman he didn't want in his life anyway. He doesn't want to listen to me."

"Liz," I interrupt, "if I don't hurry the van will leave without me. Perhaps we could get together another time."

"Oh, I'm sorry," she apologizes. "I have to go, too. My husband gets worried about me driving at night by myself. Besides, he's at home cooking dinner, making a mess of the kitchen!"

"That's the cook's prerogative," I reply.

We laugh and she gives me a hug. It seems a fitting way to part, even though we have only just met. I'm relieved that I haven't offended her by cutting the conversation short and a hug seems an appropriate response to the difficulties she faces.

Suzie drives us to the park. She is looking forward to the holidays. It has been a long term at school with too much still to get done and several of her colleagues off work, sick. She asks me about my day. For me, it has been one of those piecemeal affairs where nothing of substance seems to have been achieved and yet I have been constantly busy. Suzie recognizes the feeling; the busy professional classes, under pressure, but at least they have work.

We meet Debbie at the park and set up for the night. Three guys appear in the distance, first one and then two more following a few meters behind. Lucas, the first to arrive, has been to the van before, but it takes his companions, Bill and Owen, some convincing that a free meal is on offer in the park at night. Together with Liam, who arrives about an hour later, they occupy our entire shift. We dispense the food in double quantities. Most have not eaten today, Lucas not for two days, and they are appreciative of the hot meals and drinks. Savory sausages replace the spaghetti bolognaise on the menu and warm coffee scrolls lavished with custard complete the feast. Debbie is heavy-handed serving the food and as she pours the custard I wonder whether she will ever stop. It is indicative generally of the generosity with which she engages with the kids who visit. Bill is amazed that we should even be in the park at night. He tells me of another mission in another city that distributes free soup and bread rolls, but during the day. Although, he recalls, they also offer coffee and buns for those who attend their Wednesday night church service, "as a kind of inducement," says Bill.

It is early days but already I discern a pattern emerging on these slow nights: they are busy with talk that traverses a range of issues about life. I am being schooled in the "cultural capital"—the knowledge, tastes, and ways of thinking and acting—of the streets. I learn, for example, that a driving lesson for a learner driver with the required permit, can cost between $30 and $50 per hour at a driving school. Yet the same learner can drive around all day unaccompanied by a licensed driver—perhaps longer if not caught by the police—and only face a $30 fine. The economics of this seem far more attractive and it is an option particularly enticing to those who already know the rudiments of driving, as many on the streets do, and who just want access to the roads. Of course, there is a catch: having the $30 to pay the fine. Not paying within the designated period triggers a warrant, arrest, a court appearance, a further $200 fine, and often a stint in jail. The string of events seems reminiscent of *Monopoly*, so much so that Lucas selects an imaginary card from the "Community Chest"—the top slice of bread on the pile—and reads its inscription: "Go directly to jail. Do not pass go. Do not collect $200."

It is an amusing and clever comment and I am reminded again of the "games of society," as French sociologist Pierre Bourdieu calls them, and people's relative ability to play.

Lucas, 19, and Owen, 15, have carried the conversation thus far but it is Bill, in his 40s, who continues it. There is a mathematical relationship, he intimates, between the amount of the fine and the number of days to be spent in jail, which varies from one jurisdiction to another. Time "inside" can also vary. In some districts a person can be arrested and jailed at 10 p.m., be freed the next morning, and have their overnight stay count as a day. Yet in other counties the same debt cancellation requires a full 24 hours behind bars. For the poor, spending time in jail becomes a way of paying one's bills. For example, Bill—and it is around about now that the irony of his name strikes me—has recently 'cut out' $1700 worth of fines by spending a few weeks in jail. That is another classroom altogether and it appears that he has been a good student. As Bill continues, I recall from last week that sometimes debts to society are paid with stolen money.

"You can get a 'black' licence with a different name for about $17 and then you're a clean skin," Bill informs us. "But you're just doing your money if you don't pay off all your fines first, 'cause the police pick the false ID straight away when they pick you up on a warrant under your real name."

Suzie interrupts our lesson to ask Lucas about his new accommodation. He has been sleeping in the park for the past two to three weeks before moving into a local hostel.

"It's good," Lucas replies. "It's got polished wooden floors."

"What do you get for your money?" I ask, having been told that after paying for his new room he is left with $4 from his weekly $70 social security payment. I learn a few days later that he is also entitled to extra financial support for rental assistance, which would make the economics somewhat more conducive. I reflect on whether he is aware of this or whether the story is embellished for our benefit to secure our sympathy and perhaps something more tangible. At the very least, it throws some doubt over Lucas's account of things.

He lists the amenities in his room: bed, wardrobe, chest of drawers, and access to the kitchen down the hall, but no food. I try to think back to when I was 19 and decide I was probably a lot less self-sufficient than I would have credited at the time. As for Lucas, he left home at 16 and, until recently, traveled the carnival or show circuit, working the sideshows to pay his keep. Akin to running away to join the circus, it conjures up images in my mind—about which Patrick Danaher (1998) writes in *Beyond the Ferris Wheel*—of a "shadowy world" of itinerancy. As an outsider to the show culture, it is for Lucas a life for a time. Now he sleeps in till noon—sleep provides some relief from the hunger and the cold—and spends his afternoons at the local amusement arcade before the night sets in and he begins the search for food once again.

"Have you nicked that?" Bill asks of Lucas, referring to the blue sleeping bag he has draped around his shoulders.

"No, Debbie gave it to me; but I told her I didn't need it. I've got enough blankets in my room."

Lucas enjoys his misleading reply, the opportunity to tease. Debbie had indeed given it to him, although not to keep, at least not initially. She had noticed that his short-sleeved shirt provided little protection from the night air that now envelops us, and she simply meant to help him fend off the cold. "You can have it if you want," Debbie offers, but Lucas declines, this time in more believable tones. He is, however, seeking money and Debbie advises him to go to the church office in the morning where he can obtain some vouchers. Bill offers to wake him in time to get there but it is also a dig at Lucas's propensity to sleep the mornings away. Owen is amused by Bill's jibe and by the sleeping-bag exchange. He laughs the laugh of schoolboys who have just pulled off some mischievous prank; spontaneous and then restrained as if to avoid giving the game away. It is more endearing than sinister and comes at regular intervals throughout the night, dispersed with a seriousness that is almost naive.

"Do you go to school, Owen?" I ask.

"No."

"Why not? Don't you like it?"

"Oh, yeah. It's good."

"Why don't you go, then?"

"I got kicked out."

"What for?"

"Selling drugs."

His reply is unexpected and in it I recognize my own naïveté. I am at a loss as to how to proceed or whether I should. Bill breaks the impasse, informing me that Owen's younger brother, Mitchell, left school at 13.

"How did your mother feel about that?" I ask, now with something new to pursue.

"She didn't know for about a month," says Owen.

"He'd pretend to go to school but then go to his cousin's place," Bill adds.

"Yeah," Owen chuckles, his words and laughter intermingled.

The two of them continue their commentary on Mitchell.

"He lies his head off."

"Yeah."

"He's out of bed for two minutes and starts saying, 'I've done this and this and this,' but you know he's only just got up."

"Yeah."

"And he's as mad as a skunk. He went fishin' once, down by the bridge. He bought a new lure but when he cast out his line it got stuck in his knee. At first he thought it was a fish so he pulled and it got worse. He ended up hobblin' in to a private hospital to get it out. He was dark on them 'cause the lure was new; they cut the end off it before cutting out the bit in his knee. Then they stitched him up but they didn't say nothin' to him about paying. I said to him, 'Don't you know it's a private hospital?' He's gone in there looking for "Casualty." He's lucky they didn't throw him out 'cause he didn't have any money or any ID or nothin', just a hook sticking out of his leg!"

"Yeah," laughs Owen.

Talk of hospitals reminds Debbie about David, a regular visitor to the van who now lies in hospital on a dialysis machine. He has damage to his kidneys, liver, and lungs, sustained from inhaling the toxic substances contained in spray paint, and has been given about six months to live. Debbie directs her comments to Suzie and to Liam who has just arrived. Liam, too, is a long-term visitor to the van and knows David and Craig, to whom Debbie now refers.

"Craig says David's getting his just deserts for introducing his brother to chromin' but I told him, 'How would you like it if your brother ends up the same way and people said that about him?' I argued it that way."

"Do you think it will be a deterrent to the others?" Suzie asks.

"Maybe," Debbie replies. "They all know him."

Lucas has finished his third helping of food and is restless. "Let's cruise," he says, but the others don't seem to hear. They are busy talking with Liam, arguing the relative merits of buying loose tobacco compared with conventional cigarettes. It prompts them to roll a couple and light up. Liam has just moved to a property on the edge of the city and talks about the possibility of growing some tobacco of his own.

"I hope that's all you're going to grow," Suzie chides.

"Of course," says Liam, but his tone is deliberately satirical, for Suzie's benefit.

Owen laughs. Liam and Owen know each other; they have worked as fruit pickers in previous seasons. Bill and Owen say they plan on picking fruit tomorrow. "Luke's not coming," says Bill. "He won't be out of bed in time!" They also plan on applying for jobs at the local meatworks. Bill has worked in one before, in another city.

"What about you, Owen," I ask, not thinking he is old enough to have been so employed.

"Yeah. I was a whiz kid."

I almost miss the significance of his reply. At first I think he is referring to his skill level but then I learn he worked a handheld circular saw, used to cut the meat from between the carcass ribs. I check to see whether he has his full complement of fingers.

"Let's cruise," says Lucas. Bill and Owen rise to leave. Debbie packs an extra meal in a plastic bag and gives it to Lucas, having first inflicted a sizable whole in the bottom of the bag. "Just in case you have ideas of using it for other purposes," she explains. "We know you won't use it for chromin'," says Suzie, "but we have to do it for everyone, just in case." Plastic bags are used by kids on the streets for sniffing paint. They depart, leaving Liam to finish his meal. He is upbeat and it is clear from his rapport with Debbie and Suzie that he has known them for some time. After a while, he slips into a more thoughtful mood.

"I might be a father. I don't know yet."

"Why? Are there some problems with the pregnancy?"

"No. She's already had the kid. She says I'm the father but it could also be another guy."

"That would be hard to find out, wouldn't it?"

"They can do a DNA test. It costs around $400 but I want to find a way of doing it without her knowing."

"How are you going to do that?"

"Don't know yet. I think they can find out from the saliva in its mouth."

"Is it a boy or a girl?"

"A boy. His name is Ethan. He's two and a half."

"What will you do if you find out he's yours?"

"I'll probably end up moving in. She's all right, I guess. I couldn't have moved in a couple of years ago, though. I was going through some serious stuff then."

It is late and we begin to pack up. Debbie is reminded of packing up last Saturday and retells the sight of a horde of kids running down the hill, chased by the police doing their best to grab whoever they could. The kids had been throwing stones from the hill at passing cars, to which one of the drivers had taken exception and phoned the local police station. Suzie speculates on the distance from the hill to the road and suggests that some of the kids should try out for the Olympics, at the very least the ones who got away!

The story prompts me to recall a research paper presented by a colleague earlier in the day, concerning the hordes of street kids in Brazil and the police who are paid $20 for every one they can shoot. Fortunately, we have different ways of solving problems on our streets, but it still seems focused on dealing with problems after the event. I am reminded, too, of a second research paper given to me by Debbie earlier in the evening when I arrived to load the van. It describes an educational program for disadvantaged kids offered by The Exodus Foundation in Sydney, Australia. At the time, I scanned the paper and noted the following in the conclusion:

What we have created at Ashfield, I think, is a blending of a highly structured university centered learning program in a warm fuzzy church/welfare environment. Obviously, at times those cultures clash but it is in the juxtaposition of these two cultures that the magic occurs. We now honestly feel that we have a world-class program that could help disadvantaged children in many countries. I have learned that working with young people must include a significant education component. It may be more sensible to place work with disadvantaged children under an educational rather than a welfare banner.

Debbie is thinking about the feasibility of doing something similar. I tell her I will read the paper and let her know what I think. At first glance it reminds me of Paulo Freire, the teacher-activist whose work was directed at empowering the poor, illiterate, and disenfranchised peoples of Brazil and Chile. I decide to reserve judgment for now but I am attracted to the idea of thinking differently about welfare. I reflect again on how the small government strategy of neoliberals has meant their virtual abdication of responsibility for the poor and the greater involvement by welfare agencies stepping into the breach. Many welfare agencies now report a doubling over the past five years in the assistance they provide people in the community, despite improvements in the nation's economy.

"You've got to be careful about what Liam tells you," Suzie cautions, as we make the return journey in the van. "He's told us so many stories that contradict each other that you're never quite sure when he's telling the truth. He's a compulsive liar."

"I wonder whether he's just trying on different stories to see how they fit, to see how others respond to them."

"Yeah, maybe," she replies. "It's almost a way of getting out of here, out of the city, to somewhere else where things might be better."

An envelope awaits me when I return home. It bears the imprimatur of a government department and I recognize the handwriting as my sister's. The letter is written from her offices while she takes a break from a difficult case. She lives some distance away and doesn't write often, once a year perhaps, so I open it with anticipation of the casual news it contains. More serious news usually comes via the telephone. She tells me about her children, and how they are faring at school and church. Michael, the oldest, has recently commenced his secondary schooling at one of the country's oldest and most prestigious private schools with its long history of producing the nation's political, business, judicial, and religious leaders. By all accounts he is enjoying the experience and performing well in his new surrounds, being one of only four selected to represent the school at a coming French conversation competition and finishing sixth in a recent athletic event. I am pleased that he is enjoying success but I can't help think back to Owen and his experiences of school. I wonder how Michael and Owen would fare if their circumstances were reversed. I am reminded of the role of schooling in the reproduction of privilege.

My sister seems occupied with similar thoughts although, for her, the traditional connections between position and privilege are no longer certain. In particular, she is concerned for our older brother who lives overseas:

> We have been waiting anxiously for news of Tony. It puts a bit of a cloud over family affairs to have him without a job for so long. It really is a terrifying world nowadays; there is no real security in employment for anyone anymore.

I share her concern although I am conscious that my brother's usual income puts him in the highest tax bracket in one of the world's advanced economies.

It is difficult to reconcile the feelings aroused by tonight's events. I think about the circumstances that place us on different sides of our social systems; the boundaries that mark out our different experiences of schooling, employment, and life expectancies generally. I decide for now at least that what concerns me is that young people go without—without food, without shelter and without opportunity. I am concerned too at the absence in their lives of genuine love and hope.

Mostly, the marginalized in our society seem to go without impunity. They are rarely exempt from the consequences of the "errors of their ways" or for being in the wrong place at the wrong time. Stealing something from a shop can be a childish prank for well-to-do youth, which may never get to court. Whereas for the marginalized, even a first offense is said to bear testament to what everyone always suspected. Moreover, they frequently suffer the consequences of others' actions; as the direct and indirect bearers of redundancy, for example, when chief executives have made poor business decisions and need to cut costs. There is little buffer in life for them. Their practical jokes, their mistakes and follies, paint them into corners different from their middle-class peers. It is what is expected of them so their transgressions are more difficult to hide. To live without impunity, with penalties of one kind or another constantly before you, seems a burden almost too difficult to endure.

CHAPTER THREE

People like us

It's Saturday morning. Pam and I have just finished shopping for our weekly groceries and are on our way out of the center, heading for the car. Just outside the shopping complex I notice an older man rummaging around in the trash, looking for discarded delicacies. His hair and beard are white and full flowing and I recognize him as "Willie Nelson," his alias on the street. Assumed names are common among those who live the street life. They are often the stuff of folklore and can provide protection as well as status.

Willie is in his early 50s, but life has been harsh on him and he looks much older. Recently, he and a couple of his friends have been "sleeping rough" under the bridge behind the shopping center, near the city park. His visits to the van form part of his daily foraging for food and he often scavenges for more than one mouth. One of his sleeping companions has been sick recently, coughing up blood, and Willie has been supplying him with meals relayed from the van. He has also acquired a hamster, which he transports in a plastic bag, although at first glance I had thought it was a rat. "He's my best friend," he told me on our first meeting. He'd had the rodent for three weeks.

Willie is usually happy to engage with whomever is at the van, young or old. Lately, at the end of our shift, he has taken to standing and praying, head bowed but eyes wide open. In the stillness of the night with his dinner guests gathered around, his prayers ramble but often include "underprivileged kids" from overseas who don't have any food or water.

"Lord, can you help them and look after them," he pleads. "I'll come to church one day but I have to get myself cleaned up first," he once said.

"You don't need to get yourself cleaned up," Maggie had replied. "You can go as you are."

"Hi Willie," I say, pausing beside his trash can. "How are you?" He is startled at first but then his face lights up with recognition. As we shake hands and I pat him on the back, I sense passersby grimacing, their searching, incredulous expression inquiring, "Are you out of your mind?" It is not the first time the question had been raised. A friend had asked me a few weeks earlier how "PLU" could engage in such activities. "PLU?" I responded. "People like us," he said.

Outside the shopping center, a well-dressed woman is particularly annoyed that we have propped in front of her without adequate reason. Other Saturday morning shoppers steer a wide berth around us and it is then I realize that Willie would infrequently experience the buffeting of a crowded mall. People tend to keep away from him. His body odor is not one that is bottled for public consumption, although it is sometimes difficult to imagine how he might acquire one that is. He has told me of at least one visit he paid to a department store only to be escorted from the premises by two security guards. Shopping complexes provide street people with relief from weather extremes as well as access to news and entertainment on the multiple television screens in department stores. But they are not venues in which they can remain for long.

"This is not a place for you," they had told him.

"But I *had* money. Would they throw out someone who had no money but was wearing a suit?"

I introduce Willie to Pam, who greets him warmly. This is the first time they have met although Pam is well acquainted with Willie from my reports of nights on the van. In turn, Pam becomes the subject of Willie's own report at subsequent van nights; a report that receives several airings. As we say goodbye, I contemplate whether I would have stopped to say hello had I not worked on the van. I suspect that I wouldn't. Contrary to its nomenclature, the logic of "people like us" seems to be powerfully at work to keep us apart, playing on our fears and misgivings.

CHAPTER FOUR

Sitting targets

Another evening. Suzie greets me as I arrive.

"Hi. Are you able to drive the van tonight? I'm going out for dinner afterwards, so I'm taking my car."

"Sure," I reply.

The team's rendezvous before we depart reminds me of the opening scenes of *Hill Street Blues*, an old police television series that begins each episode with a squad briefing on the latest events "on the hill." In similar fashion, Suzie informs us of a girl who came to the park last Saturday expecting some Christian charity and, after loitering for a while, complained that no one had offered to clean her feet. Maggie contemplates whether someone should introduce her to Scott, a regular visitor to the van and professing Christian, but whose dubious theology casts considerable doubt over his claim. He also has a skill for ostracizing others. "They might be good for each other!" muses Maggie. It is a momentary lapse from her usually generous nature, for which she apologizes. Both she and Suzie are more concerned for Emma, who has recently dropped out of university to marry Scott and live with him in his car. "It's only temporary," she says. Scott plans to approach the local bank manager for a loan to buy property in the country and build holiday cabins. The fact that his only income is from welfare and that he has no capital to secure the loan doesn't seem to deter him. He is an ideas man.

Maggie accompanies me in the van to the park. She has been out at least once since returning from her recent trip away and mentions a new visitor, Bill. I recall him from last week.

"He's a bit older than our target range but it's hard to turn people away if they're in need."

"What *is* our target range?" I ask.

"Well, it's supposed to be from about 15 to 25."

"Is that a city regulation?"

"No, it's just based on what we felt was the need. There are other places catering for older people on the streets. We felt there was a need to do something for the younger ones."

Around ten kids on bicycles are waiting for us when we arrive. I park the van and more appear out of the darkness. It is a scramble to set up the table and chairs and unload the food and associated items to meet the instant demand we encounter. Our welcoming committee, four kids in particular, mill around waiting to be fed; the intensity of their interest in proceedings matched only by their insatiable appetites.

I read out the choices and hand out several meals, beginning with those whose curiosity seems most pressing before proceeding to the outskirts of the crowd where I meet a familiar face.

"Hi Bill."

"Hi."

Our conversation is short lived. I am confronted again by Brad, a rather young looking 15 year old.

"Can I have another feed, please?"

"But you haven't finished the one I gave you."

"That's for my woman."

"If I give you another one I might not have enough to give out later. Why don't you eat that one first?"

He tries his request on Maggie but she and Suzie are fully occupied with his three companions, supplying drinks, bread, and various side orders.

"Can I have another feed?" he persists, turning back to me.

"I'm sorry, I don't think I can give you one, Brad. Would you like a drink?" I offer, trying to divert his attention.

Maggie's interest is now aroused. "Whose is that one there?" She points to a meal unattended on the table.

"That's for my woman," he replies. "I need another one."

"No, Bradley. There won't be enough for everyone else," she says. "Here. Have a drink."

Brad takes the drink but continues his barrage of requests. He wants a plastic bag but Maggie and Suzie are suspicious of the use he has in mind for it and are reluctant to supply him with one. He insists he only has good intentions, that he doesn't "sniff." He wants the bag to carry food back to his woman. Eventually, Maggie succumbs but not without inflicting the bag with several large holes. He complains that now it won't hold its intended contents, particularly the plastic utensils, but Maggie is undeterred. Having been a nurse for most of her life, she is determined to avoid being an unwitting accomplice to youth inhaling toxic substances.

My attention is drawn to Dylan, one of Brad's young companions, whose forearm is bandaged from wrist to elbow. The contrast between the white pristine dressing and his black skin is hard to ignore.

"What happened?" I ask, pointing to his arm.

"I got cut with a knife."

"How?"

"In a fight."

"You shouldn't be fighting with knives," says Suzie.

"It's not my fault," he protests. "It was him who pulled the knife."

The "him" to whom Dylan refers is not known to us and does not come to the van. Maggie is more concerned that Dylan hasn't received treatment for the wound, and Suzie, that fighting with knives can lead to much more serious trouble. Brad takes up the reference to familiarity with the wrong side of the law. He is to attend court soon to face charges of stealing a BMW from one of the wealthier parts of the city. Recalling a similar event some weeks previous, I am again surprised by the cavalier attitude regarding his impending appointment, scheduled for the day after his 16th birthday.

"What do you think will happen?" I ask, trying to induce a more considered response.

"Don't know and don't care," he replies.

"Have you been to court before?"

"Yeah."

His criminal record consists mostly of property crime, unlawful entry, and theft, some of which is yet to be officially attributed to him. Flanked by Dylan, Kyle, and Jackson, he wears his misdemeanors like badges of honor.

Elsewhere in the crowd are two guys and a girl, recently arrived in town. Ashley and Thomas are in their mid to late teens, whereas Sally looks as if she is 13 but claims an additional three years. "We heard it was good here but so far it's boring," Ashley tells me. I mention a few of the city's highlights but they seem unimpressed. It reminds me of Maggie's counsel to Brett a couple of weeks ago, that things are not any better on the other side of the country. The three of them are looking for work and ask about their prospects as fruit pickers.

"You should ask Bill," I suggest. "He'd know more about that than I would."

They have already met him at the hostel where they now reside, having progressed from sleeping in their car the night before. It was from Bill they heard about the van. I ask about Lucas but they don't know him. They finish their meals and decide to move on. I sense that another town is on their itinerary. Maggie and Suzie are still surrounded by kids. I move through the crowd to speak with Bill.

"How's Lucas?" I begin, after reexchanging pleasantries.

"He got kicked out for bein' drunk and eatin' other people's food," he informs me. With nowhere to live, Bill arranged for Lucas to stay with some friends but within a few days he had disappeared.

"I think he's gone back to his mother's. It would've only cost him about $5 on the bus with his welfare card." I have already discovered that Lucas's financial resources, although meager, are not as dire as he would have liked us to believe, but the bus fare seems a trivial amount and I wonder why he hasn't made the trip earlier. I reflect on what might await Lucas at the other end of his journey that would cause him to put it off for so long.

"What about you, Bill?" I ask, after a while.

"I'm hangin' out for payday."

"Did you get a job?"

I register Bill's surprise at the enthusiasm in my voice, his mind trying to make sense of my excitement. "No," he says eventually. "Friday is when I pick up my welfare check."

My conception of "pay day" is now redefined and I am reminded how little I know about being on welfare. Bill informs me that surviving till next payday also means "eating out" at the van in the interim. Elsewhere in our gathering, Brad and his friends decide to leave and within minutes they are gone.

"What a whirlwind!" Suzie exclaims. We watch the boys peddle off on their bikes.

"I hope they don't throw that food." It is an outcome Maggie only entertains momentarily. "I don't think they will," she concludes. "I think they genuinely want it. How's Brad's form, though, talking about his 'woman!'"

"Has anyone ever seen this woman?" I ask.

No one has, and Maggie and I conclude she is probably a fabrication to obtain more food. For Suzie, the boys' inventions make them all the more endearing, whereas Maggie is concerned about their increasingly rough demeanor. "At least they say please," says Suzie, in their defense. The discussion sparks stories of the hardships and antics of kids who "live rough." Some have been known to sleep in the garden across the road, between the video and pizza shops. Compared with the park, which carries rumors as the haunt of murderers, it is well lit and not frequented by police.

"If I had to choose, I know where I'd sleep," says Maggie. "And it wouldn't be in the park."

Avoiding the park also means avoiding the problem of automatic sprinklers that turn themselves on in the early hours of the morning to soak unsuspecting campers. Some of these kids are also in the habit of 'borrowing' bikes to support their shuttle service between the city's shopping malls. If they are at one and decide to travel to another, it is a simple matter of selecting a bike from the racks, irrespective of whether it is theirs, and depositing it at their destination. It tends to leave the police with numerous reports of theft as well as overcrowded stores of impounded bicycles that are eventually sold off at auction.

With most of the crowd now gone, there is more room around the table and we encourage our remaining guests to move in closer.

"Are you by yourself tonight, Bill?" Maggie asks.

"Yeah. I'm looking after Owen's little brother but I've left him at the pool hall."

"At the pool hall? How old is he?" inquires Maggie.

"He's ten but he's OK. He was cleanin' the table when I left."

"Isn't he a bit young to be there by himself?"

"No. He'll be alright. He's much better there than where he was. The house was empty when he got home from school. His mother was out, probably sleepin' off a hangover somewhere or playing the pokies."

Bill tells how he saved the boy from his fear as the night had closed in around the empty house, but news of the rescue does little to console Maggie. We are also joined by David, a man in his early 30s, who sleeps in the park. By day, he hides his belongings in its trees. It is a common practice among the homeless, one that several have followed only to find that when they return their possessions are gone.

"You must have a good hiding spot, David," Suzie says.

"Yeah," he replies.

Among his treasures he has a tent that he sometimes erects to protect himself from the rain and the sprinklers. Unlike kids on the street, he sleeps well inside the park, moving from night to night to avoid detection.

"I'm going to court tomorrow," he says.

"What for?" Maggie asks.

"My friend's de facto hit him over the head. I thought I'd go along to see what happens."

I ponder the entertainment value of the law courts and whether David anticipates a repeat performance. But his visit has multiple purposes. He also has a fine to pay that was incurred for breaking the aerial of a police car; at the time, an expression of David's displeasure at the line of questioning by the occupants. "I was supposed to pay it today but I forgot," he informs us. "You better make sure you go tomorrow," says Maggie, "or they'll put out a warrant for your arrest." He is paying off the fine in installments and half of the debt has already been retired.

The next morning's local newspaper carries the front-page headline: "Vandals target more schools. Rooms wrecked, gear stolen." I recognize one of the sites as the area in which Brad and his friends frequent and I recall from the night before their tales of similar misadventures. The report identifies robbery as "a rising social problem" that requires a targeted approach from authorities. Reading the report, I tell myself that they are both easy and difficult targets. It is easy to blame street kids for their apparent disrespect for others' property; it is more difficult to address why they do it and what to do about it.

CHAPTER FIVE

Hitting home

It's Sunday lunchtime when Pam and I arrive home, having been out for the morning. The sky is clear and the sun pleasantly warm. Pulling into the drive we notice a teenage boy, around 14 years old, reclining on the front lawn outside the house directly opposite. Next to him are two bicycles. He appears quite relaxed and barely acknowledges our arrival.

"That's odd," says Pam, voicing her thoughts.

"What?" I say.

"Well, there are two bikes but only one boy," she replies.

"Maybe he's waiting for his friend inside."

"Well, that's odd too."

"Why?"

"No kids live on this street, none that I know of, anyway."

Our home is located in a small cul-de-sac in which almost everyone knows everyone else. Street get-togethers are not uncommon. Those who have children have seen them grow up and leave.

Once inside, we speculate that perhaps the boys—we see one but imagine that there are two—are grandchildren of the elderly couple who live across the road. Over the next hour we check on them—him—from time to time, through the front window, careful to avoid detection. No change. "Aren't they on holidays at the beach?" Pam muses eventually. I am at the point of going over to talk to him, to appease our curiosity, when we see a second one appear, carrying what seems to be a linen sheet. They mount their bicycles and ride off down the street. I watch from the front garden, wondering whether I should follow, still thinking it all odd. What would teenage boys want with a sheet? Eventually, I retreat to the comforts of home.

Later that evening there is a knock at the door. A young female police officer greets me as I open it. Almost before she speaks I realize what I should have realized a lot earlier.

"Evening sir. We're investigating a break-in across the road. Have you noticed anything suspicious in the neighborhood today?"

I feel an overwhelming sense of stupidity for not recognizing what was staring me in the face. I relate my observations of checked shirts, height, age, and the sheet.

"They took the covers off the pillows, to carry the stolen goods. The owners think they may have been black?"

"No, they weren't black."

I hear the same theory a few minutes later when I wander over to console our neighbors. They are distressed, naturally. The elderly lady, in particular, is mourning the loss of her privacy and her wedding ring of some fifty years.

"Did you see them?"

"Yes," I confess, sheepishly. "I thought they might have been your grand kids, waiting for you to come home." But my words are brushed aside in her pursuit of the offenders.

"I bet you it's those black kids doing robberies around town."

"No," I reply. "They weren't black."

My assurances seem to make little difference. They don't console her for her loss and they don't seem to register the innocence of the locals. Certainly, there are black offenders just as there are offenders within all racial groups, but being black does not predispose them to criminal activity. To think in this way relies on fuzzy logic invented as a short cut to explanation, in the race to apportion blame. "My house has been burgled, blacks commit burglaries; therefore, blacks burgled my house." At the mercy of such pseudoscientific "if-then" statements, they are sitting targets just as much as my elderly neighbors.

For those involved in such crimes, our adversarial system tends to position people as victims or perpetrators—you are either one or the other, certainly not both—with the marginalized all too conveniently positioned on the wrong side of this divide. Yet victims are not simply those whose property, possessions, or person have been violated. Often, they are also those who do the violating. My thoughts are more powerfully expressed by Matt Fallon (district prosecutor in Sydney, Australia, and guest on a recent talk show), speaking from his wheelchair about being robbed near Hyde Park by two street kids: "I realized that life ahead of them might be short, that the money they took from me might end up in their veins."

I think all this and yet recognize that they are unwelcome thoughts for my neighbors, at least for now. I recognize, too, that I am not on the receiving end of the boys' misadventures. I cannot condone their actions, but I am also reluctant to condemn them out of hand.

CHAPTER SIX

Matters of choice

Three guys are waiting for us as we pull up in the van. It isn't the swarm of hungry mouths we encountered last week, but Nick, in particular, is grateful that we have arrived, at last. We are here at our usual time, which surprises him. He thinks we are running late. He has been anticipating this moment for most of the day, filling in the intervening hours lying on the grass and sleeping in the afternoon sun. Now it is dark and the cool breeze that tempered the sun's rays has freshened into a cold wind. Nick hasn't eaten all day, perhaps longer, and is extremely hungry. "I think we can fix that," I tell him. We set up and organize a meal to satiate his appetite. It doesn't take him long to begin hoeing into the food. Nathan and John, the others in the queue, are here for the first time and are more reserved in their expectations of what we have to offer. "What would you like?" I ask John. The choices are somewhat diminished by the time I reach him. "You can have curried rice or curried rice."

"I'll have the curried rice," he replies, joining in the spirit of my offer.

"Good choice," I respond.

I feel in good humor tonight, more relaxed about my role and what to expect. Despite my good mood, I can't help thinking a little longer about the choices available to our "visitors." Choice is a much lauded notion in contemporary capitalist societies, sometimes I suspect, to appease more democratic inclinations. Yet, far from being informed by liberty and freedom, choices are always more constrained. We do not all have the same choices available to us and we cannot choose what is not on offer. Is it really a matter of *choice* that John and Nathan and Nick are on the streets, for example, as I suspect some would interpret their actions? My thoughts engage momentarily with this argumentative frame of mind, while I get a cup of coffee for Nathan and a second meal for Nick.

Nick is not the same Nick I met a few weeks ago. He is much older, in his mid-50s. He is a friend of David's, which prompts much of our initial discussion. "Have you seen David?" Maggie asks. "No," he replies. Maggie and Suzie are concerned that David hasn't been seen at the van since last Thursday, the day of his last welfare payment. Nick thinks he might have caught a bus to another city to visit family but he fully anticipates his return. He is guarding David's belongings, which are still in the park, hidden in the trees. Nick has also been sleeping in the park for the last three to four weeks. "I've got a few things to work out," he says, rubbing his forehead as if trying to massage his thought processes. His hands shake slightly and continuously as he resumes his meal. What can be seen of his face—beneath his full beard and long, unkempt hair—looks weathered. Like his hands, his head shakes. The combination makes eating a very deliberate exercise and seems to accentuate the tremor. I can't help thinking he looks the kind of person I probably would avoid anywhere else, navigating my way around him stretched out on a park bench or at the mall, for example—the archetypal "bum." It makes me wonder again about how genuine I really am. I think back to my recent encounter with Willie Nelson at the shopping complex when last these thoughts played with my conscience. "Getting it right" on one occasion doesn't guarantee it for all time.

A luxury four-wheel drive turns into the park. At first I imagine it has taken a wrong turn but it confidently approaches and pauses by the van, engine running. The driver is looking for David, and Nick is summoned to the window to retell his story. His absence is brief. The vehicle leaves and Nick returns to his seat and continues eating. They were looking for a different, much younger David.

"Little David?" Suzie says. "We know little David."

"Oh yes," concurs Maggie. "He was here last night."

Later I recall that his name is the same as the boy mentioned a couple of weeks ago who was confined to a hospital bed, suffering the consequences of solvent abuse. I wonder whether they are one and the same person. "Who were they?" I ask, returning to the events at hand. Neither Maggie nor Suzie has seen them before but Nick is familiar with their work. The driver is from another voluntary organization that watches out for young black kids on the streets.

Nathan and John have been relatively quiet until now. Suzie attempts to draw them into conversation. "Have you had a busy day today, guys?"

"Haven't had time to scratch ourselves," says Nathan, his acrimony clearly audible. Both are looking for work but there are few prospects. Maggie picks up on Nathan's sarcasm.

"That's the problem with being unemployed, isn't it?" she observes. "What to do with all that spare time."

"What kind of work are you looking for?" I ask.

"Anything we can find," is the standard reply.

John has experience as a builder's laborer but work has been difficult to find since the downturn in the market. Unskilled labor is the first to be discarded in difficult economic times. Nathan has previously worked as a motor vehicle detailer and as a DJ. Similar work is out of the question as far as he is concerned. He recently rejected an offer to detail motor vehicles when the remuneration effectively would have left him worse off than collecting the dole. "If you haven't got an education, they can pay you anything they like." It is an assessment for which I am sympathetic but I suspect the situation is probably worse than he realizes. An education does not necessarily grant people access to employment and high wages either. Maybe once, but not now. The recent jobless-led recovery in the US economy is a case in point. I also recall my brother's recent bout of unemployment, despite his qualifications.

"DJ-ing sounds like a glamorous occupation," I comment, exploring other parts of Nathan's curriculum vitae. "Where have you done that?"

"I've DJ-ed all around the country but the problem is the lifestyle."

Amidst the glamour, Nathan reveals a life of drugs and drug addiction. His own experience began early in life with speed and then moved to heroin. Six months in a "detox" center relieved him of the addiction, but he is back on speed. He is here to escape the drug scene of a nearby city but has found that it is alive and well here, too. Among other things, he tells me about his loss of appetite, a consequence of taking drugs. With my attention drawn to his physique, I also notice the tattoos creeping down his arms from under his clothes and the obligatory four characters—L O V E—one of each inscribed on the back of his four fingers. I contemplate the irony of having love with you wherever you go but for it to be so far out of reach. "I've been dry for four days," he tells me, but he is going it alone. There is little ongoing sup-port here for drug addicts who want to kick the habit. "Maybe you need to go to a city where you can get some help," I suggest, but he is not interested in pursuing that as a possibility. John is also here escaping a previous life in another city. "There is value in taking time out of difficult situations," I tell him, but I am conscious that some problems are difficult to leave behind.

"Is this food van run by a church?" Nathan asks. "I've tried to live God's way," he continues, "but I'm not at the moment. I'm usually the one leading others astray." He claims time spent studying in a theological college but I am unfamiliar with the one he mentions. I tell him he is welcome here but the air is now considerably colder and he and John decide to move on. Nathan takes with him the meal he is yet to finish. We wish them well and they merge into the night.

Suzie and Maggie are in conversation. It gives me opportunity to speak further with Nick. He has recently moved here with his partner, Phoebe, to be closer to her family. Yet, it is this closeness that is causing problems. Their house is continually filled with the to-ing and fro-ing of people; some have taken up residence with them in their already crowded home. Every day is a celebration of sorts, accompanied by alcohol, and Phoebe and Nick are often drunk. Money has also become a problem. They have fallen behind with their rent and their electricity bill is now overdue. Disagreements have developed between Phoebe and her adult daughters and verbal fights are a regular feature in their interactions. Nick wants to move on but his de facto is unconvinced of the seriousness of their situation. He has taken refuge in the park but says he is getting too old to be "bummin' around." Yesterday he stubbed his toe—his sandals provide little protection—and he has been unable to get around to the city's other sources of food and shelter. He will try to get across town tomorrow, he says, to a mission near the local hospital, which supplies a hot lunch. There he will seek some relief for his injury, if it is still causing him pain. In the meantime he hopes Phoebe will decide to leave with him. If she doesn't, he is unsure what he will do. "I might go and find a warm spot to sleep in," he says, finishing the last of his curried rice. He gathers his belongings together and leaves us to ourselves.

It is still early in the night and Maggie is concerned that we will have food left over. The meals can't be reheated so we either have to find someone to give them to or dispose of them. We watch the horizon but no one approaches. Nick's departure reminds Suzie about the Nick we met a few weeks ago. He was back at the van last Thursday. Apparently, his girlfriend might be returning soon so his relocation to the other side of the country is on hold. Suzie hopes his girlfriend doesn't return. She is unimpressed with Nick's views on women and how he relates with them. Maggie thinks that he is probably just goading her, looking for a reaction, but her analysis provides Suzie with little consolation. "I hope Brad and Dylan turn up tonight," she says, changing the subject. "I really like those guys and we've still got all this food." Thinking of them reminds her of a book she is reading about street kids in Brazil. "It's about the kind of things we face on the van, only ten times worse." She tells us stories of children living in abject conditions and the author's work among them. The book has captured her imagination and she admits to reading it at every opportunity. It reminds me of similar work by Urban Neighbours of Hope (UNOH) in Klong Toey, the southeastern slums of Bangkok, Thailand.

A figure approaches in the distance; I recognize it as Bill. Maggie and Suzie are less sure that it is him, but they are pleased that at least some of the remaining food won't go to waste. "Would you like to take a couple of extra meals with you tonight, Bill?" Maggie asks, now that he is closer and easier to identify. "Sure. That's why I came late," he explains. He has been coming to the van for a few weeks now. He knows our routines and has learned to turn them to his advantage. On some nights it could be a risk to arrive at the end of our shift but lately we have not been overrun with custom and there is generally plenty of food. I set him up with some curried rice. Maggie prepares some bread while Suzie makes him a cup of coffee.

"The kids think it's worse than watchhouse coffee," she says, "but it's all we've got."

"It's not as bad as that," he replies. "I'm sorry to say I know from experience what watchhouse coffee is like and this is nothing like it."

I recall his account of "doing time" and wonder whether he has had any more bills to pay. I also remember that he is remarkably knowledgeable about what happens on the streets, so I prime him for information.

"How's that kid you were looking after last week, Bill?" I ask. "Owen's little brother."

"Oh, he was real happy. Someone bought him a bike so he was jumpin' all over the place when I got back. But then they sold it a couple of days later. They must've run out of money for the pokies." To me, it has "stolen" written all over it.

"Have you seen Lucas?"

"No, he hasn't shown up."

"So you think he's gone back to his mother's?"

"Yeah, probably."

"Where are those three you brought along last week? We haven't seen them tonight."

"Don't know if they're still together very much. I think Sally's startin' to wise up to 'em."

"Why is that?"

"Ashley and Thomas keep on walkin' off and leavin' her but they don't tell her where they're goin'. The other night I came across her at a phone box. She called out when I came past 'cause she was too frightened to leave and didn't know how to get back. They'd just taken off while she was on the phone and left her there. I walked her home and got the manager to let her in. She doesn't have a key to her room; they've got it. On other nights she can't get in 'cause the manager is out and they've taken off somewhere. I think she's thinkin' about goin' home."

The conversation moves on to other things; Bill always has a few stories to tell. Some seem extraordinary. Even though they are technically possible, they border on the edge of credibility. I sense that Maggie is frustrated by them, by their suspect authenticity, but she tries not to let her misgivings show. She is uneasy generally about Bill, that he seems to know so much about the kids on the street. I don't share her intuition but it puzzles me to see Bill's blend of middle-class values and street savvy.

"How's the search for work going?" I ask. He has been to the meatworks today to fill in an application for work.

"It'll be hard to get work there," Suzie remarks.

"Not really," he replies nonchalantly, "not if you know how the system works. I've worked at a meatworks before. You just have to get on to their casual list."

"How long will that take?" I ask.

"About two weeks, after the physical and all the blood tests. They check you out all over before they'll give you a job."

As Bill talks, Maggie begins to pack up. It is late and time for us to leave. Suzie prepares a parcel of food for Bill to take with him, enough for another four meals.

On the return journey Suzie and I chat about her work, teaching at a local school. She has a student in her class who deliberately separates herself from her peers, sitting at a distance from them during class work. The girl also refuses to answer questions and Suzie catches herself constantly chastising her. Meetings with the girl's parents have not improved the situation and Suzie fears she is simply making things worse.

"I've told her I'm here to help but it doesn't seem to make any difference."

I listen and sympathize with Suzie's situation before speculating about whether a solution might lie in how we name the problem.

"It's tempting to view it as a behavioral problem," I tell her, "but I wonder what the solution might look like if we understood it as a structural problem."

"What do you mean?"

"What if you were to change the way students engage with learning in your classroom, the sources of knowledge and the conditions under which it is accessed? Maybe your students could be involved in deciding how to arrange their activities and even what is to be learnt and for what purposes. What if you were able to give prominence to the particular knowledge and skills this girl already has, to give them importance within the classroom?"

I have let my academic discourse slip out. Still, I see Suzie's mind mulling over the possibilities and the difficulties that such an approach might entail. She appears interested in the ideas but maybe she is just humoring my lack of knowledge about what happens in the "real world" of classrooms and schools. My mind returns to the real world we have just left behind in the park and the conditions that constrain the choices people are able to make in society. I think about Nathan's commentary on education as the gatekeeper to higher wages and "better" lifestyles, and then about the way schools are structured to privilege certain ways of knowing and being. As in classrooms, choice only seems to figure in this account if you are willing and able to accept the constraints.

CHAPTER SEVEN

Behind the scenes

It's Saturday morning, the only mutually convenient time in the week for the team's monthly meeting. Entering the room, I recognize Maggie, Suzie, Debbie, and Liz, but the other four are new to me. Debbie initiates the introductions.

Gary, Liz's husband, is in his late 40s and has a back injury that keeps him out of full-time work. "I'm the handyman," he says. "If anyone wants anything fixed they usually ask me." Graham is a pilot for the local air rescue service. The emergency nature of his work doesn't allow him to get out on the van very often. "He's my fill-in man," says Debbie, "when I need someone urgently and he's available." Cynthia, Graham's wife, also works on the van and is studying music and art at university, between caring for her grandchildren and doing other things within the community. Then there is Angela. "I've never come across people who are so supportive of each other and of the kids on the streets," she tells me. "I just mouth off about it everywhere I go. It doesn't matter whether they want to hear about it or not!" She has recently cut back on her hours at work in order to spend more time learning about drug addiction and how to help addicts kick the habit. Ray arrives just as these introductions conclude. He has been finishing off a few chores around his home and apologizes for being late.

"Well, what we'll do first is to talk about any problems that anyone has with how things are going," says Debbie, opening the meeting.

Ray—last to arrive but first to speak—seizes the opportunity to express his disquiet. He tells a story about three young boys, around ten or eleven years of age. They arrived at the van recently, expecting a feed while waiting for their mother to finish her shopping nearby. It troubles him that we are being treated as a childminding service. "What do you usually eat at home?" he asked them. "Steak, fries, vegetables," they reply. They see no reason to hide their regular diet or even its regularity. He resolved to hand over drinks but instructed them that the food was reserved for "the poor and needy." "Go and get your mother," he advised them on their departure. "If she is happy for you to have some food, we can give you some." They didn't return.

Ray's account reminds Gary of Gavin, a 13-year-old boy who appeared at the van one night claiming that his mother and father had moved house without telling him where they'd gone. To add to his story of woes, he'd been expelled from school and was living in a burnt-out house somewhere. But then, the following Saturday, Gary saw him again, this time at McDonalds conversing with people with very similar features to his own. "They might not have been his family," Gary says, "but they sure looked like it." By all accounts, Gavin hasn't returned to the van either.

"It sounds like something Cassie would do," says Maggie.

"Oh, Cassie's doing well," interrupts Cynthia. "She's doing really well now. I saw her the other day heading off to school on her bicycle."

"I saw her on her bike, too," says Maggie. "She was parked outside the amusement arcade and it was 10.30 in the morning."

"Sounds like you've been taken for a ride, Cynthia," says Suzie, making a clever pun but also voicing an emerging theme.

I recall a similar theme expressed by my younger brother recently while we walked the streets of the nation's capital, in search of a restaurant. Our respective work commitments had placed us there overnight so we decided to meet up for dinner. As we strolled from one closed eatery to another—it was early in the week and few restaurants were open—a young guy approached us from the shadows. "Can I have $2 to buy a burger?"

"I've only got $1," I told him, my wallet bursting with plastic but short on cash. "But you're welcome to that."

He took the dollar, along with another offered by my brother, and then faded into the night. "I'm never quite sure what to do in those situations," my brother confided. "I always feel like I'm being taken for a ride."

"You probably are," I replied. "But I think it's a risk worth taking."

Actually, there was little risk. Those two dollars prized from our pockets had no impact on what we eventually ordered and ate that night. Still, there remains a fear of being sold a lie, which can loom larger than the financial loss. A similar issue now appears to weigh on the minds of some members of the team who want to "make a difference" but are worried that their efforts might be subject to abuse.

"Do we serve everybody and that's it, or do we just hand out food to young kids or homeless kids?" asks Liz, expressing what some are now thinking. "Because they're not all young kids anymore. Where do we draw the line?" Liz refers to the team's initial plan to invest their energies in addressing the needs of street kids rather than replicating the work of other agencies assisting an older group of disadvantaged people.

"We should give to anyone in need," replies Angela, drawing her own line in the sand. "Homelessness is not just a function of age," she counsels.

"And it depends on what we mean by homeless," says Debbie.

She launches into a story of a young guy who has recently sought food at the van, arriving in a near new car. "To look at him," she begins, "you might think, 'why can't he feed himself?'" But the car had been secured on time payments just before he recently lost his job. After paying for his rent and car from the dole, he is left virtually penniless. Not to make the payments would mean the car's repossession by the finance company as well as restricting his access to future work opportunities. Maggie expresses her sympathy for his predicament and that of others who arrive in motor vehicles, some whose car doubles as their bedroom. But she is also mindful of how this looks, how others—particularly the van's benefactors—would view the sight of vehicles pulling up at our "diner."

"What if we invited the local politician to see the work we are doing and then all these people arrive in cars?" she asks. "I can imagine him asking himself why he's supporting us."

She is also uneasy at the prospect of having to explain all this—the childminding, the deception, the motor vehicles—to those who cook and donate meals for the van, free of charge. Maggie's ruminations and the team stories give the group cause to reflect on the difficulties of determining who is worthy (and who isn't) of receiving assistance. Several argue that the complexity of people's lives on the streets needs to be made more widely known, particularly to those who provide support to the van. It is a new educative element to their work that they now contemplate, directed at an audience not living on the streets. And it raises the level of the discussion to a more complex understanding of needs.

"It's not just food and shelter they need," asserts Angela.

"I agree," says Graham. "I had a friend once who had no material needs but ended up committing suicide because he had a whole lot of emotional needs. People come to us to get a meal but actually it might be just an excuse to have someone to talk to. They can be in need without being homeless." His comments receive thoughtful nods from around the room.

"Apparently Craig has returned home to his parents' place but he only goes there to sleep at night," adds Angela. "There's virtually no conversation going on and it's really tense. He doesn't really live there. It's just somewhere to sleep. So in that sense he's homeless. It's not his home. It's just a house."

I recall a similar definition offered by Jordan (see Chapter 16), appearing on national television talking about his personal experience of living in a homeless shelter: "If you can't walk around in your kitchen half naked cooking dinner or something like that, well you really haven't got a home."

"Bill's in a similar position," observes Ray. "He's got a roof over his head at the hostel but during the day he can hardly find anyone there at all. People only go there to sleep at night."

"Besides," says Suzie, "there's no point sharing his problems with those people if they've all got the same problems as him. They're not going to have solutions and they might not even be interested in hearing about his problems."

I'm not so sure I agree with Suzie's assessment. I ponder the potential in it to render Bill, and others like him, dependent on us and others like us. All of us need support at various times in our lives but the idea that professionals and paraprofessionals are the only ones who have "the answers" and that others in the same predicament don't, strikes me as a little paternal. In fact, we—that is, those we represent—may well have contributed to the problems ascribed to Bill, and those he represents. Nor are we without our own problems. I weigh up how best to go about raising these concerns but, thankfully, Debbie interjects and moves the conversation on.

"I ask people from time to time, 'What would you do for food if we weren't here?' Some say, 'We'd steal it.' Or, 'We'd go without.' So, we are really meeting a need. But I think their emotional needs are more important, whether or not they can afford to buy their own food. They won't change unless they've got the emotional support to change. By us being there, we provide much more than just food. We provide them with someone to talk to, someone who's interested. The homeless and least advantaged in our community have problems far bigger than where their next meal is coming from. They need people to talk to as much as they need food. We'll probably get taken for a ride or used by people from time to time, but handing out food also presents us with opportunities to talk to them. We wouldn't get to see those people otherwise, if they didn't come to the van."

"I agree," repeats Graham. "But I'm not sure how we can do it. Some nights I feel as if we're like a train stop in their journey, on their way from one place to another. Along the way they take a short detour. The train stops at the station, which is us, they all get off to eat before they all get back on again and away they go. One night, they were all talking about whose place they were going to and where everyone could sleep, who was going to have the sofa, etc. Then, the next night, they'd be at someone else's place. It's like they're on a runaway train and we're just a whistle stop along the way. I'm not knocking the lifestyle. I'm just not sure how we can break in and contribute anything else apart from the food."

"Oh, I think it can be done," says Ray. "But we need to be more sensitive, particularly on the slow nights when there's only one there or even just a couple. If one of us is talking to that one person, then probably the other two need to be talking to someone else or doing something else, because otherwise it's a bit like an interview for a job or a police interrogation. They can feel like they're being grilled!"

"Suzie's usually the policeman on our shift, asking everyone what they're doing," says Gary.

Suzie appears oblivious to Gary's chastising. Instead, it reminds her of something she recently heard and now shares. "The charges against Liam have been dropped," she says. "He still has to go to court for the previous offence, though."

"When I first went out, not many of them told me anything but after a while they started to open up to me," confides Cynthia.

The meeting's narrative momentarily loses its structure. Some quiz Suzie further about Liam and the charges he faces. Others continue with how best to engage in conversation with those who come to the van. And some attempt a reconciliation of the two. The groups' attention is finally united around Debbie's account of police recently arriving at the van, in search of someone to "assist with their inquiries." She has since been to the station to complain. "If they think the police might turn up, they won't come," she says, referring to our regular visitors. It raises another dilemma for the team—how to handle situations on the fringe of the law—and it diverts Ray's attention to his encounter with a young black kid, probably David, inhaling toxic fumes. "I'm not giving you any food while you're chromin'," he had told him. The boy then walked off, not far away, where he sat down and continued to draw in through his nostrils paint fumes emanating from his plastic bag. After a while, Ray went over to him and said, "You really shouldn't be doing this. It's not good for you." "Why?" he answered. "No one's interested in me. No one loves me. No one cares about me. No one's going to be bothered whether I do or don't."

There is an audible pause in the conversation at the end of Ray's story. Even though helping these very people is the reason the team exists, each feels a degree of impotence in knowing how best to respond. Eventually, Maggie acknowledges, on the group's behalf, that it's tempting in these situations to say that we care. I add that I think many of us do in our own way, but I'm not sure we fully appreciate what it means to live their lives and, therefore, what care really means. Is what we feel empathy or just sympathy? What is the best way to help? Is there such a thing as a "best way"? Gary notes that there is a great deal of camaraderie among those who live on the streets. The street community can be very supportive, looking out for each other, visiting each other in hospital and so on, so there is some uncertainty over how far the boy's claims of being alone in the world should be believed. According to Debbie, there is also a downside to this community spirit, which is difficult to penetrate at times. She is reminded of a boy who used to regularly come to the van and then, without warning, suddenly stopped.

"Do you know where he is?" she had asked his friends.

"He's left town," some had said, although his exact destination varied according to whom she asked. Finally it emerged that he was in jail.

"Why didn't you tell us he was in jail?" Debbie had inquired. "We could have gone to visit him."

"Well, we didn't know why you wanted to know. We were just lookin' after him, protectin' him."

"They don't always know our agenda," Debbie concludes. "And that's probably one of our biggest challenges."

"They might think we have links with the government or with the courts," ponders Angela.

The time set aside for the meeting has expired and Debbie draws the conversation to a close. She consults her notes on the issues raised, including the need for more meals on Monday nights and more hot water for coffee. Dates are discussed for the next meeting and minor amendments to the roster are announced. Coffee and cake follow, along with the chatter of small groups, most continuing conversations initiated during the meeting. By chance more than design, Ray, Debbie, and I mingle together in a corner of the room. During our own review of the meeting, Ray's frustration spills over.

"We keep having these meetings where we talk about what should be different, but we just go round and round in circles. Nothing happens. We keep on doing the same things. Nothing gets resolved. It's not only the kids on the street who don't know our agenda."

CHAPTER EIGHT

Not for profit

Two guys are waiting for us when we arrive in the van. I greet one, Nick, and introduce myself to the other. "I'm Jack," he reciprocates. "We met last week." I examine him more intently, noting his closely cropped blond hair and beard, but memory of a previous meeting eludes me. "I was here with Nathan."

"Oh, are you John?" I respond, relieved that I have remembered him.

"John. Jack. Either, it doesn't matter."

"Sorry Jack, I didn't recognize you. Have you had your hair cut?"

"Yeah. I had an interview for a job."

"As a builder's laborer?"

"No, doing some agricultural work."

We continue in conversation as I help Maggie and Suzie set up the table and chairs and unload the food. Nathan, Jack's companion of last week, has found some support for his drug problem. He has gone to a farm in the country, removed from the drug scene, in an effort to "stay dry."

"How long does he plan on being there?" asks Maggie.

"Until he's off the drugs and he finds God," Jack replies. I hand him a meal of savory sausages while Suzie makes the coffee. She is in conversation with our other visitor.

"Have you been to see David, Nick?"

"He's in hospital."

"Yes, I know. Have you been to see him?"

"No, I haven't been able to get there."

"I went to see him yesterday. He's OK but he's still very weak."

"Can you say hello to him for me. Tell him I'm minding his stuff."

"I will. In fact, I mentioned your name to him but I'm not sure that he remembered you. I think he was a little tired. But I'll tell him you're looking after his things."

"Thanks."

I hand Nick a container of curried rice and sit down beside him. Again, the deliberation and intensity with which he approaches his food reminds me how close he lives to the edge of life, not just on the edge of society.

"I feel much better than when I arrived," he says, replying to my query.

"Things haven't been going too well?" I probe.

He pauses before speaking and swallows, not just to relieve his mouth of food but also, it seems, giving himself time to think how to word his reply, even whether he should. "I've messed everything up, basically. I've messed up my life, at least the last ten years of it, and I can't change it. I can't rub out the mistakes and do it all again."

"Everyone makes mistakes," I tell him. My counsel sounds hollow even to me.

"I'm just not very good at life. It doesn't agree with me." He is amused by his own turn of phrase, at likening life to an allergic reaction or to a question of taste or ability.

"Is there something particular that's worrying you?" I ask.

"Just about everything. For one, I've got three sons, the oldest is around 30, and I've missed spending time with them. I've just made so many mistakes. I've messed up my life and I can't go back and change it."

"What about Phoebe? How are things with her?" I search for something that might provide a sense of a future but it is not the kind of future Nick had imagined. Phoebe is still not convinced of the need to move on and Nick is having difficulty relating to her "dysfunctional family," as he calls it.

"I went over there the other night and all we did was get drunk. Then her daughter's de facto walked in and said, 'What's he doing here?' I can't use the expletives he called me. He decided that I was the scum of the earth and started belting into me. He has just got out of prison so he's no angel himself. But Phoebe just said to me, 'Oh, you'd better go.' I can't cope with it. Actually, I cope by getting drunk. That's what I do." He contemplates whether he should visit his sister for a while. She lives in another city. I tell him that makes good sense, to give Phoebe some space to think things through and himself an opportunity to deal with his alcoholism. "I know all that," he says, responding to my concern for his health. "I'm just not ready to do anything about it yet."

"Anyway, what do you do for a living?" The discussion has become a little too intimate for Nick's liking and his question enables him to shift my "official gaze." It provides a welcome jolt to my thinking, reminding me again of the surveillance critiqued in Foucault's *Discipline and Punish*. I am aware, too, that this is the first question I've been asked about my life away from the van. "I've got a friend who does that kind of work," he says, taking up the theme of my reply. "We've been friends for years. We used to share a place together when she was at university and I was a taxi driver." We talk about the "good old days" of college life for a while, before the smell of fire in the air interrupts our discussion.

"It's probably in the hills on the outskirts of the city," I say. "I hope it burns down some of those rich people's houses," mutters Nick. The prospect gives him some perverse pleasure, that the rich might also be experiencing pain. In my mind, it is also reminiscent of Hugh Mackay's (1993) account of the desires of an emerging underclass to retain the middle-class dream of social egalitarianism. Nick's vision for the houses of the rich would certainly place him on more equal terms. "I can remember a few years ago helping some of our friends save their houses from fire in those hills," says Suzie. Suzie's father is a lawyer and her friends' houses are probably exactly the ones Nick has in mind. "I really miss being able to burn things in the back-yard nowadays," muses Maggie. "There are some things that are best cleared up by a small fire."

"I'm starting to worry about you, Maggie," I say, jokingly.

"It's probably very cathartic," says Nick. His comment is greeted by blank stares and Nick senses that his audience is unsure of his meaning. "You should know what that means," he says to me. "You'd have to have a good command of English in the work you do. Doesn't it mean to cleanse oneself?"

"It does," I reply, "but I'm not sure that academics are very good at doing that." I suspect it is a more common complaint.

The night is growing colder and Nick's mind turns to the whereabouts of his blankets. He recently stowed them in one of seven hiding places he uses around the city, but he was drunk at the time and now can't remember where they are. He decides he will use David's blankets tonight, given that he is in hospital and is not in immediate need of them. Suzie is concerned that Nick should return the blankets in the morning. He assures us he will and then ventures further into the park to find the tree where David hides his belongings.

Jack seems more willing to speak now that Nick has gone. He pulls a book from his bag in which he stores some crumpled photographs of his

18-month-old son. He is an attractive boy and we make appropriate comments as the pictures are passed around. They are the high points of Jack's story. Until recently he had rights of access to his son but Jack's replacement—his girlfriend's new de facto—does not take kindly to his visits. "He knows which buttons to push," says Jack, and the result is often violent. A restraining order is now in force and if Jack is to see his son again he must prove to the court that he is not usually prone to violence. I am surprised by his account, given his placid nature, and I wonder what would constitute such proof. "You don't seem like the violent type," I tell him. "It's in every parent to protect their kids," he replies, "no matter how old they are. If I see that guy hitting my son I'm going to protect my son every time, no matter what it takes. What annoys me is that the law takes no notice of that. That guy's not even his father and he can stop me getting access to my own son." I listen, recalling Nick's earlier story and wonder whether it is in the early stages of being repeated. Maggie recites her counsel of work and responsibility that she gave to a different Nick several weeks ago, as a way for Jack to demonstrate to the courts his good intentions.

The night is well advanced and we are concerned, again, about the prospect of food going to waste. A car enters the park, turns and departs, but not before its headlights outline the figure of a boy approaching on his bike. Glenn is a regular visitor, although I have not met him before. I discover later that he is 16 years old but his appearance suggests he is much younger. He is so softly spoken I am forced to move close to hear his response to my rendition of the menu. Even hearing him provides me with little direction. He is noncommittal and I feel I am making his choices for him. As he sits, it is difficult to avoid noticing that his limbs are constantly in motion. The night air is cool but his shiver seems exaggerated by comparison. "Are you cold, Glenn?" I ask.

"No." He mouths his reply more than voices it, yet his lips barely move and it is the shake of his head that really conveys his meaning.

At first, I wonder whether he is on drugs but Maggie later confirms my subsequent impression that he is incredibly shy. I try to establish conversation but later realize how much it sounds like I am interrogating him. In the interim I discover he likes to sketch. I wonder whether his interest in art is code for graffiti, although Suzie encourages him to bring some of his drawings along next time for us to see. "Jackson went to court today," he adds, but he doesn't know what the charges were or the outcome. It almost seems as if it is said just for the sake of having something to say, to satisfy our curiosity. He also tells me he hopes for a job in horticulture or as a ranger in a national park. A welfare agency is arranging an interview for him in the near future, but the prospect is not overplayed and this casts doubt in my mind over how firm are the arrangements.

His reserved nature reminds me of another one of my nephews of a similar age and disposition. I tell Glenn about him, about his recent motorbike accident and stint in hospital having injured his spleen. I also tell him about my nephew's philosophy on social interactions, at least my interpretation of it; that there is enough talk in the world and he doesn't feel the need to add to it unnecessarily. It makes speaking to him on the telephone really tricky and probably frustrated the nurses at the hospital. I know it frustrated his teachers when he was in school. My stories bring a smile to Glenn's face. So, too, do my efforts to furnish him with more food. Twice I offer cake and custard but he is not seduced. I reflect on the change from our initial encounter; me less assuming, him more discerning. Finally he agrees to an apple slice I find among our supplies. He is amused by my subsequent claims of triumph, not a Pyrrhic victory but spurious nonetheless given that he has accepted the slice, in part, to keep me quiet. With prize in hand, he mounts his bike to leave. It gathers speed quickly and I ponder how differently he moves on his feet compared with our conversation. I imagine that it would be easy for some to think he is intellectually slow, but I sense there is more going on in his mind than he is ready or willing to reveal. I contemplate how he might have fared at school and how he does now, now that he is subject to the strictures of other institutions. I am reminded of Basil Bernstein's (1971) account of "elaborate" and "restricted" speech codes and how schools privilege those who talk freely and eloquently while consigning others to lower status.

Scott, Emma, and Martin arrive. We are introduced, but I have little to do with them other than to hand them a meal. Maggie is soon engaged in conversation, particularly with Emma and Martin, while Scott latches on to Jack who decides to stay a little longer. Their arrival is closely followed by that of Bryce and Jake, two guys in their mid-30s. They are clearly drunk, swaggering as they make their way—just—to two vacant chairs. We serve them hot food and drinks, Suzie noting how they take their coffee. Jake is particularly taken aback by the hospitality he receives. "I wish everyone was like you," he says to Suzie.

"I don't," says Maggie.

It is my turn to be taken aback by Maggie's rather blunt advocacy for diversity. With Suzie, she joins me in laughter. "Only you could say that and get away with it," I tell her.

"That's because Suzie knows that I love her, warts and all. Isn't that right Suze?"

"Of course," she replies, with no hint in her voice of being offended.

Jake is still pondering the mysteries of our generosity. "Most people are only interested in what they can get out of you," he observes. It is an indictment on our society for which I have some sympathy, concerned as I am with a growing emphasis on individualism and self-interest, particularly since capitalist markets have come to dominate social relations and almost everything else that moves. Perhaps my mind is just fresh with the events of the recent World Economic Forum on globalization. As an antidote, I remind myself of all the things people do without any concern for financial gain.

The hour is late. We stock our remaining customers with "takeaway" food, exhausting our supplies of garlic bread and containers of curried rice and spaghetti bolognaise. I apologize to Martin that I haven't had a chance to speak with him.

"That's alright," he says. "We can talk now." He tells me he is desperate to reenroll at college, having reapplied every year for the last eight since being excluded. "I've had 21 jobs since then, and now—because I'm 45 and because I have no qualifications and so little experience in any of them—no-one will employ me." We talk as I load the van. "Perhaps we can do lunch sometime," he says, as we part. He joins Scott and Emma in their car and they drive off.

On our return trip I raise the issue of discretion with Maggie. "I felt like an interrogator at times tonight," I confess, "especially with Nick and Glenn."

"Yes, I know what you mean," she replies. "It's a bit of a trap. You want to talk, and questions are a natural way to strike up conversation, but you don't want to be prying into people's personal lives, uninvited. They need to be able to receive a meal without feeling obliged to reveal their innermost secrets and problems. And it's not as if we've got it all worked out either."

I am chastised that perhaps I have been charging for the food after all and resolve in the future to avoid such trades in the emotional economy of the street.

CHAPTER NINE

Opportunity knocks

Pam and I are out walking. It is one of those balmy summer evenings on which the sun refuses to set. We are drawing close to home when I spot Elvis in the distance. It is his signature black ten-gallon hat I notice first. Rather ungraciously, some at the van think he has a propensity to talk through it. His leather boots, black trousers and jacket, white shirt, and a small red bow tie complete the picture. He could have just stepped from a cowboy movie set but instead he is making his way from a nearby house to his car parked on the street.

"Hi Elvis," I say as we approach.

"Hello. Hello…Hello," he replies.

His greeting is only intended for the two of us but he has a tendency to "three-peat" words and phrases. The first two occur one after the other in quick succession, the third typically follows after a brief intermission. He is also adept at answering his own questions, a characteristic not unlike that of politicians or even academics. For Elvis, it is his way of making sense of the world, which he freely shares with those within earshot. He fancies himself as something of a pseudophilosopher and will wax lyrical about global and local politics, drawing on insights one could imagine—at least, from how he talks—he has gleaned from luminaries with whom he is personally acquainted.

Recalling Elvis's questioning mind, my thoughts wander back to one particular night when Nick had inadvertently collected a spider's web while walking through the park. He arrived vigorously brushing his hair and clothes. Elvis came in late on the performance. "What are you doing that for, Nick? What are you doing that for? Oh, maybe you're a bit cold. Are you a bit cold Nick? You're a bit cold. I know what it's like to be cold." Nick was frequently perplexed by such mutterings, induced by Elvis's mental illness, and he struggled to know how to respond to them, particularly when he himself was "under the weather." The latter was often cause for further inquiry. "How are you Nick? Aren't you feeling well? You're not feeling so well?

Why aren't you feeling well? What's the problem? Have you been ill?" On such occasions, the frustration on Nick's face was palpable. Which question to respond to first and whether he should even bother to respond at all seemed to provoke extreme mental anguish within him; a stupor that always had the potential to boil over into rage if someone around didn't defuse the situation. I have shared something of Nick's frustrations, although perhaps not so intently, and share them again as Elvis resumes our conversation:

"Do you live near here, Trevor? Which one is your house? Is that yours over there? You've got a nice garden. Is this your wife? Which one of you is the gardener?"

"We live a little further up the street, Elvis," I reply. "What are you doing here?" I ask, getting my question in before Elvis hits me with another.

"I'm looking for Gary. Do you know what his last name is? I can't find his name in the white pages. It's not there, I've looked."

There is a rule on the van about giving out names and addresses so I am a bit cagey about my reply. Besides, the barrage of questions allows me to choose the one I want to answer. There is not much time to choose, however, before Elvis resumes the conversation.

"He's got a guitar he says I can have. He said I could have his guitar. That's what he said," Elvis continues. "I've got a gig at the hotel on Saturday."

Along with philosophy, Elvis counts performing country and western music among his talents, although he doesn't let his love for the genre restrict him from engaging with a good song from another one. Predictably, Elvis Presley is both his idol and his identity on the street. In the past, he has supplemented his disability pension with small performances and busking around the city, but now he is without the tools of his trade. A companion of Elvis's and with similar demeanor, Jamie, arrived very excited at the van one night with what he thought was the solution to their idleness.

"Hey, Elvis. Elvis, what do you think? What do you think if we taught some kids how to play the guitar during the school break? All these kids, they won't have anything to do." Apparently, he'd spied a guitar in a pawnshop for $30. "I saw it in the window. It's got nylon strings and we could teach them all how to play."

Elvis's initial reaction had been pensive, weighing up his response. I also was lost in thought, visualizing the scene: Elvis, Jamie, and a herd of kids donning Texan hats and strumming $30 guitars on the city's street corners.

Seizing the break in conversation to press home the virtues of his grand plan, Jamie continued.

"What do you think, Elvis, what do you think? It's an opportunity. It's an opportunity." And then, as if to clinch the deal, "You know, Elvis, you've got to put something back into society. It's only fair."

"Listen, pal," Elvis said eventually, "I've got to take care of number one. I've been doing these free shows for too long and now I've got to start taking care of number one."

Conversations with Elvis (and Jamie) frequently had this surreal, almost comical quality. The words are familiar and yet they also sound out of place, as if they belong to someone else. I have decided that mental illness, common on the streets, seems to speak in these clichés. So too young offenders, as I encountered on my first night on the van. For me, it is the institutional speak coming from their own mouths juxtaposed with the reality of their lives that gives these conversations their hollow ring.

"I can get Gary to call you if you like," I say to Elvis. "Or I'll ask him if he can bring the guitar to the van tonight. How's that?"

It satisfies Elvis's mission for the time being but it doesn't end the conversation, not immediately. We undergo several more exchanges on politics, musicology, and perfume before we see him off in his car.

CHAPTER TEN

Troubled minds

"I drove the van last Friday, so it's your turn to do the honors tonight." Suzie holds out the keys for me to take. I am happy to accommodate her; it gives me a sense of making a contribution. She slips into the passenger seat and we depart. "How's school?" I ask. "I don't know how I'm going to make it through this term," she confides. "They're a really difficult class. I was brutally honest with them the other day. I told them I almost didn't come back after the holidays because they are so terrible. I've decided to take a few weekends off this term." "That's probably a good idea," I tell her. We continue our conversation from a few weeks ago about a student she finds particularly difficult. "How's she going?" I ask. "Terrible," Suzie replies. "She seems to have leadership abilities but she uses them to lead others in the wrong directions. She distracts the whole class simply by walking across the room! I think she could have some psychological problems but I've also been told that she is very much like her mother." They are issues I decide to let ride for the moment. We arrive, shortly before Maggie, and set up for the evening.

No one is here to greet us, although I notice in the distance a body lying on the ground under some trees. I decide to investigate and am both relieved and startled to find the man asleep but talking; relieved because his nocturnal chatter signals that he is still alive and startled because his words are so audible.

"He shouldn't have hit me. I'm a kind person. I help people."

"Are you OK, Nick?" I interrupt.

"What?"

"Are you OK? Sorry to wake you but I thought you were probably waiting for us. We've got some food if you want some or you can just go back to sleep if you like."

I am uncertain whether I have rescued him from a disturbed sleep or whether I have just disturbed his sleep. He moves as if to rise to his feet but he is quite groggy and settles for a temporary position somewhere between lying and sitting. I inquire again after his well-being and he grunts a reply I take to mean that he is not injured or in pain. Consoled, once more I extend him an invitation to dine at the van and then rejoin Maggie and Suzie who have been watching from a distance. "Is that David?" Maggie asks. "No. It's Nick," I inform her. We watch as he staggers to his feet and gains his balance. He appears to hover momentarily in one position, like a helicopter looking for a place to land. "Oh, please, no," remarks Suzie. She realizes his intentions from his body language but her request falls on deaf ears. With his back towards us, Nick finds a tree and relieves himself. It doesn't interrupt his stagger, however, and I suspect he waters more than the tree.

"You've found Nick drunk tonight," he announces, as he zigzags his way towards us. He arrives at the same time as, but not with, two others: Shane and Vanessa. We furnish them with meals, their choice of curried rice, curried sausages, or roast beef and vegetables, augmented by buttered bread and flavored milk. Shane and Vanessa are in their late teens and quietly spoken. Suzie initiates a few exchanges with Vanessa before Nick addresses the two of them, as if he has only just recognized them. His voice is loud and his tone accusing.

"Did you give that money to David?"

"Yeah," Shane replies, his voice barely audible.

"Eh? I gave you some money to give to David. Did you give it to him?"

"Yeah, we gave it to him," says Vanessa. "He said to say thanks."

"Shane. Shane," Nick persists. "Did you give David that money?"

"Yes," says Shane, this time louder and with a more definite nod of his head but still with little hint of being intimidated by Nick's verbal onslaught.

"You better have given it to him 'cause if I find out you didn't, I'll break your neck."

Maggie is concerned by Nick's demeanor and his threats of violence, and reminds him that he doesn't talk like this when he is sober, that it is not part of his usual character. She assures him that Shane and Vanessa are honest young people and would have given David the money. Nick seems adequately appeased or perhaps distracted as the conversation turns to David's whereabouts.

"He's gone to the southside of the city, near the fountain," says Vanessa.

"Shane," Nick begins again. "Did you give that money to David?"

"Yes," says Vanessa, her voice raised.

The night air is now punctured by mosquitoes, also inflicting their presence on us. Nick seems to be oblivious to them but the rest of us are becoming increasingly irritated, not just with Nick.

"I'm allergic to mosquitoes," Vanessa informs us.

"I suspect that most people are," I reply, handing her some repellent.

"I'm allergic to mosquito repellent," says Shane.

Vanessa is five months pregnant. She and Shane have no food left in the house and plan to visit the van for the next few nights until their next welfare payment falls due. News of their financial predicament raises Nick's ire again but Maggie is quick to squash a repeat performance. "Here, Nick. Drink this." Maggie hands Nick a cup of strong black coffee, laced with sugar. For now, it quenches his anger along with his thirst. Suzie also pours some coffee for Shane while I tempt Vanessa with something more to eat.

"Would you like some yogurt, Vanessa?" I ask, after she turns down everything else I offer. My younger sister, of similar age, is a big fan of yogurt and I imagine that it could go with the territory.

"What's it like?" she replies. At first I'm taken aback, surprised that she has not had yogurt before, but then I realize she is referring to this particular kind. "The last one was a bit lumpy," she adds.

"Well, this one says it's extra smooth."

Vanessa takes the yogurt and, with Shane, decides to leave. They are pleasant young people and, on departing, express their genuine appreciation for the food. Nick continues to harbor some dislike for them but it seems unwarranted, at least from our brief exchange. I have become quite fond of the kids we meet on the streets. Most are grateful for the food and the company. They seem to respond well to the interest taken in them, the time spent in listening to their stories, however far fetched, and regularly reveal their resourcefulness and wit. For me, it has become a pleasant way to spend an evening, although I am mindful that we approach this encounter (and leave it) on very different terms.

A car arrives, its panels furnished in various hues and stages of disrepair. Now stationary, its engine continues to run, lurching from one rotation to another and to such extremes it appears in danger of stalling. Finally, the driver accepts the inevitable and turns the engine off. Its headlights remain on, however, and continue to illuminate the park around the van. Two figures step from the vehicle, bringing with them their own fold-up chairs. One is barely seated when he launches into his usual verbal torrent.

"What's the story? What's the story, Trevor? What's a story we can tell Nick? What story can we tell him?"

Nick is nonplussed by Elvis's barrage of questions, particularly since he seems to be the subject of them and that they are unconnected to anything he has said or done, at least as far as he can determine. While Nick rummages around for a response, his hand movements endeavoring to aid the process, I tell Elvis that I can't think of any stories right now and hand him a meal instead. Undeterred, Elvis continues to scratch his head in search of possibilities, mumbling likely storylines that he first tries out on Jamie, his companion, before eventually creating his own diversion.

"What about a song? Let's sing Nick a song. What do you want us to sing, Nick? What about this…'And I said to myself, what a wonderful world' … 'somewhere, over the rainbow, you'll find me'…'everybody, loves my body, sometime'…"

Egged on by Jamie, Elvis is now in full song, delivering one-liners, sometimes more, from his personal rendition of the "greatest ever" pop songs. He moves seamlessly from one to another rarely missing a beat, only to provide commentary on the acts which made them famous and when they debuted on the world stage. The knowledge he demonstrates on the subject and the speed with which it is delivered is impressive and rivals Dustin Hoffman's *Rain Man* although much of it I accept on face value, not being fully conversant with the material. Throughout, Jamie claps his hands and joins in on the lines he can remember and even on some of the ones he can't. He laughs in appreciation of the wit he perceives in Elvis's variations to the lyrics and at one point contributes one of his own. "Strangers in my nightie," he sings and then bursts into laughter again. Nick, however, is not taking too well to being serenaded. He has sobered up some since the night began, but still finds it difficult to interrupt Elvis's performance. Frustrated by his unheeded attempts to make himself heard and to restore some semblance of sanity to the occasion, he finally rises to his feet and advances on Elvis. As he approaches, Elvis senses the danger and falls silent.

"Watch out, Elvis," Jamie warns. "Watch out. Watch out. Oh sorry, sorry… sorry."

Just at the point of grabbing Elvis by the collar, Nick baulks. "Phew. You stink!"

The scent—or at least its detection—is enough to repel Nick back to his seat and bring Elvis's musical performance and associated commentary to an end. But it doesn't silence him completely. Now with the spotlight on his odor, Elvis feels compelled to defend himself, to dispel any false impression of foul smells emanating from his body. In between diversionary asides—about the problems he is having with his car, his dole payments going astray and his parents' restrictions on his career—he explains that the aroma is derived from the mix of fragrances he has been sampling at the local department store.

"It smells like the country," he explains. "It's 'country cologne.' I've got a gig on Saturday. I have to smell the part, be ready for my audience."

Jamie laughs in appreciation of Elvis's preparation. In others, his laughter might appear exaggerated given its raison d'être, but Jamie's eyes are wide open and his whole body joins in on the act.

"Elvis, have something to eat," I say, adding some bread to go with their meals.

He and Jamie obediently turn their attention to the task, cramming their mouths with as much food as possible, although some escapes down the side of Jamie's face and onto the ground. It is as if they expect the supply to run out, like children in large families scrambling to ensure their share of the delicacies before they disappear at the hands and mouths of their sibling rivals. I am concerned for the two of them. In days gone by, both would probably be resident in institutions or in special homes under 24-hour care. Now they fend for themselves, in receipt of disability pensions and various kinds of community support but, by and large, alone and isolated.

Tonight, Jamie wears a bicycle helmet, the peak of his baseball cap protruding from underneath. Two thin electrical cords extend from each ear and join at his chest where once there was a jack but now are bare wires.

"Have you been out riding, Jamie?" I ask.

"Oh, no, no," he replies, dribbling ketchup onto his left shoe. "Sorry, sorry…."

"So, why the helmet?"

"Oh, I wear it everywhere." He tells the story of his recent assault in the park, prompting him to seek protection under his helmet from repeat occurrences.

"What about the cord?"

"That's from my walkman. Hee hee hee. Oh, sorry, sorry. Ha ha ha."

While I have been consumed by the antics of Nick, Elvis, Jamie, Suzie, and Maggie have been attending to Joe and his companions; ten to fifteen guys in their mid to late teens. Joe has recently been discharged from hospital, having had his stomach pumped after taking an overdose. He has found it hard to keep down much food since. He is also distraught over the suicide of his friend who recently hung himself from the branch of a tree in the park, the spark for Joe's own suicide attempt. Few in the group seem interested in conversing about the suicide, or much else. They eat their fill and depart. Trent, however, lingers behind, looking for a conversation.

"Hi Trent," I say.

"Hi."

"What have you been doing?"

"I got engaged."

"That's great. When?"

"Last week. We're not really engaged yet. The ring doesn't come till Wednesday. And the party's on Saturday."

"When's the wedding?"

"I don't know. I don't want to get married."

"OK. So you just wanted to get engaged?"

"I didn't want to get engaged either. It was her idea. She wanted to get engaged to me."

"What's her name?"

"Olivia. I can't remember her last name."

Trent usually comes to the van accompanied by his carer. They change daily, working on 24-hour shifts, but the carers as a group are also temporary company. The work does not seem to sustain them for long before they move on. It is difficult to get to know them, not just because of their transience. Some will join Trent sitting around the van but most hang back, waiting in the agency car. Trent is alone tonight. He has slipped the gaze of his carer on the pretext of walking to the shop to get some milk.

"This should corroborate your alibi," says Maggie, handing him a container of milk. "But you really should head back. Your carer will be really worried."

"Elvis, Elvis," says Jamie. "What do you think? We could give him a lift. It's an opportunity!"

Elvis takes the opportunity not only to "make a contribution to society," as Jamie puts it, but also to escape Nick's simmering dark demeanor. For his part, Trent is pleased to have the company. With extra meals in hand, the three of them head toward Elvis's car, Jamie now contemplating the prospect of offering it to Trent for use as the bridal car. He recalls seeing some white ribbon at the $2 shop, which would make ideal decoration. Elvis has some empty soup tins at home that he could also attach, along with a sign. He also offers his musical services for the reception, at a reduced price, of course. To the surprise of all except its occupants, the car starts without incident and they depart, still in conversation about plans for the wedding.

The evening is drawing to a close when Frank arrives. I am almost certain we haven't met, but I ask just to make sure.

"Hi, I'm Trevor. I haven't seen you before."

"No, I haven't been here long."

"What brings you here, then?"

"I'm here by accident."

I can't help smiling at his response. I imagine it fitting in well into a stand-up comic routine that begins something like: "A funny thing happened to me on the way to the park...." I refrain from sharing my amusement and am thankful later that I did.

Frank is in search of his daughter. He is being given the "run-around" by a government agency about her whereabouts and the search has him shuttling from town to town. He produces a photo from his wallet. It is worse for wear but still reveals a pretty young girl of 11 years of age. Her mother, Frank's partner, has recently died and the girl, experiencing the onset of puberty, has been forcibly "transferred" to her mother's sister by a child welfare worker. Frank and his wife's family do not get along. He recounts their allegation that he chooses to live on the streets and that it's no place to bring up a young girl. In his defense, he argues, "No one wants to live like this. No one wants to live on handouts. Some might, but I don't."

His thoughts are distant, perhaps focused on the girl in the photograph, and his words are slow and deliberate, as if he is on medication rather than under the influence of alcohol. In the course of our conversation he reveals he is in receipt of a pension, although he doesn't elaborate on why he qualifies. His circumstances remind me of the film, *I am Sam*, but I suspect in this case a similar outcome is outside the realms of possibility.

"If they're not careful, I'll do something they'll regret," he promises.

"Well, don't commit yourself to doing anything that *you* might later regret," I respond. "Maybe you can ask them to allow you to talk to her on the phone, so you know she's OK."

It is a truly sad story but I am also aware that sad stories are not always accurate, although I have no reason to disbelieve him. Neither are sad stories easily resolved. The prospect of Frank regaining custody of his daughter seems remote, given what he has revealed about his circumstances.

As we pack up for the night and our visitors depart with our remaining rations of food, I note that in many ways it has been a troubling night. Mental illness and anguish do not sit well on the streets, yet they feature in the lives of more than some might expect. I suspect we are ill equipped to adequately assist them at the van, beyond the food and company we provide, and this in itself is disconcerting. I am reminded again of the troubling conversations at our recent team meeting and the lack of answers we have to many of these questions.

CHAPTER ELEVEN

Means of escape

A crowd is waiting for us when we pull up in the van. There are more than I have time to count and it is another scramble to set up and distribute the food. I fall into my usual pattern of waiting on our guests as they make their selection from our menu, while Suzie makes a note of their names and Maggie sees to the drinks. At the end of my round are two young boys, Mitchell and James, 13 and 12 years of age, respectively, although, like others I have met on the streets, they look much younger than the ages to which they admit. James, in particular, could easily pass for 10. Their youth makes them stand out even though others around are young themselves, in their mid to late teens. We sit on the ground and engage in conversation while they eat. They talk freely, James in particular.

"What brings you guys here tonight?" I ask.

"We just want to get away from our older brothers," they reply.

They tell familiar stories of the hostilities exchanged between siblings but I sense that being on the street is something of an adventure for them, more than just a means of escape. We talk about school—both should have advanced to higher grades but have been "held back"—and about what they want to do when they eventually leave. Mitchell hopes to be an artist. He prefers painting landscapes on canvas although he has recently been sketching some native fauna. James wants to work on the land, riding horses and herding cattle.

"I want to follow in my grandfather's footsteps," he says. It sounds an odd phrase from someone so young.

"Have you ever ridden a horse?" I ask.

"Yeah, at my grandfather's place," he responds, but he is vague about the equipment and skills involved. He tells of his grandfather's expertise at breaking in horses and of his uncle who works as a clown at the rodeo, distracting the bulls to allow their fallen riders to escape. "My grandfather gives me lots of things," he says. "I'm the spoilt one in the family."

His adult account is amusing but I am also taken by his efforts to impress on me his privileged position, particularly within his family. It seems to spark Mitchell into similar accounts of prosperity. He tells about a painting of mickle proportions that his father sold to the local hospital for $20,000.

"He's got more than that now," he says. "You can make a living out of painting, you know."

"It would be good if you could," I reply.

It is difficult to know how much of these stories to believe, given that their circumstances do not seem to match the wealth they claim; doubts which Maggie later confirms. Yet I sense they want to be taken seriously. I decide the smattering of adult phrases in their discourse is a function of this, irrespective of the truth of their accounts.

"Are you here every night?" James asks.

"The van is," I reply, but I am aware he has been before and I suspect the intent of his question is slightly different. "I'm usually here on Mondays," I add. "Maybe you could bring some of your sketches sometime, Mitchell." I recall suggesting something similar to Glenn some weeks ago but as yet without result.

My attention turns to two other young boys, Stuart and Cameron. Stuart is in Grade 6 and Cameron in Grade 7, although as yet he hasn't returned to school after the summer.

"So, what are you doing instead?"

"Oh, just hangin' around."

"Don't you want to go back to school to be with your friends?"

"Nup."

Our conversation is cut short by a slightly older Brad, who interrupts us with his insistent plea for a plastic bag. He reeks of paint fumes and his speech is slow and deliberate. A spray can protrudes from his pocket and I am fairly certain of his intentions.

"I need a plastic bag."

"What about something to eat instead?" I reply, knowing full well that his appetite is likely to be depressed because of his solvent abuse. It is as if my question has halted him in his tracks. His gaze is in my direction but is focused past rather than on me. His pupils are unusually enlarged, over-compensating for the night light. He gives the impression that his mind is deliberating on my offer but I am inclined to think otherwise. After what feels like an eternity, but is probably no more than a minute, he responds.

"I need a plastic bag."

"Don't give him one," says Timothy. "He wants it for chromin'." Timothy is one of the throng of youth still milling around the van. He is a little older than Brad, about 16 or 17, and seems to enjoy the respect of his younger charges. Perhaps the beginnings of a moustache under his nose commands their admiration.

"Yes, I think you're right," I reply.

"I need a plastic bag," says Brad again.

"Here," I say, holding out a container of food. "Have some of this."

He is unimpressed by my offer and retreats to the outskirts of the crowd, seeking from other fringe dwellers what is not forthcoming from me. Suzie is there, making her usual inquiries among the crowd.

"Hi Brad. Have you seen Dylan?" she asks.

"I need a plastic bag," he replies.

"Don't ask me. I'm not giving you one. Have you seen Dylan?"

Brad mumbles something, perhaps discernible to Suzie but not to me, and then seeks solace away from our enclave, under a tree. I have moved on, too, offering food to those in the crowd who want it. In my travels I come across Joe who seems brighter this evening, perhaps because he is in the company of Kirk and Amy. He has recently acquired a tattoo and, with Kirk and Amy, they display their finery much like birds pruning their feathers in preparation for an elaborate courting ritual. Together, they constitute their own mobile art exhibition, which would have appealed to Mitchell's earlier interest in painting landscapes if he was still around.

"How much does it cost to get a tattoo?" I ask.

"We get 'em for free," says Kirk.

His body is a living canvas for his girlfriend who offers her creative skills free of charge in exchange for the opportunity to trial new designs. But Kirk has almost outworn his usefulness, his body offering few remaining spaces. The tattoo now decorating Joe's upper arm is a new design, developed by Kirk's girlfriend, in search of creative expression. The skin is raised given the recent addition and Joe offers me the opportunity to feel its texture. My interest in body art prompts Amy to flaunt her new lip ring. My attention has already been alerted to it, clashing with her spoon while eating.

"You should put it on the other side of your lip," I remark. "Given that you're right-handed. Is it hard to take out?"

"Brooke took hers out when she went to court," she replies. "But she forgot to put it back in. It's closed over now so she'll have to get it done again."

Amy's lip ring is only her latest in a line of bodily adornments. Earrings, forbidden wear when I attended school, are now passé by comparison to her tongue and nose studs and navel ring. I decide not to ask if or where she has plans for others, deflecting attention to the ring through Joe's eyebrow. In the ensuing conversation they tell of a friend who connects chains between his nose and earrings. Till now, I have been mesmerized by tattoos and body piercings—the attraction that others see in them as much as the things themselves—but then, in my peripheral vision, I am distracted by a glimpse of Brad standing near the front of the van, camouflaged against the dark backdrop of the park's trees. It is clear that his earlier search has been successful. Periodically, he buries his nose into a plastic bag and inhales. With him is Kyle, also inhaling.

A commotion now erupts between Brad and Timothy, recently arrived on the scene. He confiscates the offending baggage from Brad and Kyle and, with Maggie's help, stashes them under the van's front seat. Dispossessed, Brad lunges at Timothy and the two of them roll around on the ground's rough stony surface. Others are now on the scene, egging them on. I yell at them to stop but it falls on deaf ears. Brad has gained the ascendancy and sits astride Tim with his hands clasped around his throat. With Tim gasping for air, I decide now is the time to intervene. I grab Brad under the arms and pull back. His grip is surprisingly easy to dislodge and I suspect he was happy for the altercation to end. It is easier to save face when someone else stops the fight than if you stop it yourself. With some persuasion from Maggie and Suzie, the crowd disperses, returning to the food and blow-by-blow descriptions of the fight. Suzie leads Timothy off to find him a drink and a comfortable seat.

"I'm cold," says Kyle.

"Yeah, we're cold," Brad concurs.

Maggie unlocks the side door of the van and produces a box of sweaters. Rummaging through the box, Kyle is unmoved by the selection until he happens on a woollen vest. To taunts of "Hercules," he strips off his jacket and shirt and wears the vest as an undergarment. Brad, however, is not enticed by the clothes on offer. "I want a blanket," he says, looking through the van's passenger window. I suspect it is a rouse to gain access to the front seat, to regain possession of the plastic bags.

"We don't have any blankets tonight," says Maggie.

"I'm going to sleep in the back of the van, then," he replies.

"You've got no chance of doing that." They are Maggie's words but they also reflect my sentiments.

"It's all right for you," Brad continues. "You've got a house to go home to. You've got somewhere to sleep. I don't have anywhere." The truth of his words cut right through me. I feel an overwhelming sense of guilt. Sleeping rough holds no glamor especially on cold nights like tonight.

"All I meant was, this van is full of stuff. When we pack up everything, there's nowhere to sleep."

"He's sleepin' at my place tonight." Timothy has returned to the scene of the scuffle, to take charge. "They both are."

Their drama resolved for now, Timothy, Brad, Kyle, and several others leave. All except for Brad, they thank us for the food. In his usual style, he expresses gratitude to no one. From those who remain, I recognize the girl I met on my first night on the van, the 15 year old with the 2-year-old daughter. I learn that her name is Brooke. She says she has been hanging around on the street with her brothers and cousins for protection against her stepfather.

"How's your little girl?" I ask.

"She's got eyes you can't refuse," she replies. "But she reminds me of the past. If she lived with me I'd probably cut her up or cut myself. She's better off with my aunty."

Our conversation ranges from the weather to whether her stepfather should go to court. Included are her plans to escape to the coast—somewhere safe—to live with relatives who are professional fishermen. After some time her two companions decide to leave and invite Brooke to go with them. She decides to stay, to talk with Suzie. I recall Ray's counsel from our recent team meeting and leave the two of them alone. While Brooke and Suzie chat, Maggie and I gather up our belongings and pack them into the van.

The night has been arduous and I am ready to make my own escape. I look around the park, one last time. It is quiet now, not the commotion that first greeted us when we arrived. The kids from the streets have dispersed, out of sight, out of hearing. I have learned a great deal over the past few weeks, not just about those who live on the street and what that means but also about myself. "Few, save the poor, feel for the poor," writes Letitia

Landon in her poem, *The Poor*, but I wonder how to increase the numbers of the few without creating more of the poor.

PART TWO

Professional opinion

I remember thinking that I'd become a "screaming mother" but that's because I was a mother; I wasn't a paid professional. I hadn't had the education to be a professional. I always expected a lot more out of them than what I received. (Jenni)

CHAPTER TWELVE

Contemplating life on the streets

You need to be aware that kids don't live on the street for nothing. Kids don't do drugs for nothing. Kids don't harm themselves for nothing. There's always a legitimate reason. Otherwise they wouldn't do it. (Welfare worker)

In this first simulated conversation among professionals working with youth living in the shadows of society, the focus is squarely on what the young person's life entails: what their home life is like, what drives them onto the streets, the dangers they encounter there, and how they fare at school. There are attempts at explanation as well as description although both are offered through the eyes of onlookers, albeit with considerable experience. For the most part, each provides a sympathetic and sometimes heart-wrenching account of the considerable difficulties encountered by marginalized young people and, at times, they point to the influence of issues outside the control of those concerned. There is considerable agreement in their stories but also subtle disagreement. How these professionals understand and explain their own involvement is also explored. The chapter concludes with a case study of Thomas: an illustration of the complexities in negotiating a difficult life.

Driven onto the street

What do you think it means to be homeless? Why are there kids living on our streets?

I don't really think that there are many people who don't have somewhere to go. They might not want to go there because they might have had a fight with a family member, but it would be very unusual to come across someone who genuinely had nowhere to go. There are a lot of people who stay with friends for a couple of weeks and then move on and stay with other friends, but in terms of being someone who does not have a bed for the night if they really wanted one, there are not all that many people of that description. There are not that many people who are genuinely homeless. (Magistrate)

The way the legislation is written, we shouldn't have any homeless kids living on the street. We shouldn't have any because governments make provision for them. However, you still get kids who can't be at home and don't want to be involved with the department or who don't want to be in care and run away. So, while there shouldn't be any homeless kids—while there should be a place to sleep for all of them—they are still out there. (Welfare worker)

We get kids, particularly in the 14 and 15 age group, who will sleep at a friend's place for a couple of nights and then another friend's place for a couple of nights. They're doing the circuit. They have a place to lay their head each night but they don't have a home, even though they might go home to where their parents live maybe one night a month. (Youth worker)

With the kids I work with, if they have a choice they will always go home. Most of the time that's their first choice. But if they can't be at home, then most would prefer a foster family to being in residential care. Residential care drives kids onto the streets time and time again. (Welfare worker)

People will tell you that kids go into group homes and become wards of the state because they want to. I've got to say that over the 20 years that I've worked with kids in that situation I have only ever come across two kids who really left home voluntarily. In most cases, home had left them. The situation at home was so appalling they could no longer safely stay there. (Teacher)

Some young people come to me and say, "Oh, it was my choice. I wanted to leave." But you have to ask, "Well, why? Why did you want to leave? What was so wrong at home? What's wrong with your relationship with mom or dad or your brothers and sisters that means you don't feel connected to home?" I think that's probably a key issue for a lot of them, just that lack of connectedness. (Social worker)

Many have very sad stories to tell about why they are where they are. A lot of us don't comprehend what they have been through in their lives to get them where they are. We might see a dirty old man on the streets who is shabbily dressed, but we don't realize just what that shabby old man has been through to get him to that point. (Youth worker)

Some of the young guys I talk with have experienced abuse from their parents. Their father might have beaten them up. Other times they've had a reasonable upbringing but they have just made huge mistakes. Then they get caught up with alcohol and doing drugs, things to take their minds away from their problems. You can see that they would have struggled at school, which hasn't helped them gain employment. They don't have a high opinion of themselves, they don't have high motivation and they experience cycles of depression between drinks, drugs, and broken relationships. (Community worker)

Very common in a lot of the women that I see are relationship issues related to broken families, single mothers—a lot of them are single mothers—domestic violence and a history of abuse. Many have experienced trauma in their childhood, particularly domestic violence including sexual, physical, and emotional abuse. A number also have grief and loss issues that they really haven't been able to deal with properly before coming to prison because they've been self-medicating with drugs and alcohol. (Psychologist)

I first meet them as young adolescents from single parent homes, living with mom or dad, and there are issues around divorce or separation impacting on their relationship with mom or dad. Their behavior can be quite inappropriate and mom or dad will say, "I'm not putting up with that anymore. Get lost." For some it's not a problem because they just weren't connected with home anyway whereas others will go kicking and screaming because they really want to stay at home. It's all very scary for them. Mom and dad are saying that they can't be at home or they don't want them to be at home. Then they tend to fall into two different categories. Either mom or dad will say, "No, you can't come home now," or they'll say, "No, that's it. You're never coming home." We've even had parents who have packed up and left. So, when the kid gets home from school, there's nothing left except a note saying, "I've gone. I've put $500 in a bank account. Don't bother trying to find me." That's happened probably three times since I've been here over the last two-and-a-half years. (Social worker)

I know of cases where kids have been told not to come home that night. Maybe mom's got a boyfriend staying over for a while and wants a bit of privacy. Maybe there's some sort of party going on. Maybe there's been an argument and the child's been told to get lost for a while. (Youth worker)

There are a lot of kids that are out late, that do what they like. They don't even bother going home after school. They just stay on the street, hang out with friends, smoke a few joints, and do gangy things. Their parents really don't know where they are a lot of the time. I see a lot of that with the boys that I'm working with. It seems to be quite a pattern with kids that truant. (Welfare worker)

A lot of them say that they go out on the street to get away from their brothers and sisters or because their parents are going out. So they have the freedom to go out as 14 or 15 year olds and get together with friends. They start with things like smoking and then try to get some alcohol. They'll get an older person to go to the bottle shop to get them something to drink. (Community worker)

Most of these kids come to our attention in adolescence because that's when parents decide they can't handle it any more. No one wants to lose a 5 year old but parents are much more prepared to say, "Get out," when you're 14. Often these kids haven't had a history of severe abuse, it's more a history of neglect. At 14, they're on the street, dumped out of home, feeling that, "No one loves me, no one cares about me." All of a sudden they have to look after themselves. (Welfare worker)

I think a lot of my clients have experienced homelessness at one time or another and certainly a number have said that they've lived on the streets, supporting themselves through prostitution. But really, the women that I meet, some of them in particular, tend to seek out other people to look after them. Most of their partners are older, sometimes quite older, and are also in prison or have been in prison in the past. It's a fairly common thing for these women to have partners who are maybe six to ten years older than they are and when you inquire further you find that the relationship often began when they were 15 or so. Some of them can be quite reliant on those relationships, which explains why they don't leave them even when they become violent and why they intend to go back to them after they get out of prison. (Psychologist)

Crime is also a major part of their lives, often triggered by boredom but also as a way to survive. A child who is 11 years old and wandering the streets at night is naturally going to get into some sort of mischief with that many hours to fill. Maybe the first couple of times he's out there he might just hide somewhere, cowering, frightened, but then he'll get a bit more adventurous and that's when he can get into trouble. Often younger ones like that are picked up by older ones who will encourage and support them but then they'll also use them as the one to put through a window to perpetrate a crime. (Youth worker)

The youngest I've ever dealt with was 11. He was assaulted because he'd been holding drugs for a dealer who came back to claim them, to find that they had been smoked and they were no more. So he belted the crap out of this kid and the police were called and they called us. (Welfare worker)

They tend to commit crimes in order to be able to support themselves, to get the money that they need. For the majority it's things like theft, armed robbery and property offenses, and a good proportion of those would be committed with the intention of obtaining money to pay for drugs. Actually, there's a lot of drug possession and trafficking offenses as well. (Psychologist)

There are other concerns on the street you've got to be aware of, too. There are people seeking to take advantage of kids on the streets. The most at-risk kids on the street are those with intellectual disabilities. Many of them have a history of trauma and abuse because they don't have natural protective instincts and people just take advantage of them. Often adolescent girls who have an intellectual disability are very provocative and will attract perpetrators like you would not believe. I know quite a few girls with mild intellectual disabilities and social and emotional problems who are on the streets. They are at high risk because they really don't understand. And they're not likely to. (Welfare worker)

At various times there are also assaults and bashings, so there can be a real fear on the streets that something big is about to happen. Almost every week they talk about it. Sometimes things do happen. When we go out on the streets we talk to the security guards to find out about what's happening. (Community worker)

Life on the street has a culture of its own, I think. It has its own language. It has its own rulers or dictators and its own laws. For kids, I think it provides a sense of family. It's different from everyday life because there are different rules and different players, but it gives them a sense of security. A lot of the kids that I work with have a long history with street culture and know who is who. They have worked their way up in status, have a sense of belonging, and go there for consoling and comfort when things aren't going well at home. Because they make the rules, it also provides the young person involved with a sense of justice. "An eye for an eye" is common in a lot of the street talk that I've heard. "You do that, this happens. You do this, they'll beat you up." Whereas in their families and in the institutions they encounter, they can't always see justice. Justice can be a very difficult concept to come to terms with as an adolescent, especially for those who experience extreme circumstances. They can be the victims of abuse but in real life it's the parent with the power. It's the parent who has to be proven guilty before anything happens to them. For kids, "It's unjust that I have to go to court, sit all day and wait for a magistrate to tell me what's going to happen in my life." "It's unjust that my mom takes my dad's side, not mine." "It's unjust that mom's boyfriend can tell me to leave." There's a lot of injustice in the real world for kids. But on the street, "This happens to me and I see results." "I have people that look after me no matter what. I have people that watch my back. I have people that provide my needs. I feel happy. I feel safe," often with the help of substances. (Welfare worker)

Substance abuse

To what extent do drugs and substance abuse play a part in the lives of street kids and marginalized youth? What is the impact on their lives?

At some particular point they have been introduced to an addiction and then they've got to support the addiction and they don't have any way out of it except to continue on in it. Heroin is so cheap now—it's cheaper than marijuana—that most kids who want to get involved with drugs just go straight to it. I haven't had much to do with speed. It's more of an issue for middle-class kids, I think. Most kids are just into heroin. They may be involved in marijuana but they seem to go straight into heroin. (Magistrate)

We give out needle packs for drug users and diabetics but you don't see as many overdoses as you would expect, in proportion to the number of packs we give out and we give out a lot. You would think we would have more overdoses given the needles we give out. However, we do have lots of people who come in suffering the effects of drugs. One of the biggest is alcohol. Speed is also common, but not heroin. We have heroin addicts who come in but they're not usually having any problems from that. Typically, the heroin addicts we see are trying to get off it rather than being under its influence. (Nurse)

Alcohol and probably marijuana are quite prevalent in schools and are socially acceptable among students. Glue sniffing and aerosol sniffing aren't so widely accepted. None of them are acceptable to schools, of course, but among students, drinking and marijuana and smoking are quite widely accepted. They're almost like symbols of peer acceptance, you could say. We have had students who have said they've experimented with inhalants and they might experiment with them a couple of times but that's generally it. The ones that are very seriously doing it, we either don't know about because they're quite good at hiding it or because they're not going to school. I know of about nine or ten students over the last three years who we have spoken to about it and there's probably about three that we have supported through the struggle. Each of those young people had other quite serious issues to deal with and predominantly they have been black kids. It has a dramatic effect on them. They just lose the plot. They don't go to class. (Teacher)

We see some kids who have been sniffing paint, but not a lot. They're also young black kids but that's not to say they're the only ones doing it. They're the only ones I've seen. We had some recently who came in with paint all around their mouths and all over their clothes. They were just off their heads, displaying bizarre inappropriate behavior, and they couldn't sit still for very long. One claimed he had a dislocated finger and then that it was burnt but there was absolutely nothing wrong with it. His finger was perfectly normal. (Nurse)

I don't know whether many people have seen someone who's on paint, just the way they can't function properly. Apart from the visible signs of having the paint on their hands and carrying a plastic bag, they have a really distinctive smell about them, about their breath. When they're inhaling paint the breath that they exhale isn't quite normal. I remember one guy who was continually sniffing paint, chroming as the kids call it. He'd sometimes wildly swing a chair around and at other times he'd be just really dopey-eyed. His eyes would be wide and unfocused. I've seen his father a couple of times and he looked quite a respectable sort of man but his two sons and his older brother had absolutely no respect for him. The older boy was into harder drugs whereas the younger one was on the paint. His life was quite a mess and he was constantly in trouble with the police. They could quote his name, date of birth, everything, just off the top of their heads simply because they had arrested him so often on various charges. (Youth worker)

There's almost no case that I can remember where a person's got into trouble with the courts without being involved with drugs and when there is one, you make a big thing of it. You almost never send them to jail if they haven't already been involved with drugs because they're just going to get into more drugs when they go to jail. Their addiction fuels the crime to obtain the drugs. Generally it's burglaries or armed robberies. (Magistrate)

When I worked on the streets we knew there was a big drug problem especially with crack. It was well known that there was a lot of crack being sold and that was part of the reason for the fights because they were just bursting for one once they'd had their dose. Everyone knew there were drugs involved and that the kids hadn't been drinking. You could just tell. You could talk to them normally for a while about their problems, what they've been going through, what they've been to Court for or their problems with their family, and then they would be off. All of a sudden their demeanor would completely change. Their eyes would glaze over, their whole body would tense up and they'd want to fight some person going down the street. It's quite scary when you see what happens, how they can relate to you so well one minute and then they just completely change and want to tear their shirt off. They were just not in control of their emotions. Either they would be very high or very low, very physical or very calm. (Community worker)

In my experience, people on drugs are much different than homeless kids who are not involved with drugs. They are much less able to be relied upon to engage in any initiatives their counselors might want them to undertake for a court case or anything. Just turning up in court is a big achievement. (Magistrate)

It's the same with the ones who are on alcohol. They can change so quickly. They can flare up over nothing and then five minutes later they don't even know that they've done it. They're just sitting and talking quite normally to you, then something might trigger them again and you have no idea really what's done it. All of a sudden they've changed again. Whether it's something that's been said or some thought process inside their own mind that sets them off, I don't know. (Youth worker)

They're too drunk to tell you anything anyway. They're normally lying there in their own vomit or throwing up or they're that drunk that what they're saying doesn't make sense. Normally, the only ones who tell you about their stories are those who have overdosed and they're usually relationship problems. It's because they're down and out. It's because they had a fight with their partner or something. (Nurse)

There's one young boy named Matthew whose father is constantly drinking. Because he's in that state most of the time and he's so disruptive, he's often not allowed into the accommodation where Matthew's mother and two children are staying. It's particularly affecting Matthew's life. He's become a firebug. He's very angry and deals with it by destroying things. He's very rarely at school and when he is there his teachers find him very hard to cope with, but maybe they don't know what the home situation is. It's easy to say, but there needs to be some understanding by the people around him that his situation is different than theirs. Not many of us have to live in that situation with a father who is constantly drunk and is absolutely comatosed on the ground, not knowing what's going on around him. At other times when he's not in that position, he's yelling and carrying on. It's very rare that you see him in a really sober frame of mind. Matthew will be ten this coming weekend. Already he's a very angry young man that I can see in prison in years to come if something isn't done to change his life now. (Youth worker)

By the time they've got to me, all of these things are much less important than what they've done. To get into my court they have to have committed some very serious crime. All I really hear is the history of addiction, which is generally just a progressive history, and the fact that they've got no real way out. I never hear about them when they're in the beginning stages of addiction, or very rarely would I see anyone who's just in the beginning stages. (Magistrate)

Without the comforts of home

What's home like for young people at risk? What can they reasonably expect?

Most people see home as the house that they live in, but a home is a lot more than that. A home is somewhere you feel loved and wanted and accepted, and where you can talk to someone about your problems and get some feedback. When you're in a household as a child with adults who are providing a house to live in rather than a home, I think they're as homeless as the actual ones who are out on the street. (Youth worker)

That's where most of my kids are at. You might have a house to live in, but that's not necessarily home. Even though they have a bed, they're definitely homeless. (Welfare worker)

I know of one young girl, four years of age, whose mother had a whole lot of friends around one time. Now, this little girl was the only child there. The adults had stolen some drugs and they'd been drinking prior to that. They came back and mixed the drugs with the drink. Later, the girl rang a friend of mine actually, who knew them very well, and said, "I think Mommy is dead." This same child saw one of her mother's boyfriends try to hang himself because the mother had said she didn't want to see him again. Her boyfriend tried to hang himself in front of her. (Youth worker)

A little girl arrived in my class one day with tears in her eyes. She'd obviously been howling her eyes out all night or for quite some time. Kids can cry for something as trivial as, "My best friend isn't my best friend anymore." So I said, "What's the matter?" And she said, "Daddy tried to kill himself." She was living with her father and two younger siblings. Her mother was a drug addict and was undergoing detox at a farm on the other side of the city. Dad had gone out to visit her and said, "When you're straight, I want you to come home." But she said, "I'm not coming home. I'm using dope because I hate you." He came home, got drunk, swallowed all of mom's sleeping tablets and passed out. There was no extended family. All the relatives lived interstate somewhere. So this kid organized the ambulance and the police, got the other two off to school and then fronted me, quivering and hysterical. (Teacher)

Because I work with the extreme end of the kids in schools, the home environments I see tend to be noncommunicative. There's not a lot of communication between parents and kids. They are often single-parent families with mom being the primary care provider, and mom also has to work to care for the family, so she's not often there. (Welfare worker)

Many of the ones I see live in small, box-like housing or apartments. Even though there are so many people there, they're very isolated because there's a fear of the antisocial behavior in the area. A lot of these kids would be perpetrators of that antisocial behavior. So, people don't venture out much and there's not a sense of community, which I think puts pressure on the family. They are also on very low incomes, which creates a lot of stress for single-parent families. Some of the kids have blended families and there's added stress for the young person there, too. Because of the environment they live in, from when they're young they're exposed to a lot of high-risk behavior such as drugs and crime. They know about that early on and they're very much in the middle of it because that's where it all happens. Then there's basic stuff like nutrition. The kids that I've seen and know, eat really poorly. They eat rubbish—high fat, high carbohydrate, not much fresh food—and a lack of sun. (Welfare worker)

Generally, they don't really have a very stable family life. Very often the parents are separated and there's no one really who's particularly interested in the child. I don't know whether it's true to say that they don't go very far at school because there are lots of kids who actually have gone quite well at school. (Magistrate)

It can be really hard for them to cope with the academic expectations of school like, "Why haven't you done your homework?" Well, quite often, there isn't anywhere to do it. They might have eight people living in a house that's designed for four. They all work shifts and they're up at various times of the day and night. Or the kitchen table is part of the factory and they're all doing piecework and sewing shirts. The kids could come home from school and have to do eight hours of work because piecework goes on in the house 24 hours a day, and various members of the family take it on and keep it going. You don't have to buy Nike to exploit minorities. We have people in western countries working in substandard conditions in their garages. So you can give a kid an assignment, but there might be nowhere for him to do it at home or he has no time to do it. (Teacher)

One of my Grade 8 boys rang me one night from the local railway station. His father was a paranoid schizophrenic who used to sit in the front room with a .22 and take pot shots at Patrick when his dinner didn't come quickly enough or something like that. It was one of those nights and Patrick had escaped the house but didn't know where to go. So we picked him up but couldn't get him into emergency accommodation and he slept the night on the floor at our place. The next day we met with his mother who needed to get out of the house too, because her life was also in danger. She wouldn't leave her husband and so Patrick stayed too, until he was just a little older. Then he ran away onto the streets. There's only one way you can earn a living on the streets and because he couldn't bear prostituting himself he developed a drug habit to block it out of his mind. The first year he was working the streets, he would come to school and try to study but, of course, he couldn't because his life was such a mess. Eventually, he got AIDS and died. (Teacher)

A lot of people in that situation just can't help themselves, even if a restraining order is taken out. They'll turn up the next day at their girlfriend's place and scream abuse at the de facto or they turn up at the school. They are so used to confrontation that they will engineer confrontation. And it's really not unusual for people subject to restraining orders to break those just because they know that they've been told not to do it. It almost seems to be an incentive for them to do it or they'll go to the same butcher shop and look glaringly but not say anything. There are enormous numbers of situations where restraining orders are taken out where the people have been shadow boxing for years against each other. Half the time, both sides are equally at fault. Often you've got restraining orders taken out by both sides, two sets of restraining orders and they're really just taken out as a vindictive exercise, I think. They're taken out regularly and they are regularly violated. People just can't stop themselves. They get a fixation about something. They can't go away and just do normal things. (Magistrate)

Fitting in school

How do these young people fare at school in their studies and relationships? To what extent do they fit in?

A lot of young people with different life experiences find it very hard to fit in with their peers, which makes school a pretty frightening place for them socially. (Social worker)

Numerous times I've been told that someone didn't fit in well at school and got in with the wrong crowd. (Magistrate)

Some of the prisoners I work with were quite isolated at school. They weren't liked at all by their peers. I'm basing that on what they've told me and also how they present now. Some are quite isolated people and I can imagine that they would have been quite similar at school in that they didn't associate with their peers and were bullied. (Psychologist)

One of the biggest problems I've seen in schools is bullying. It's a huge problem. A lot of the boys tell me stories about when they've been bullied. (Welfare worker)

I think at their age, developmentally, being one of the crowd is really important. On one level they want to be individuals, and they do and say things just to shock people, but on another level it's about what they need to do to fit in. If they've got a really big problem like domestic violence hanging over their head, then a lot of young people feel very isolated. They think their peers won't understand what they're going through—if their peers see the bruises, if somebody knows they've been sexually abused or that mom's kicked them out of home. They think their friends will ostracize them. They find it really hard to develop strong peer relations with others apart from those going through the same things. The only other young people that they will associate with are kids with problems as well. So their role models are quite limited in that respect. (Social worker)

Because of their home environment, a lot of these kids don't flourish socially. So then you get that whole cycle of them not getting along with other kids and struggling to build friendships and relationships, which sets them up to be a bad kid. It's a snowball effect where they become bad or they develop a bad reputation. They get bullied so they start bullying. That's not conducive to anything. You can't learn in that sort of environment. (Welfare worker)

But then there's a whole lot of times when people overcome problems like a parent dying and that sort of thing, and go well until they get to a particular stage and something sends them off the rails. (Magistrate)

If a young person has no home to go to, that's *the* issue for them. If there's domestic violence at home, that's the center of their focus. So whatever it is—it could even be an eating disorder—it makes it really hard for them to be able to go to a class and sit there and absorb and process the content they're supposed to. (Social worker)

In those circumstances, education is not a priority for these young people. As much as you want to believe that they're at school to learn or not at school because they don't want to learn, the reality is these kids don't often have a choice. When you're dealing with so much trauma and emotional baggage and hurt and rejection, to be at school to learn is not possible sometimes. (Welfare worker)

I guess it really boils down to survival for them. It's very much about them and what they need to survive. Things that are taken for granted by schools—for instance, that lunch time will be a valuable peer experience, that being in class will be a valuable social experience—just cease to be important for these young people. I guess this is a generalization, but whatever's going on in their lives is just so huge for them that it becomes the center of their lives and education takes a back seat. (Social worker)

There's a lack of enthusiasm for education by parents, I've found. I don't know where it stems from but there's almost a noncommittal attitude to their kids getting educated. (Welfare worker)

I think the families that they come from are quite chaotic. I'm not blaming the parents here. I'm just saying that they've probably had to deal with a lot. These children, who are now women in prison, have been in fights and conflicts in and out of school. I think they're probably quite rebellious against their parents as well. I think that it would be quite difficult to keep those kids at school if they don't want to be there and most of them say that they didn't want to be there. (Psychologist)

I've had quite a few people say, "My son was doing really well in elementary school, but it all went wrong in high school and we couldn't control him any more." Even with my own kids, I've noticed that they had friends in elementary school who came from backgrounds in which academic learning was not valued but who themselves were quite bright and were doing really well. Some of them did much better than my kids, in mathematics or whatever, but crunch time seems to come when they get a little bit older. I think it's because a lot of parents don't have very high ambitions for their children. They don't expect them to do very well. So if you don't expect them to do very well, they don't do very well. I'd say that for most of the people I see in the courts, it's not a valued thing to do well at school. (Magistrate)

Another major reason for them not liking school is that they felt they weren't able to complete the work. They didn't feel competent in mathematics or English or weren't able to do the assignments and felt ashamed of that. So that became one of the reasons for dropping out. (Psychologist)

Most had troubles at school, although they weren't always expressed but you could just tell by their speech and their ability to learn. You'd decipher it from how they conducted themselves. (Community worker)

A lot of them aren't good at school. A lot of them struggle academically. (Welfare worker)

Schools need to meet students' educational needs by looking at the inequities that exist, which prevent students from succeeding. I think a lot of teachers expect that young people enter their classrooms at a similar level. From there, teachers have the attitude that what students get out of class depends on what they put in, but it's not that way at all. Young people come with all different ability levels, which schools don't appreciate. So many young people fall below the entry level the system anticipates. (Social worker)

Only a small proportion of them are totally illiterate. I'd say that a lot of them have trouble with reading and writing and they don't feel as confident as they would like to be, but there's only a very small proportion that actually can't read at all. (Psychologist)

Some people who come to the courts and have particular learning problems just give up and endure school. The problem with that is they never really get jobs other than those on the edge of criminal activity. Yet there are a lot of people who seem to have done quite well at school and still come up before the courts. It's a bit hard to tell now because they say, "Well, I completed secondary school," but you don't really know what standard they completed it to. (Magistrate)

A lot of the people that I meet have said that they've been expelled or suspended on numerous occasions. The majority of them say that they didn't like school. There are some people that have done quite well at school, completed university, and been quite successful, but the majority of them have left school around 14, 15, or 16 years of age. Very few completed secondary school. (Psychologist)

I suppose you'd have to say that kids who don't do well academically are more likely to end up in the courts because they generally go on the dole and then they can't afford the things they want and get depressed and introduced to drugs. But I don't know whether it's universally so. There was a boy from a wealthy private school who appeared before me last year. His mother had separated and remarried, and there were other children from the new relationship, but the boy didn't get on with his stepfather although the stepfather paid his school fees all the way through. When he got into Grade 11 he started getting involved with recreational drugs and then got to be a high drug user, but that couldn't be discussed at home because his mother was so ashamed. When his stepfather found out about his drug habit and criminal activities, he said, "Well, that confirms what I thought. He's not much good." The boy had committed an enormous range of burglaries but was really a middle-class kid otherwise doing well at school. Then there was another boy who appeared before me from a similar sort of school. He had a very bad background but was given a scholarship to the school because he was so academically talented. He was incredibly bright. He had been a homeless kid so the school had found accommodation for him. Everyone knew his background and he was really supported. Then, during the course of his secondary schooling, he reverted to doing burglaries he'd previously been accustomed to and eventually the school had to expel him in Grade 11 or Grade 12, when you would have thought he'd just about got there. (Magistrate)

Getting personal

What do you say to those who denigrate young people living on the edge of society? How do you rationalize your involvement?

I certainly didn't come from a rich background but I was privileged in that I had a good education and I had parents who cared for me. I had limitless opportunities and I think it should be that way for everybody. I think it's really unfair if a person doesn't have access to opportunities just because their circumstances are different to the norm. I was always encouraged when I was younger so I always seek to encourage now. (Community worker)

I went to a very small private school and later, for the first time in my life, found myself teaching in an education system I'd never been in. I'd never been in the government school system and it was a complete shock to me. I had kids in my class with weird names who ate really weird food and kids from socioeconomic groups that I never had anything to do with. Some of them even had things like ringworm and lice, which I had never come across. A few had stripes up their arms and personal hygiene was very low, but they were terrific kids. (Teacher)

I just look at them as being no different to me except that I've had some advantages in life that they haven't. One thing that I'm very grateful for is that I had two parents who are still alive and still together. They've been good parents to me during my lifetime. My husband's experience is the same, although his parents have passed away now. We both have good families that are there for us if we need them, whereas a lot of these kids haven't had that advantage. For instance, my husband is in a job that could disappear tomorrow and being middle-aged he would find it very difficult to get another job. But I know that we would have the support of friends and family to emotionally deal with that type of situation. That's what happened some years ago when he got chronic fatigue syndrome. He was sick for eight years, we lost our business and our lifestyle changed dramatically, but because we had the support of friends and family we made it through. That's why I feel that friendship is very important, that people know that somebody cares. That was a traumatic time for us, but if I didn't know that there were people who cared about us, I can imagine myself going off the deep end. (Youth worker)

It's much easier to criticize than be constructive. When people write off this person and put them in that bracket, they don't have to do anything about it. They say, "This person is this way because they're a drunk, they're a drug addict, they're a criminal." (Community worker)

Often it's ignorance on their part. They'll say things like, "Why don't they go and get a job? Why don't they go to school? Why aren't they doing something with their lives?" It's very much a blaming attitude. (Welfare worker)

The general public might feel some sort of justification that these people have been sent to prison because they've done the wrong thing. On my first exposure to working with male offenders I, too, was quite disgusted, scared I guess, quite blaming of them. And at first, listening to the women's stories, it was a bit new to me. I'd been exposed to television and seen the trauma that people go through, but actually meeting someone who has been raped or beaten up constantly is quite a confronting experience. But from working with them, from hearing people's stories about their life circumstances, inter-acting with them on a personal level, I now find that I have a completely different view. Now, when I see someone on the news convicted of some offense, I immediately think to myself, "What's happened in their life that has led them to make the decisions that they have?" Maybe that's something teachers need to do, to take a broader view of their student's behavior. I think that people are responsible for their actions, but I also think that there are a whole lot of reasons and little steps along the way that have led them to that point. That's how I view it now. They're responsible but they have a history and background that was probably quite traumatic, quite different from mine. (Psychologist)

Thomas: A case study

Thomas's story is illustrative of many told by professionals about at-risk youth. In this story, school and family are the main social institutions addressed, although similar accounts could be given of hospitals, prisons, law courts, government departments, and so on. Indeed, the welfare worker that tells this story is very mindful of institutional matters and the challenge to them that Thomas's story makes. There are challenges here, too, for all professionals about what constitutes good practice.

Thomas was brought to my attention maybe a month after I started at the school. The reason he came to my attention was that he had been causing a lot of problems in class—throwing chairs, abusing teachers, using bad language, swearing at other students, and things like that. There was also a non-attendance issue. He's in Grade 8 so he would be 12 or 13 years old. The teachers had put him on a list for a special group of young people with behavioral problems, which met once a week for some character building, type stuff. He came to my attention soon after because he couldn't get into the group that he wanted and his teachers wanted him to be in because there was no room. So someone approached me about spending some time with him weekly. I'd been told a little about his background before I met him, mainly that there were some problems with his mom. There were some whispers about mom needing to detox, which is why the family had gone away, but I didn't know much else. I knew there were two younger brothers and that he was the eldest and that he had some family problems, but I didn't know what. There was quite a big period at the start of the term when he wasn't at school. He'd been away for several weeks and no one knew why for sure, so I was asked to follow it up.

Initially, I met with him to have a bit of a chat. He's a very elusive kid, really closed, very private. From there we spent some time together every week and we would talk about what's going on in class. He would tell me which teachers he doesn't get along with and we would talk about how to make that better, what things he could do to improve the relationship. Most of the time he would say such things as, "She doesn't listen to me. She blames me for everything when it's not even me that did it." His view was he copped it just because he had a bad reputation. So while I couldn't do a lot about his relationship with his teachers, because I don't have much power or control over them, we would talk about how he could make it better. He would tell me about his father who had been to jail and how he can't help the way he acts because he's exactly like his dad who deals with things the same way; things like getting angry and lashing out and throwing things. So we talked a lot about how he was not his dad and that his actions were separate from what his dad did. I'd say things like, "We often have similar traits to our parents but we don't have to act the same way," or "That's our responsibility," and stuff like that. He's not really responding to that yet. He's still very much convinced that he's the image of his father. You can imagine, can't you, his mother saying, "My God, you're the image of your father."

I met his dad a few weeks ago and he's a lovely man. He came in and filled me in on a bit of the story. Apparently mom hadn't detoxed, although she was quite a heavy heroin user, and the family hadn't gone away but she had left her husband and three boys two months before. So now dad is a single parent, recently out of jail himself, with a very difficult life of his own to cope with and with three young boys to bring up on his own as well. Things were very chaotic at home. On top of this, mom had been seen around town with her new guy who had kids of his own and she'd also been seen at their football games but wouldn't even ring her own kids to talk to them. So, there was a lot of anger and it climaxed with this kid trashing mom's market stall and her new house, really severe behavior of that kind. His trauma was expressing itself that way.

I still see him weekly and we're talking about all those things and trying to get him to a place where he's coping a bit more, but the reality for him is he's not learning in his classes at the moment. It's enough for him to survive the class, to stay in for the whole class. With one class, in particular, he spends most of his time outside the room. He says things to me like, "I hate the teacher." So I'd say, "Alright. Well, why?" And he said, "Miss, I don't know what to do." This is a 12 or 13-year-old boy and he really was at the end of his tether. He didn't know how to act in this class. He was at a loss because whatever he did he was picked on. If anything went wrong in class, it was his fault. One day he said to me, "I've got her next. Can you please come with me and just see what happens?" And I said, "I'm sure it's not that bad. Come on. I'll go with you." So I walked him down to his class.

When we got outside the room he said, "Watch this." Two seconds after he walked in he was out again and the teacher walked out after him screaming and shouting at him like there was no tomorrow. "What the hell do you think you're doing in my class? I don't even want you in here. You're not supposed to be in here." She was screaming at the top of her lungs and this kid looked at me as if to say, "What on earth is going on? Help me." So I said to this teacher, "Listen," (I was tempted to say something rude but I didn't) "I'll sort this out." So I took the young person and we went and found his correct class. His timetable had changed unbeknown to him and he had a different class but he wasn't aware of that.

I was livid. I was so angry with the way this kid had been spoken to. I thought I just can't leave it there because this is a young person who is actually trying really hard. He comes to school every day. He goes to all of his classes. He sees the mentors weekly. He comes to see me at lunchtime and he is really responding to the support that's been put in place. Yet his teachers, one in particular, are still working on his reputation and not giving him a go. So I went to see the deputy principal and I told him exactly what I thought and we had this conversation.

"Well, I can't get personal."

"I'm not expecting you to get personal, but what I do expect is that you hire professional teachers that don't treat kids like they're dogs."

"No, I agree with you."

"Teachers are there to be role models and positive influences."

"Maybe it's because she doesn't know what his circumstances are. Maybe if I told her."

"I don't care whether she knows or not. No child deserves to be spoken to like that, particularly after I've just spent the last hour talking with him about positive behavior and how to be a good student and how to work with this woman to build a good relationship. Her response just blew that all out of the water. I might as well not have bothered."

Her behavior just cut my legs out from under me and totally ripped the boy apart. This is a young person who's trying. He's not even truanting or trying to get out of school. He wants to be here because it's stable and safe, except when people yell and scream at him for nothing! School provides him with clear boundaries and he knows what's expected. That teacher hasn't been back since. I don't know what happened to her but it solved my problem and it solved his problem. He's in Grade 8 now. This is a great time for us to be intervening and trying to support him because we have some time and we have some opportunities to make a difference. But he needs a key relationship. His dad's struggling and his brothers have really been hit hard by mom going. His life is in chaos. School's safe, school's stable, he knows what to expect at school. And it's the teachers who are spending the most time with him, not me. I see him a few times at lunchtime. There's a real opportunity for a teacher to actually invest in him.

I think it's really interesting, too, because this is a school that is very confused about the number of kids who truant, who don't want to be there. It's very obvious to me that they don't want to be there because they don't like it and they're not given a reason to like it. Whereas the teachers are very clear that they're there to teach a curriculum. Their attitude is they are not there to befriend students or invest in them. They're there to teach a curriculum and if students want to learn then they learn. If they don't, then leave. Yet the school's still confused about why young people don't want to be there. I've got several Grade 9 and 10 boys who refuse to come to school, point blank; don't care what you do. This is a school of seven to eight hundred, and on my caseload I've got close to one hundred boys with non-attendance issues. (Welfare worker)

CHAPTER THIRTEEN

A helping hand

We're like an ambulance at the bottom of the cliff helping young people who have fallen off. At some stage we'd like to be at the top, preventing them from falling. That would be lovely. But at the moment the need is at the bottom. (Youth worker)

There is a degree of overlap in this chapter with issues introduced in Chapter 12. Its point of departure is a focus on the involvement of "the helping professions" in the lives of at-risk youth. Rejection, anger, and trust are some of the issues for young people that the professionals in this pseudoconversation argue require patience, calmness, openness, and understanding. Again, while there is considerable coherence in their discussion of what is required and when, there is some disagreement. Advice for other professionals working in the field, particularly for teachers in regular contact with young people, is also freely given. The chapter ends with a case study of one teacher's efforts to help a young boy in need. The emphasis is on "working with" rather than "working on" young people in developing solutions to the problems they encounter.

Confronting rejection

How do young people at risk deal with rejection? What kind of support do they need?

Kids, particularly those in care—all kids who are homeless in that broader sense—very often leave home with nothing. It's quite traumatic at that point of separation from home and if they're running away, even more so. They grab what they can find. Most of them don't even have a proper bag so they carry their belongings in plastic bags. This is while they're also confronting all those big life questions like who I am, what I am, what I want to become, where I'm going. (Welfare worker)

That's the nature of a crisis situation. If there's a house fire, people think about getting what they can out of the house so at least they can save something. It's the same with young people when they have to leave home. They focus on the material things first. They'll say things like, "I want to get my belongings." And, "They've got no right to keep my CDs." Once all of that is sorted through, the focus shifts to the emotional issues. We find that if we can keep hold of young people at school while that initial crisis is happening we have a lot better chance of holding onto them and helping them. But once that initial crisis period is over and if the young person still hasn't found appropriate accommodation, then it becomes very difficult to keep them in the education system. We just lose them. They don't come to school any more and who knows what happens to them after that. (Social worker)

For a lot of kids on the street and in care, it's so important to wear the right things because they believe that what you own is a reflection of who you are. When I went overseas I lived out of a suitcase for six months and I didn't particularly need anything else. I don't place much importance on things and probably that's just the type of person I am. But for some of these kids, material things are so important. They have nothing else so they dress well to make themselves feel better. Street culture is about presenting a façade. (Welfare worker)

Some of them use pseudonyms to try to disassociate themselves from the terrible things that have happened to them. They take on another name to move into another world away from the one that's hurt them so much. There's a new identity that goes with the name, which makes them feel more acceptable. One guy, "Prince," used to wear a hat over his green or purple or red hair. He'd delight in taking his hat off and shocking us with what color it was that night. It's a release for them, a way of getting away from the stress of being James for a while. (Youth worker)

Denial is a common way of dealing with rejection. There's a young woman I'm currently working with who is just 18. Her dad left the family home when she was quite young, around 2 years of age, and her mother died when she was about 8. She has quite a lot of brothers and sisters, none of whom really looked after her, although some continued to live in the family home after their mother died. Then, when she was 13, she was left to look after two of her younger sisters and didn't have any real contact with her older siblings after that. At some point she was placed in foster care but ran away and took her two younger sisters with her. She found a place to live with a drug dealer who was quite a lot older and who took the place of her mother. That was where she was introduced to marijuana and, later on, heroin. So she grew up with a mother figure but a different kind of role model than she might have otherwise had. Even so, she felt terribly isolated and very rejected. Yet, when I spoke to her and asked her about her family, she was quite protective of them and of their actions in leaving her. She admitted that she felt abandoned by them but she seemed to take on all the blame for that herself. She convinced herself that they left her because she wasn't good enough, that she didn't deserve anybody to hang around her, to look after her. Now the only people that she has in her life that might potentially care about her are her family, her brothers and sisters, and if she blames them for abandoning her, if she's angry with them, she's left with nothing. By blaming herself she's able to keep them in a good light in her eyes. It would be quite devastating for her to admit that she's not to blame for being left alone when she was 13. (Psychologist)

A similar thing can happen with kids in residential care. Placements can break down and often it has absolutely nothing to do with the kids. Carers become tired and worn out because they're living and relating to such difficult young people. And they often have families of their own with their own family issues so providing quality care to others can be difficult at times. I've also had kids who've been in abusive foster homes where we've had to remove them for duty of care reasons. So there's a multitude of reasons why they have to move and most of the time it's not the young person's fault, which is really hard for them to accept. They read it as being their fault because they're so down on themselves already. They think that the reason they're out of home is because mom doesn't love them anymore. On top of that, they feel rejected by the foster family that they have to leave. That sense of rejection can build until you've got young people who attempt to kill themselves, overdosing on drugs or throwing themselves off bridges. (Welfare worker)

A lot of the women in prison say to me that they've been neglected, that they have been virtually left on their own during their childhood, allowed to do what they want. They didn't feel that they were particularly important or cared about by anybody. They feel that they were put down by their parents or by others close to them and told that they're not good enough. (Psychologist)

We often support kids charged with criminal offenses by accompanying them through the court process. We do it mainly to show them that somebody cares about them, that even though they've done wrong somebody will still try to help them get back on the right track in life. A lot of them have never had that experience of somebody caring once they've done wrong. Usually, people throw their hands up in despair and say, "Well, I've tried and that's it." (Youth worker)

They become so used to people's derogatory comments that when somebody does try to do something nice for them, it's not always received very well. They think, "Well, why are they doing that? What's in it for them?" That was the attitude of a lot of the kids when we first started going out on the streets. The first time some of them accepted a meal from us, they said, "What do you expect us to do now that you've given us this?" They're not used to a world where you get something for nothing, where somebody's just doing something out of the goodness of their heart. (Youth worker)

The reason you give food to them is because you have compassion for them, you care about them, and you want to help them. To charge money for it, even if it was a small amount, would make them suspicious because they would think it's a moneymaking venture. Whereas they really know it's special if somebody's out there giving it away. They start asking questions about why anyone would do that for them and they start to listen more. (Community worker)

I've always seen the food as the tool that we use to get to know them because if we just went and sat in the park we wouldn't have met half of these people. It's the fact that we offer them something that encourages them to come and talk to us and allows us to get to know them better. Now, I don't think by any means that we're going to change all those lives, but I do think our being there has changed some lives. We've had some that have come back and said, "Thank you," for the help that we've given them. They've gone on from where they were. I think the thing that most people need is someone to care about them and often those who come are the ones that feel nobody cares. To me, friendship, someone to talk to, is something that everybody needs in life. I know if I talk about a problem I'll often see something that wasn't clear before I actually verbalized what I was feeling. Maybe we can give them some material assistance to help get them where they're going. Maybe just by being able to talk to us about their problems, some of these young people will be able to see a way out. Maybe just by being there and caring about them prevents them from taking their own life. (Youth worker)

Young people's experiences are different, but no matter what, they all want to talk. They really want to communicate with somebody to tell them their problems. It seems they have friends but nobody they can communicate with personally, not on deep questions or about their emotions. Often their problems are about relationships, things like how to communicate with their girlfriend. One guy said his girlfriend would regularly take off with somebody else but then come back to him. He felt like he was being used, that the girl only wanted him there for protection or until she could find someone better. (Community worker)

Some avoid relationships by constantly moving around. I can think of one person in particular who left home when she was 13 and moved from one relative to the next and then between friends. She constantly moved from place to place. Her explanation for leaving home and moving around is that she got different jobs and made friends with people; I guess the normal reasons why people move. But the frequency of moving is just quite extraordinary, quite high. She has developed a way of relating to people that doesn't help her to maintain long-term relationships. I'm talking about same sex relationships here, her friendships with girlfriends. She told me of conflicts that she had with people who she considered were close to her. Typically, those conflicts were concerned with her commitment to the relationship and how honest she was being with them. In most cases it would get to a point where she would feel that she wasn't willing to offer any more of herself to those people. For her, it just wasn't worth remaining in that situation, having her commitment to those relationships constantly questioned. Now she has trouble getting close to people and expressing her emotions, which are fundamental to some of her problems at the moment. She sees moving and getting new friends as the solution to those problems. She seeks to develop new relationships with people who have no idea of her past and have less expectations of her. (Psychologist)

I worked with one young girl from a single-parent family who just had no boundaries. Her mom didn't have a clue how to discipline her. Mom also had a drinking problem and her daughter was also regularly drunk and regularly using drugs at age 12 going on 13. The girl was also in the habit of going off to live with friends for extended periods—months—before returning home. Apparently her mother thought that was OK; it was part of their normal family life. Finally, though, mom told her not to come back. She had acquired a new boyfriend who didn't want the girl around and because she didn't have a close connection with her daughter, it was a lot easier for mom to kick her out than it was for her to kick the boyfriend out. In the end, the only support this girl was receiving was from school, from me, and from a teacher she just adored. She would probably attend one class a day and the rest of the time she bounced between this teacher and myself. She had immediate material and psychological needs that needed to be met and school was where she received that unconditional, positive regard. Our attitude was, "I like you because of who you are. I'm not going to say leave my office because you come high one day." That was what she needed, which is what we gave her. We didn't give her one-hour appointments once a week to sit down and work through issues. We were there for her when she needed us and her level of need was extremely high at that time. In that period she even got herself off sniffing glue; she did it cold turkey, all by herself. Then, one day, one of the school administrators decided that we weren't a baby-sitting service. That's exactly what he said. "You're not a baby-sitting service. If she doesn't go to class, she has to leave." I fought tooth and nail to try to get them to change their minds and, when they wouldn't, I tried to get her referred to an alternative school, but they wouldn't take her either. In the end they excluded her from school; she wasn't allowed on the premises. I told her that I would still support her. I tried to link her with other services but, basically, school was her whole life. It was what she felt connected to and when that was lost, she starting abusing glue again and twice attempted suicide. She had been rejected by her mother and rejected by the school. I spoke with her just the other day and she had been to stay with her dad but he had just kicked her out. I guess she just has no way to adapt to a family situation now. That's just one example of a young person looking for more than just academic support from school and it was denied. (Social worker)

If kids don't learn anything in their day at school other than they're wanted and that somebody cares about them, that might be all that they can cope with. Just feeling that somebody cares might give them self-esteem to then be able to sit in class and learn. I don't think you can expect these kids to learn at the same rate as other kids, but I don't know that it's any good either to put them in a separate class or school because that just makes the differences more obvious. We need to show them community support. It's not just about individual teachers or schools; it's about the community supporting these young people. If kids feel wanted and respected, I'm sure that they'll react differently in time. (Teacher)

It would be unusual for me to hear a plea in court and not have a member of the family or close friends available to give evidence. It would be unusual if you didn't have someone to say, "He lives with me and he's a good boy." The defending counsel might want to have someone from the family to say those kinds of things anyway, but there's a limit to what you can do if it's just not there. You can't make something out of nothing. (Magistrate)

Anger management

How do you manage the anger that some of these young people have? How can we support them?

I had to explain to one colleague that if you literally backed a child into a corner, there was only one way he could get out of that corner and that was through you. And he said, "What do you mean?" So I said, "Stand in that corner and have somebody stand in front of you. How do you get out of there?" It happens psychologically as well. If you back a child into a corner, he will come out through you and he'll probably do you as much damage as you've just done to him. Then there are two people who are hurt and humiliated instead of just one. (Teacher)

You need a certain space to be able to cope with life when you've been kicked out of your home and when mom's effectively rejected you and chosen her partner over you. There are so many unresolved issues, so much anger, so much hurt to deal with, that you can't see much else. (Welfare worker)

We need to stop and think what that child's been through to get where they are. Even though they go to school angry or upset, obviously they've needed to be there for the company or whatever. We've got to recognize the effort that they've gone through to get there. For us it might be a matter of getting in the car. For them it's about dealing with their drug addiction or other forms of abuse. We need to look at what that person has been through to get to where they are and be prepared to help them take the next few steps. (Social worker)

I know particularly with young David, when he was in a really aggressive mood, I'd just sit quietly and talk to him, which calmed him down better than saying, "Now, sit down and behave yourself." I remember another night there was a young guy who was so upset he was trembling. A couple of the other guys had told him that he was stupid and he was shaking with rage, so I just sat and stroked his head. Just me just standing there stroking his head while he sat calmed him down, and the trembling stopped. Then there was another young guy, Darren, who was ready to kill Grant because he had called Darren's sister a slut. So Darren was out to get him. He was so angry he couldn't string his words together. I gave him a meal and actually fed him a couple of spoonfuls to try to get him thinking about something else. He said to me, "Well, you have some too." So I picked up a bit of food at the opposite end of the plate and put that into my mouth and just kept spooning his from the other end. He looked straight at me and I'm sure he saw acceptance in me doing that. Within five minutes he'd calmed down a lot. (Youth worker)

I think it's important for teachers to learn how to manage conflict within classrooms and within the school. If teachers simply punish students for fighting, for example, their level of aggression and their resentment is just going to escalate. I think traditional methods of punishing students—I don't mean physical punishment but things like sending them to the principal or making them stand in front of the class—simply generate resentment and more anger in them, and don't necessarily address the problem. Conflict resolution is very important. (Psychologist)

A lot of the programs in jail are reserved for long-term offenders. So if you've got someone who needs anger management or counseling, there's not much point sentencing him to three or four months in jail because he just won't get it. They don't get anything until they're sentenced for at least twelve months. There is a tremendous amount of courses you can do in jail but you don't even get a look in on them unless you're in for a substantially long time. It's a real pity because if you've got a young person who's a heroin addict and you're thinking of sentencing him to under six months in jail, you know that they may not even get transferred to a permanent prison location. They might do the whole six months in a holding unit. You don't actually get good conditions until you are sentenced and unless your sentence is a sentence for a long period. You're much better off to say to someone, "I'll give you four years jail," and then you know that those programs are going to kick in during the time they're there. The system is designed around that. It's not designed around putting people in jail for short periods of time. (Magistrate)

There's one young boy, Matthew, who regularly comes with his family. He was much calmer last time compared to what he is usually like. Sometimes he throws his fists around but last night he was just throwing stones at the trees. I was watching very carefully because I thought any minute now he's going to throw one at a passing car. He was some distance from his family although close enough to hear his father telling him to come back. Watching him, I just got the feeling that he was deliberately separating himself from them. I think it's a learned behavior from when they're young. They go into their own world as a way of escaping and it makes it very hard for them to concentrate on anything for any length of time. One of the big problems he has at school is that he's unable to concentrate on anything for more than five minutes. That's really difficult for teachers who have him in their class. I've never had an actual conversation with him. Even when I hand him his meal he just shakes his head, he doesn't actually speak. There isn't any verbal communication. I don't think I've ever actually heard a word pass from his mouth. It's the physical communication, the lashing out, that's more prevalent, like throwing stones or throwing his fists around. Once he threw his bike into the river. He was angry with his father who hadn't been home for three days, which was simply because he was drinking in the park. He wanted to visit his father but his mother wouldn't let him because she knew what condition he was in. So Matthew threw his brand new bike into the river and it smashed on the rocks. He also wrecked the apartment that they were living in so they were forced to shift out. Then they went to a van park and he burnt down the dry grass in the adjoining vacant lot. The owners moved them out of there very quickly because they could see more problems on the horizon. While you can't blame the owners of these properties for evicting them, it puts the family in a situation where they're not acceptable anywhere. It's really difficult. (Youth worker)

Reading between the lines

To what extent are their needs genuine? How do you know when to offer support?

The general joke around the department is that after their evening meal they'll get the family together and come up to Emergency because there's nothing better to do. The things they come up with are just ridiculous. We check them out fully, but most of the time there's no foundation to their complaints. One man always turns up at mealtimes. As soon as he gets there, he says, "I'm a diabetic. I need to be fed." Then he whines about his family not feeding him. We alert the social workers but we end up giving them some food anyway. If we don't, they complain about us. But there's no reason for them to come for food. You can get free meals from any number of places. (Nurse)

Older men sometimes exaggerate the position that they had before they were on the street to try to give us a certain impression of themselves. They don't realize that they're acceptable to us even if they were just a laborer in the car factory. But no, they've got to make themselves out to be the foreman. There's a certain amount of talk that they do to try to present themselves in a better light. (Youth worker)

You can say to kids charged with drug use, "Look, you need to work at this place for three months so you'll have that to say to the Magistrate by the time it comes to trial." Or if you've got a drug-addicted mother and she wants to keep the child, you say, "Now, these are all the things we'll do. You've got to have urine tests and they've got to be drug free. You've got to have a clean house." And they'll agree. "Yes, that's fantastic. Thanks for helping me." But they won't do it; they just don't follow through. That's why it's so hard dealing with people involved with drugs because there's that unreliability, which just seems to be built into the whole thing. They just can't do it. It must be so frustrating being a lawyer now because you can have all these counselors sitting around organizing programs for people but you can't rely on them. (Magistrate)

Some of the women in the prison try to relate to me more as a friend. They think that by presenting themselves as "normal," as not having had too many terrible experiences, I might identify with them more. By "normal" I mean what they think I think is normal. Others are quite open and honest and really appreciate the opportunity to tell their story, because they haven't been heard before. A lot of the people I see for the first time describe their childhood as being very good, no problems. Their parents were great, their childhood was happy, and so on. It's partly about not wanting to admit that bad things have happened to them in the past, but it's also about gauging me, who I am, and how much they can trust me. Later they open up with things like, "Things weren't so good. My Dad used to hit me," which would seem to be quite significant things but at the start they won't tell you. Several have experienced things that are quite traumatic and very distressing, and they tell me their story in such a way that I get the impression they're trying to shock me with all the gruesome details. Part of that is because if it's shared with someone who appreciates how awful it was, they might get more sympathy, perhaps more help. Then there are people who don't want to tell me anything that has happened to them in the past because they think I might not be able to cope with it. I might not have heard anything so awful and I might be so shocked or disgusted that I won't come back. (Psychologist)

One young boy told us recently he was going to sleep the night in the park. Now, we can't register shock or horror when they tell us these things.

We just have to accept that that's where they've planned to sleep tonight. Sometimes though they will say, "Can you find me somewhere to stay?" I can remember one young boy who had been on the streets for some time; he was living in a condemned building. One night he said, "Look, I'm sick of it. I can't take it any more. Can you find me somewhere to stay?" So we searched around that night and got him into some accommodation. If we'd tried to push him before he was ready, he probably would have run a mile. We had to wait for that time when he said, "Can you help me get out of this?" (Youth worker)

You can be sitting in your classroom, marking an essay or something, and a student will describe to you what has happened at home. Your first reaction might be, "What do I do with this?" But they're not telling you just to pass the time of day. They want you to take it somewhere. They may say they don't but usually when they've decided to tell you something, the burden has become too great for them and they want you to do something about it. They want you to step in. (Teacher)

A lot of young people put up barriers to avoid being vulnerable. They say things like, "Well, I don't want to do that anyway. I'm not going to see a social worker. What's she going to do for me?" or "Oh, f__ school. I'm not going to go to school. Who needs it?" That sort of thing. Ultimately, I think it's a self-protection mechanism. They are taught that if you don't succeed, then you're a failure. They quickly work out that if you don't play the game, you can't fail. If joining the system means you've got to be on the bottom of the rung, who'd want to join? (Social worker)

The sports teacher came in to my office one day, white as a ghost and absolutely shaking. So I said, "What's happened?" He said, "Young Sam." That was all he could say, "Young Sam." I thought he was about to cry so I said, "Look, come into my office." This kid had been in detention for weeks because he wouldn't do sport. He wouldn't go into the change rooms to change and he wouldn't participate in sport no matter what it was. Eventually the sports teacher got sick of this so he confronted the kid. "There's a reason for this, isn't there? You don't hate sport that much. What's going on?" The boy burst into tears and said, "I don't want you to see my body." "Why? What's wrong with it?" Eventually the kid took his clothes off and all across his back, his buttocks and down the back of his legs were long welt marks given to him by his father who had been beating him with the cable from an electric appliance. Now, we had been giving this kid detention because he wouldn't do sport not realizing that he didn't want to take his clothes off because people would see the scars. (Teacher)

I was sitting in my office one day when a kid ran in, a very tough girl but she was absolutely spun out. She said, "My father is outside the school," which is amazing because she was from interstate and he'd tracked her. She'd seen the plate number of his car and run around to the back of the school. "What am I going to do?" I said, "Just calm down, we'll fix it." I rang the local police and said, "We've got a guy sitting in a car outside and there's an apprehended violence order out against him. I'd like all the bells and whistles." It was Friday morning and everything was really quiet when all of a sudden it was NYPD Blue on the school grounds. This guy took off at 150 miles per hour with the police after him. They arrested him because he wasn't allowed near his daughter. The mother had gone off with somebody else but the father thought that the girl knew where her mother was so he kept tracking her. This kid was bringing herself up and she wasn't doing a bad job of it. Now, we're expecting that child to cope with her final year of school! (Teacher)

Demanding help

What are the demands that helping puts on helpers? What advice do you have for the helping professions?

There was one guy who turned up one night who was extremely demanding. He didn't seem to be happy with any of the food we offered him. The thing that really frustrated me right from the start with him was that I watched one of our workers bend over backwards to give him a meal that he liked. I think he must have been offered three or four different meals. Then he decided he didn't really want that meal. I was frustrated because I thought we were doing everything we could to include him. When he put the meal in the trash, "Grrr." I was angry because I'd just seen somebody else throw a meal away and it really annoyed me. So I told him what I thought. Then he apologized and apologized and apologized. After he'd apologized for the third time I said, "Look. I'll get over it quicker if you stop apologizing." But he kept on and on and on. When I thought about it, after I'd gone home, I realized that that's not normal to apologize to that extent. I don't know enough about him to know whether he's had an abused life, whether he really feels unwanted. Maybe he has really suffered. I don't know why he behaved the way he did and I guess I should have been more understanding. (Youth worker)

I have had people question my presence in prison. They see themselves as being stronger and see me as being quieter. They think that if I were in their situation I might not be as strong or as aggressive or able to survive as they are, and they're possibly right. Some ask me what I would know about their experiences. I haven't been in prison and I haven't used drugs before. How can I help them if I don't fully understand what they're talking about? That sort of comment is not uncommon, particularly from those who refuse to speak to me or are difficult to interview to do an assessment. I generally agree with them, that I don't know what it's like to withdraw from heroin. I don't know what it's like to be in prison. I don't know what it's like to be abused. I tell them that that's a fair point. They are the experts on themselves. They know a lot about themselves and how they have felt in their life. They know all about their life experiences and I don't. But what I can do is bring the knowledge that I have about how people have effectively dealt with these kinds of problems and we can work together. So it's not about me solving all their problems. It's about them bringing their knowledge and combining it with my knowledge to see how best we can actually help them. It's really a process of them helping themselves with me providing what knowledge I have. They don't all respond particularly well to that and I think that that's more about the reasons why they bring up that sort of issue. I think that it's about sabotaging the actual process of the interview, rather than actually questioning my ability. (Psychologist)

I think that's what makes a good protective worker, when you can separate the issues from the person and when you're able to remain positive and upbeat and concentrate on the young person's strengths even in situations where they're trying your patience and when things are never going right. It's so important to concentrate on the positives and to really help the young person see the positives. (Welfare worker)

I knew that there was a need to go out on the street to address some of the crises that were happening. I could see the problems appearing in the courts but I wanted to know what was behind them. You don't know the "whys" when you're working at the courts. You just know how it happened and the consequences of it. You don't know what caused it. So I thought, "Maybe I can address it before it happens and get an idea of why it's happening." When I went out onto the streets, what struck me first is that people just wanted to talk. They really were open and asked me lots of questions about why I was doing what I was doing. They found it strange but they were also really curious and wanted to know why I did it. It was interesting. I'd gone out onto the streets to find out why they did the things they did and they confronted me with the same question. (Community worker)

You cannot make any sort of difference and you cannot hope to help kids learn or mature and develop properly and well, unless you invest in them. Without investing something of yourself, you run the risk of abusing them more and causing much more hurt and havoc in their lives. I think first and foremost you've got to be passionate about what you do. Even if you're not that good at social work or you're not the best teacher in the world, if you believe in the young person and you reflect back to them the positive things about their lives and who they are, I think you're going to make an impact. And who doesn't want to make an impact as a teacher or as a social worker or any one of the helping professions? That's why you do the training. You want to make an impact. If you want to make an impact, you need to invest personally. You cannot remain impartial and separate. I heard all the way through my social work course that you've got to have your boundaries. And yes, you do have to have boundaries, but you've got to put yourself into your work. It doesn't work otherwise. (Welfare worker)

You need to be careful not to overextend yourself. A lot of teachers feel pressured into having to do everything themselves; to be a counselor, to bring food for students who don't have lunches, and do their core work of teaching as well. It's just not possible to do all that. (Social worker)

I know that if you don't have a heart for doing this type of thing it would be very difficult to do it. It's even difficult sometimes to remain patient when you do feel you've got the heart for it. If the wrong type of person was on the team they could probably do more damage than good by being there. At the same time, people don't know the needs unless they're told and even when people are told it's very hard for them to visualize the needs unless they've actually been there. One of my helpers said to me recently that until she went out on the streets she had no idea what people went through. I think we've all experienced that shock because none of us on the team have been used to that kind of lifestyle. (Youth worker)

When I was a child, a Polish family came to live next door and they didn't speak English very well. My brother and I taught the two boys how to play cowboys and Indians but they wouldn't play properly. When we shot them they wouldn't lie down. Instead they would cry and run home. Years later, I realized that they had just come out of the ghettos of Warsaw where the last people who had pointed guns at them were the Gestapo. At the time we had no idea because nobody told us. We couldn't understand why these kids cried every time we pointed our toy guns at them and shouted, "Bang. You're dead." I hate to think how traumatized those two were. We do things out of ignorance. When we got the first wave of Vietnamese refugees into the country, we put all the kids in classes together because we thought they'd be really good company for each other. In our ignorance, we didn't realize that there were different ethnic groups in Vietnam with a racial hatred that went back hundreds and hundreds of years. So, every time they went to ESL lessons, there'd be a fight in the classroom because they were competing against each other. (Teacher)

I have had some of my clients tell me that they were harassed by teachers and picked on. I'm not saying that what they're telling me is true; just that's what they tell me. They felt persecuted and that's probably brought on by some of their behaviors, too. (Psychologist)

We have had situations where teachers have refused to let a student into their class because they've got six rings in their nose and an eyebrow ring or they're not wearing a sports uniform. And I say, "Well, how does their physical appearance affect their right to learn and to be here if they want to be here?" (Social worker)

Teachers need to be very aware of the backgrounds that students come from. They might not share with you the problems they have at home, not specifically anyway, but they need to try to work out if there is a problem at home because that can really limit their potential. When they've got problems at home, they're not thinking about what they are studying. They're going to be thinking about their parents' problems and be distracted by them. If they're hungry and you try to teach them, they're only going to be thinking about eating. (Community worker)

A lot of these young people have so much going on in their head that learning about triangles and angles and logarithms is not a priority for them. What is a priority is knowing that they have someone that cares about them. A teacher can be a very significant person in a young person's life. I think teachers have a really important role in creating key relationships with young people. The teachers who have made an impact in my life aren't the ones who taught me the most. They're the people who invested in me, in who I am, and taught me more about myself. A good teacher is someone who has a passion for people, I think. (Welfare worker)

There are some teachers who are very good at connecting with students. Students feel comfortable in going up to them to talk. They just respect young people and are open to saying, "I'm here for you to talk if you need to." They are the teachers that I find get through to students because of their openness and understanding. And yet their workload is the same as other teachers. (Social worker)

Teachers should try to develop good peer relationships among students, particularly for those who feel they are disliked by everybody and spend most of the time by themselves. I think big differences are possible in their lives if there is some way of connecting them with someone else. Even one other significant person can make a huge difference in someone's life in alleviating the feeling that the entire class hates them or is picking on them. (Psychologist)

Some of their problems at school can be because they're in a group by themselves or they're in the bottom academic group. A lot of teachers focus on that as the problem but being in that group isn't the problem. Sometimes they can perform better because of that; they try to prove themselves. But to extract the best results out of them teachers need to make an extra effort to include them in mainstream class activities, to get their opinions on things, to value those opinions, to demonstrate that they have things to offer in class conversations. Sometimes because kids are quiet and don't say much, others automatically think that they don't know much. It just takes that extra effort to demonstrate how much ability that person has. (Community worker)

You can't group all young people the same. You have to be open to individual experiences, listen to what they say, and meet those needs as best you can. But you also need to be aware of some of the broader issues that young people face. One is that there are not many employment opportunities out there for many of them. Some don't want to be in schools but they've got no other option. They can't get a job right now so they're just there until something comes along. (Social worker)

You also need to be aware of the limitations that have been placed on them by their expectations of themselves and by their parents and friends. Sometimes there's pressure from their peers to remain with the group, to not distance themselves by furthering their education. There can be lots of people pulling them down. (Community worker)

Beyond recipes: A case study

This is a case study of a professional, a teacher, as much as it is about the boy he seeks to help. It illustrates the value of adopting a particular disposition, a way of thinking about troubled young people, rather than implementing a set of predetermined procedures irrespective of the young person's particular circumstances and individuality. It is about the nature of help and a conception of welfare that takes a long-term view; providing support for solutions constructed by individuals themselves rather than solutions imposed by others.

There's a young guy in Grade 9, with an older brother at the school, who comes from a very violent family. It's nothing for him to come to school with a black eye. Getting away from home is a viable option for him and the school is only holding on to him by a thread. He's at risk of self-excluding. In my experience there are two ways in which kids deal with these kinds of issues. One is to act out, the other is to become introverted. Those who act out are the ones we tend to come across more; they get sent to my office or they get expelled from school. Whereas those who don't say anything—and this young guy is one that doesn't—are never referred to me. He wasn't referred to anybody because he was just assumed to be quiet. People would ask him things like why he had a big bruise on his arm but he was quite good at explaining that away. He didn't draw too much attention to himself in class although he did develop a relationship with his sports teacher. This teacher would joke with him when he came in and say things like, "Don't you talk too much in gym today," and he just made him feel like he was accepted. This is a young boy who was very closed to everybody else but he started opening up to his teacher. I guess part of it was the teacher was another guy and he wasn't pressuring him. He wasn't saying, "Come on. Talk to me." He was just letting this boy know that he saw him, that he was aware that he was there, and that he thought he was a good kid.

Then one day this sports teacher came to my office and said, "I'm very concerned about Will. He doesn't concentrate very well in class and he was dizzy the other day." The teacher had invited this young guy to walk around the field with him when he was doing a lunch session and noticed that he didn't have any lunch. So he came to see me.

"I think this kid doesn't have any lunch. How can he concentrate in class if he doesn't have anything to eat?"

"That's a really good point. How are we going to find out if he doesn't have lunch?"

"I might bring him up to see you."

"Well, if he wants to come he can, but I'm not going to force him. We need to be pretty careful here."

In the end the teacher opted not to bring him to my office and instead we talked about what he might be able to do to support him. Without rushing him, the boy started to open up a little to this teacher, telling him about dad and mom's violence at home and was quite open in saying that most of the time he wasn't in the firing line. He wasn't being physically abused but I'm sure he was being emotionally abused, experiencing the trauma of a child witness. As well as the violence, dad was taking all the money and gambling it away, so that mom wasn't able to buy the family enough food. But the teacher didn't say, "Oh, we've got to get you out of your home. We've got to tell the authorities." He understood that this was the reality for this young boy, that he couldn't do anything about it and he was at risk of losing him if he tried.

The teacher just continued to talk with him whenever an opportunity arose and one day said, "I see that sometimes you have a burger for breakfast. How much money do you usually get?" "Oh, mom gives us $5 and we have to spread that out for lunch for the week." Now, instead of saying, "Well, you shouldn't be eating burgers for breakfast," over the next few weeks the two of them decided that they would make a list of food to buy from the supermarket. Because the boy couldn't do it himself—he wasn't permitted to miss classes—the teacher would go over in his lunch break with the boy's money and buy some bread, butter, honey, and a bag of apples. There's a room that students can access during their breaks and it has a small refrigerator. The teacher would put the food in there and this young guy and his older brother had sandwiches and apples for a week, basically, until the next lot of money came in. The boy's life hasn't changed profoundly. His parents are still engaged in domestic violence at home. He still hasn't got books to take to class and things like that, but he's now got some food in his stomach to help him concentrate on whatever he's doing. Previously he'd been fainting because he just didn't have any food and the other kids were staying away from him. Now that's all changed. Now he can go out during breaks, run around, and play football because he's not going to faint.

It didn't take up much of the teacher's time. He didn't have the kid hanging around him twenty-four hours a day, seven days a week. It just happened when he saw him, when he got him involved in activities, and the boy formed a connection with him. He followed a sound process. Firstly, he was aware, he was aware of what was going on around him. Secondly, he didn't impose on this kid his own expectations of how to live life. This is a teacher who comes from quite a well-established, middle-class background. He hasn't experienced in his own life what this boy has. Thirdly, he moved slowly. All of this happened over time. And fourthly, he provided this young guy with a role model. He wasn't saying things like, "I'm telling you what you've got to do." Instead, by being himself, by being a role model to this young guy, he taught him some really valuable life skills. Through what he did the teacher was saying, "You don't have to beat somebody up for their lunch money," which is what his older brother was doing and how his dad got money from his mom. It was about helping the boy make some choices, to choose what he wanted for lunch within the constraints of budget and nutrition. The temptation would have been to say, "I'll put in $20 and we'll easily get enough for your lunch for the whole week." Instead he just worked with the $5 and said, "This is what you can get for $5. You can make it spread over that period of time."

Also, the teacher was supported and he knew he was supported—that I was able to give him some support if he needed it. He'd regularly come and bounce ideas off me. He made no pretensions about knowing everything and neither did I. We would just agree, "Well, let's just try this and see where we go from there." That worked really well. It wasn't a recipe response. "When this happens, do that. This is what you do with kids who are in domestic violence situations." It was more about being aware and working it out as you go and stepping slowly through that process while allowing space for the boy to contribute to that. He had ownership of the whole thing. It wasn't a matter of saying, "Come with me and I'll fix you up. This is what you're going to do." And it wasn't, "Yes, OK, you've got all these problems going on. Let's shuffle you up to the social worker or to the guidance officer," or someone like that. I don't have a problem with people who genuinely feel that's the best thing to do, to refer students on when they don't know what to do. I just think a lot of the time you lose young people when you move too fast and that's with anything, whether it's the curriculum or anything else. We lose them very quickly when we move too fast. I also think those situations provide opportunities for us to learn and, with support, it really doesn't take that much time or take teachers away from their job of being a teacher. In fact, I think it helps them to become better teachers. (Social worker)

CHAPTER FOURTEEN

Working the system

I think the systems are OK as far as systems go…. You're going to get abuse in any sort of system….It's bound to happen because people aren't perfect and there is no way to make sure everyone's doing the right thing. (Welfare worker) The government as a whole, including the education system, has a lot to answer for….It's a real dog-eat-dog mentality and young people just don't have a voice to stand up and say, "This is what our needs are." (Social worker)

This chapter considers the systems that young people in need encounter. The professionals who constitute this conversation are aware of the manipulation of systems attempted by young people but they are also cognizant of the ways in which systems are themselves manipulating and at times insensitive to the needs of individuals. Through their exchanges, they recount the experiences of youth and their families who feel the full weight of the justice system, as well as their endeavors to comply with systems that don't seem to understand them and which they in turn fail to understand. The professionals herein argue that it is people who make systems work and the case study at the end of the chapter provides an extended exposition of how one professional seeks to find "a way out" as a strategic approach to negotiating outcomes of benefit to individuals.

System abuse

In what ways do young people on the fringe of society abuse the system? How can we excuse such behavior?

Children who have been coached and children who live on the fringes of society will lie with an ability that you would not believe. (Teacher)

One of the skills that you need to live on the street is being able to lie without anyone knowing that you're lying. Some kids are seasoned liars. They can look you straight in the eye and tell you something that definitely isn't right. They are not always as innocent as they try to make out. (Youth worker)

I can remember one boy who absolutely thrived on attention and he was an expert liar, which he used to great effect. He decided one day to convince our principal, who was not particularly socially aware, that he was a drug addict. We teach them all about drugs at school now, what to take, what it does to you, and how bad it is for you. It's a brilliant idea! You take kids who have no idea about drugs and teach them all about it! Armed with all that info, this boy had the principal completely convinced that he was a heroin user of quite some considerable size. He even managed to produce some marijuana once, which he stole from his father and then sold to his friends to keep up his image. I tried to get the principal to see reason, but he wouldn't listen despite my best efforts. I couldn't get him to explain to me where this child got the money to support a habit the size that he said he had. The other thing that let the story down was he didn't have any track marks. In the end I had the kid tested for drugs and brought the results back and said, "Look, there's nothing. There's no cannabis. There's nothing. The kid is pulling your leg." But the boy had achieved his objective. He received enormous status among his peers because the principal believed he was a druggie. Now the kids are always asking him to get them some stuff. (Teacher)

One of the things they do in court is to accentuate their bad circumstances and sometimes they even manufacture those, so that I might treat them differently. A rapist appeared before me the other day. I put him in jail for a week before I heard the plea. When he came back to court he said it would be terrible if he had to stay in jail because he couldn't get medicine for his bad back and he was just in absolute agony. So, I said, "Oh, that's terrible. I'll ring up the governor and find out what's happening." So I got my associate to ring up the governor of the jail and found out he'd been offered all the medication he needed but he refused to take it. He obviously refused to take it so that he would seem to be worse for the plea. I've also had others say they have been bashed and often men, in particular, say that they've been raped in jail. Sometimes it happens and sometimes it's just to make me feel sorry for them so I won't send them to jail. (Magistrate)

They come to the emergency department of the hospital all the time because it's free. They don't use the doctors around town because it costs them too much. I'm not sure how much it is but you have to have the money up front. If you're a single mother with four kids, that's a lot of money. They even come to us in the middle of the night because they think they'll get seen quicker. They'll get their kids out of bed at one or two in the morning and come then because they think it will be quiet. Apart from the fact that they can't afford to go to a doctor, they'll say they've only just arrived in town and haven't found one yet, or they don't like the one they're going to, or the one they're going to is on vacation. Then they claim they don't have transport home and want us to pay their taxi fare. We're very reluctant to do that because they'll want to do it again and again. In the end we have to and they know we have taxi vouchers anyway. Some people genuinely race to get to the hospital and don't have any money with them so we help them out with a voucher—whereas others will never get out of the department if you don't pay their fare. Sometimes they'll use an ambulance to get there and then say they can't get home. They'll tell the ambulance guys that they've got something wrong with them and then when they arrive they change their story. They'll register and then leave. They don't even wait to be seen. Presumably, they just wanted a lift to somewhere near the hospital. Often the ambulance guys get a different home address to what we get, so they don't know where to send the bill and it gets written off. It's obvious it comes down to money, but people get housing assistance, they get the dole, they get children's benefits. I think there is a lot of misuse of those benefits. For instance, a packet of cigarettes is not cheap and they always have them. They all smoke and claim they have no money. And the kids are always eating junk food. That's not cheap. (Nurse)

My mom's a nurse and she often complains to me about people abusing the system. But it's easy for people to be dismissive of their problems and say, "Little animals. How can they get away with it?" Some young people can manipulate the system extremely well. They are adept at it. But I would say that's not the majority. A lot of kids get a bad wrap because of the few that do it. I'm not a bleeding heart that says, "Well, they obviously need to do that to survive." I don't condone it, but I am concerned for them, too. They're not learning the valuable skills that they need to make any sustainable change. They're always going to need to mug somebody, literally and figuratively, to get what they want. Others who live with domestic violence are very good at hiding that too, or they find excuses for it, which is about shame and stigmatization and not wanting to be different. They are very good at manipulating their circumstances to give the impression they have their lives under control. The problem is they then don't access the support systems and resources that they need to learn other ways of solving problems. (Social worker)

I think kids are really smart, particularly street kids and particularly when it comes to getting what they want. A lot of kids in care would have assigned to them a protective worker, someone from an agency who looks after their accommodation, a worker at their residential unit, and a drug and alcohol worker with an outside agency. They can have up to six key workers really involved in their day-to-day life. If you are a kid who doesn't have a lot, it's tempting to get as much as you can from each of them. So you often have a dynamic where the child plays one against the other. Welfare organizations are very aware of it and I think most of the time they only let it happen when it suits them. That's the sort of situation that I've been in anyway. You're always very aware that young people are going to try you out, which is no different to any adolescent really. "Mom, can I go here?" "Only if your father says it's OK." "Dad, mom says it's all right." Adolescents manipulate. It's a fact of life. (Welfare worker)

One young girl said she wanted to go to a respite hostel for girls (aged 12 to 17). We managed to get her accepted but she just didn't have the skills to interact within the family atmosphere and left. It caused considerable controversy because before she left she stole the sheets and the canned food, and news about it got out. People were saying, "How could she bite the hand that feeds her?" They made a big issue of it. Now she moves around from place to place, staying with older men. She says that she's not having sex with them but she just gets them to take her out for a meal. Then she spends the night with them and goes on her way the next day. She does that on a very regular basis. I'm sure some of their things go missing occasionally as well! That's the way she's learned to survive. In a lot of ways her boundaries are very open and in other ways they're very closed. She has experienced quite serious abuse for a large period of her life, which has led to her drawing some very tight boundaries around herself. She doesn't let anybody in emotionally but she's quite free with her body and her money and possessions. That's the way she survived out there. She uses people to get food and accommodation when she could very easily say to them, "I haven't got anywhere to stay. Can you put me up?" From where she stands, that's not very self-reliant. She sees herself as very self-reliant in being able to con a meal out of others. She eats on her terms. She's opposed to putting her hand out for charity, which is a big issue for a lot of young people. It's very embarrassing for them to have to admit that they need help and that they can't do it on their own. (Social worker)

Abusive systems

To what extent are our systems at fault? How much do they take account of the needs of individuals?

For particular groups, schools are very oppressive places. I've come across some absolutely brilliant teachers, but they're individuals up against a system based on competitiveness. It's based on your ability to access resources. A lot of young people from low socioeconomic backgrounds just don't have the ability to access those resources. They don't fit the role of good students who come to school in nice clothes, who smell nice, who are pleasant to look at, who are widely accepted by teachers. For them, school is a very lonely place. They're not getting what they need out of the education system, so eventually they just don't go. They try to meet their needs in other ways. (Social worker)

I think the systems are OK as far as systems go. You're always going to have problems because the individuals who work in them aren't perfect. For example, I've had really significant problems with police. There are some police who beat up young people and we've had to try to deal with that. You're going to get abuse in any sort of system. When you're dealing with people, you're going to get some abuse of a system. It's bound to happen because people aren't perfect and there is no way to make sure everyone's doing the right thing. But generally, the majority of kids I've worked with have had OK relationships with the police and have quite a positive relationship with the courts. (Welfare worker)

The system probably isn't designed with this intent, but the outcome is to take away people's individuality. For example, a lot of the women that I work with have had their children taken away, put in foster care, or placed on custody orders and things like that. The department, as it rightly should be, is quite focused on the needs of the child. That's of paramount importance. But when their children are taken away, the individual woman, their circumstances, their needs and wants, aren't exactly taken into account. They feel that they're not their kids anymore. They'll say, "Somebody's taken them away and I have no say in what's going on," which isn't always the case. One woman, in particular, just doesn't understand why her kids have been taken away from her or what she has to do to get them back. For a while she didn't even know their address or where she could write to them. Another woman that I know still has guardianship powers over her children so she can make the major decisions that need to be made for them, but she just feels like they're not hers any more. She thinks that when she sees them again they won't want to know her and they won't want to live with her any more. The focus is on the child and the parents miss out, really. They aren't really kept properly informed about what's happening to their kids. (Psychologist)

There were two sisters who I didn't work with directly but every time they had to move out of their residential care I was the worker on duty. I was never their case manager, I just happened to be on duty. I happened to be the person that somebody called to help out. That happened three times. It was so traumatic for those girls. They were just 14 and 15 at the time. I particularly remember the third move. We stood at the front door of their new foster family and they cried and cried for half an hour. All I could do was just hug them both. It was so traumatic for them, being uplifted and moved to yet another family they didn't know. It was just not conducive to making them feel good about themselves. They felt like, "We're a burden. No one loves us. Why doesn't anyone want us?" All I could say was, "You have to do this but there are people around you who want to help you and support you." That didn't do anything to help them of course, when they have to meet a new family and confront a new bedroom. It's really traumatic. There's no stability, nothing. I consider that system abuse at it's worst. It makes me really cross. (Welfare worker)

The government as a whole, including the education system, has a lot to answer for. Why aren't there more special-needs teachers there to go into the classroom to work with students? Why isn't there more support to address the issues that they have and to help the teacher work with other young people who don't have special needs but need some extra support anyway? It's just not happening. It's a real dog-eat-dog mentality and young people just don't have a voice to stand up and say, "This is what our needs are." (Social worker)

The system that I've seen in operation in schools doesn't really support the kids who have academic problems. There are measures that they put in place, such as extra support in the classroom, but in terms of the way students get ahead, the system, the institution, just isn't made for kids who struggle academically. You find a lot of boys just hang in there until Grade 10. Then they really struggle and that generally is the end of their schooling. (Welfare worker)

Schools cannot be there to meet the needs of every individual student. It's just impossible given the very limited resources in most government schools. A lot are understaffed and, particularly in disadvantaged schools, there is high staff turnover. One of the schools that I worked in last year lost 16 teachers in one year, about a third of the entire staff. Those who came to replace them were virtually graduates, still coming to terms with what teaching is all about. Schools generally do the best they can with what they've got and they contribute or don't contribute to the needs of young people through some quite rigid inflexibility that seems to be built into the system. (Social worker)

I've spent many weekends in the hospital with young people who have overdosed on a cocktail of drugs, so they're not even sure exactly how much they've had and what they've had, or they've fallen unconscious from chroming. The hospitals don't respond well at all. In the majority of cases, the kids are left just to be observed. Because there isn't a lot they can do and because these young people are doing these things to themselves, the attitude can be quite negative. They are seen as a waste of resources. That's the feeling I've got. Not a lot of respect has been shown to them in those circumstances, which is why it's important to have a key person as an advocate for the young person. Kids in that sort of circumstance don't respond well to being patronized. When they're high or they can't breathe properly, they don't respond really well to being treated like dirt and as a drain on the system. (Welfare worker)

Young people go through a developmental stage where they challenge the system. It actually teaches them some very valuable life skills. It can start with, "Well, why do I have to?" Then, depending on how people respond, it can become a real power struggle. "Because I said you do and this is the rule." "Well, I couldn't care less about the rule." And then the whole purpose of the exercise gets lost. It becomes a matter of me against you. A lot of young people's conflict resolution skills aren't great. They get themselves into fights and it just escalates and escalates until it becomes very personal. And I think that kind of interaction is not uncommon in schools. As much as schools might tell you it's about the good of one versus the good of all, it's really about, "This is what I want and this is what you want, and we're going to fight it out until one of us gets what we want and that's going to be me." (Social worker)

Order in the court

What happens when young people encounter the justice system? How well does it work for them?

As far as justice goes, they're often scared. Not scared of the police so much, although they do refer to them as bullies. That shows the relationship they have with them. They see the police as there to push them around, to impose their will upon them. And the police do things like shine their spotlights on them at night on the streets and talk to them from a distance. It's quite intimidating. (Community worker)

Often young people refer to the police behind their backs as pigs. They'll say things like, "Do you smell bacon?" But when they're face to face with them, generally the kids that I've worked with, even really difficult young people, respect the authority that police have. And I've found the same thing, too, when I've gone with young people to court. (Welfare worker)

There is often a bravado when they are outside the court. Their friends are there and it's almost like a carnival atmosphere sometimes. But when they come into the courtroom, when they are on their own, you can see they are very afraid. They are uncertain about what will happen to them and they don't always feel that their counsel is listening to what they want. They are told to be quiet. When charges are read and they're asked, "Are you guilty?" Some answer, "Yes," but sometimes it is really said out of courtesy. They don't really mean it. They don't understand the courtroom. It moves too quickly for them. They don't understand the language or the process. They just go along with it and pretend that they understand although they have no real idea. (Community worker)

There's often a real fear associated with being in court. Adolescents know enough to understand that the magistrate has a lot of power over what happens to them. You might get a really obnoxious adolescent waiting out front for a court hearing; mom and dad are anxious and stressed while the young person is mouthing off. Then they walk into that courtroom and something happens. It's quite odd. Some kids don't care. They've been in the system long enough not to be affected by it anymore. They don't care what the magistrate says, or they act as if they don't. They'll do what they like anyway. You do get that sometimes. But generally, young people walk into the courtroom and suddenly become very quiet. (Welfare worker)

A lot of times the defending counsel is just there out of duty. They just get the facts of the case. "Did you do it or not?" They don't go into, "Why did you do it?" or "Why do you think you're accused of this?" or "Do you know what's going on? Do you know what the police have charged you with? Do you understand the charge?" They begin with the crime. "Did you do it or not?" And from there they try to work out the best outcome. So they'll say, "If you plead guilty it might be better for you than if you plead not guilty. If you plead not guilty and you are convicted, the penalty could be more serious. You could get more time. But if you plead guilty from the start you can get that taken into account and you might get a lesser penalty." They just want a guilty or not guilty plea and then they plan from there how the magistrate will respond. They don't help their clients understand the charge or the seriousness of it. And it seems as if they just want the best result for themselves, what would be quicker for them. It's aimed at the outcome they can get. (Community worker)

The fact that someone has been brought to the attention of the court once for doing something generally demonstrates that they've done it many, many times before without having come to court. We only see the tip of the iceberg. So if someone comes to court on a drug-related crime—they may be charged with four counts of theft, for example—that doesn't mean that's the only time in their life that they have stolen something. It just means that those are the ones that the police have managed to get enough evidence on to convict them. And that's one of the reasons, I think, that it's so difficult for drug users. They almost, always reoffend. They're just totally unable to be cured because they've got into the habit of it, and they've just been unlucky once or twice to come before the court on those offenses. (Magistrate)

I think the court system works quite well with young people. It's not too austere. It's not too high and mighty that the kids are too intimidated, but it has enough respectability. I've found most of the magistrates to be really compassionate. There are exceptions but most make every effort to make sure the young person knows what's happening and understands what the decisions are. There is quite a nice feel to it even though it's a stressful place. (Welfare worker)

Sometimes if you give them too short a sentence, it's not an advantage to anyone. My very first culpable driver was a kid on a motorcycle who had killed a young child in an accident. I didn't send him to jail. Instead I gave him an intensive corrections order because I was sorry for him. He was 18 or

19. I found out later that he was picked up by the police five or six months later, again driving an unregistered vehicle in a dangerous manner. He obviously thought, "That was a stupid sentence. I didn't get adequately punished for it. I don't need to worry particularly." You've got to take that into account when sentencing, what the impact of the sentence might be and what his counsel has told him. Often they'll say, "Now, listen, you're in really serious trouble here. The magistrate is going to give you a really serious sentence, so you've got to really start thinking about what you're doing with your life." Well, after being told that, if a person gets a suspended sentence or something that's really minor, the effect of what he's been told by other people is not going to sink in. (Magistrate)

When they get a good result they seem to belittle the crime. They think, "That wasn't so bad. The system didn't do very much to me. The magistrate was quite lenient. I was really scared, but it's all OK." That's how they respond when they are put on probation or ordered to do community service. They don't feel as though they are paying for the crime. Then their counsel will shake their hand and say, "You did really well," as if to say, "I'll see you next time." When they get off lightly you can't wipe the smirk off their faces. One minute they are very matter of fact with their counsel and then when they get outside you see the huge relief on their faces. But when they are put into prison, you can see the devastation on the faces of their families. (Community worker)

Sometimes I get the feeling that the police have set the situation up to solve the family problem. They'll charge the offender with something like armed robbery and they'll come to court and say, "Well, this person has really learned his lesson and has really changed since." You get the impression that they're hoping that you will reinforce what they've done. If you've got a young teenager committing armed robberies, then sometimes it's the best thing in the world for him to be caught and for the family to go through all that agony associated with their son being in jail. Often the police will put them in jail for a couple of weeks, which is a terrifying thing. By the time they come to me, which might be six months later, the problem is already solved. That's the problem in sentencing because then the community says, "Why did that person get such a short sentence?" Yet often the reason is that all the work has been done before the young person has even come to the court. (Magistrate)

The courts and the police have a really important role with young people because they set really clear boundaries and young people usually respond well to that. Even if they don't do what they're supposed to do, they usually respond well to a clear set of values. (Welfare worker)

There's a phrase that some use: "If you do the crime you do the time." It's not common. I have heard a couple of people say that and they tend to be the people who have resigned themselves to the fact that they're going to be in jail for a long time. They can see it as a bit of a cliché as well and I don't know that it really means a lot to them, but they say it to me sometimes. I think it's to mask how they're really feeling about being in prison. I think they think that maybe that's what I think and maybe what society thinks as well. I don't think they're really resentful about being sent to prison. I know that they don't like it and they say to me it's a horrible place to be, but they do accept the system that puts them there. There are always people who say, "I got far too long. Look at those other people who did much more than me and got a lesser sentence." There's a lot of that that goes on. (Psychologist)

The serious criminals, the armed robbers who really intend to do it, they expect a serious sentence. I had two men who intended to hold up an armored vehicle at a local supermarket. They had guns and balaclavas and were about to do it when they were caught by the police. The reason they didn't do it was because the van didn't arrive on time. They were quite OK about their sentence. They pleaded not guilty but when the jury decided they were guilty, well, you know, that's it. What can they do. They're used to it. They get used to a certain sort of tariff. If they've been in jail or connected with people who have been in the same criminal area, they know what the going rate is. And they really do not appear to me to bear any ill will toward the magistrate at all. (Magistrate)

Red tape

What are the obstacles that systems place in the way of young people on the edge of society? How can these be overcome?

A lot of families don't want anything to do with child protection, the police, or the courts because it implies that something is really wrong. Whereas you go into social security and into hospitals expecting them to help you. (Welfare worker)

Often these government agencies don't treat people as individuals because they see themselves as having a duty of care to the larger community. "If we do it for this one, if we let this person through, then we'll have chaos and we'll have to do it for everybody and things won't be good for anybody." I guess the dilemma is, "What's good for one person versus what's good for all." (Social worker)

I think the difficulty is they have to be accountable for what they let through the system. That's the biggest pressure on them. On the other hand, kids who live on the street are struggling to feed themselves or trying to get ahead when everything is against them. It's a clash of purposes. They are coming from different perspectives. Whereas a professional like me, who doesn't have to worry about where my next meal is coming from, can appreciate that the person behind the desk is doing her job and is constrained by her tasks and job responsibilities. For the average 15 year old who just wants her welfare payment so she can eat or get her next hit, that's not going to make two hoots of difference. She's just going to be really frustrated because this person wants her identification or something to tell her that she's the right person and she's entitled to the money. (Welfare worker)

They struggle constantly with government assistance. And when they don't get the money from welfare they think they deserve, they take it very personally. They take out their frustrations on themselves by getting drunk or on others through physical violence. (Community worker)

They often get the runaround when they go along to the department. They have to have this form in and if they haven't got that form, they can't see anyone then and they've got to go somewhere else to be able to see them and so on. It would be a big deal to go there because you had to have everything ready, and that's not often a priority for young people who are struggling to find a place to live or don't have a really nice home life and they've got all those pressures as well. (Welfare worker)

There are a lot of circumstances where they miss out because they don't fill out all the forms or they thought they'd filled out the form and something else has come in the mail but they didn't understand it. They might have thrown it away but it was something requiring more information. A lot think the system is up against them and they view it with suspicion. They see it as a conspiracy against them, to put them off. The department will ask them for things, they'll give it to them but then they'll come up with something more. They feel as though the requirements are put in place to trip them up, so they'll give up part way. And often it works like that. People give up because they just can't keep up with the paperwork. (Community worker)

I think there are increasing difficulties the more and more schools become institutionalized. When you enroll your kids at school you have to fill out all these forms; you have to organize uniforms; you have to pay for books and if you don't have the money you have to fill out another form to get assistance from the government to pay for them. It's made as simple as possible, I know, but it can be very intimidating for disadvantaged families. On lots and lots of occasions I've done that for a mom because she hasn't been able to cope with that. (Welfare worker)

When I worked at the counter, I was often called on because the others where I worked thought I knew how to speak to them or sometimes because they didn't smell very nice. I would just let them speak even though sometimes it would be slow. When I did the talking or I tried to rush them through a document—"Just fill out this and this and this"—they wouldn't understand. So I'd go through it with them, even asking the exact same question that was on the form. Then the lights would turn on, even though they might have read it themselves. I suppose a lot couldn't read very well. You'd hear them reading sometimes and it would be very slow, one word at a time, and they'd make mistakes. But when you got them to fill in the form themselves, they were able to write. They were just really confused about having a document to fill in. They seemed to have the view that because they weren't educated, "I'm not able to do that. I don't know what to do." (Community worker)

If you're an average worker at the local hospital or at the counter in a welfare department and you try to deal with these young people reasonably, it doesn't work. Often they're not reasonable because they've got other priorities in life. For me, the key is to make sure that the young person has a key relationship with an advocate. If they can establish a buffer like that, you can often get where you want to go—in hospitals, welfare departments, and institutions generally. It's very difficult to work with these young people but bureaucrats need to understand that young people see them as having all the power and that they're just being told, "No." Or, "No." Or, "No." Or, "You can't do that." Or, "You can't." Or, "You're being bad." All that negative stuff is all they hear. (Welfare worker)

There have been principals who I've worked with who have been very open to sitting down and exploring the issues with young people. Others find it more convenient to say, "No. This is the rule and that's the way it's going to be." I think we all have the capacity to do that when we're under pressure and we're feeling we don't have the time to explore a situation more fully. (Social worker)

Looking for a way out: A case study

Of particular interest in this case is the way in which the sometimes con-flicting demands of the system (in this case, the justice system) and the needs of individuals are reconciled through a strategy of "looking for a way out." It is not so much that the system is ignored or abused but that various ave-nues and opportunities within the system are explored in order to find one that satisfies the particular circumstances at hand. In this it has similarities with the cases presented in Chapter 12, which also is mindful of an institu-tional-individual dialectic, and in Chapter 13, which expounds the benefits of avoiding a one-size-fits-all approach to solving problems.

I recall one woman, in particular, who had been introduced to drugs by her boyfriend before he left her. She was continually high on drugs and had done the rounds of the city agencies and worn out her welcome at all of them. With nowhere to go, she ended up in a psychiatric hospital. She also had a baby from an earlier relationship, which was taken from her at birth and given to her parents who lived on the other side of the country. Her drug habit inevitably led her into a life of crime and eventually brought her to court. She had committed some dreadful armed robberies using a syringe that all her victims thought contained HIV-infected blood. She actually pricked somebody with the syringe although there wasn't anything in it. Now, while they are very serious crimes, you try to look for the way out. You look for the solution that will get them out of that place.

The people from the psychiatric hospital said, "If she goes back to where her parents live we can organize a residence there and she can start having something to do with the baby. That relationship might be enough to break the cycle." So, instead of sending her to jail—she'd already been in jail for six months—I said, "All right. I'll give you three years' jail but I won't im-pose it on you now. I'll let you go back to your hometown. If you don't commit another offense for two years then that will be the end of it. See if you can make a go of it. But if you do commit another offense, you'll have to come back here and I'll sentence you to three years in jail and you won't see your baby again." She was really upset and said, "Oh, no. I won't do anything wrong again." Now, I don't know whether she will or not but in every situation, that's what the best lawyers do. They look for a solution. They look for a way out.

Some Christian organizations are good for that, although some are really naïve. There's a farm run by one group somewhere north of the city. They take on drug addicts and criminals, give them a farm lifestyle and spend lots of time talking to them. They're not trained counselors but they just talk to them and get to know them. One guy who went there after being charged with armed robbery had people from this farm come along to court and say, "He's a changed man. He's terrific. He'll never do this again. He's learnt the error of his ways." But the problem for me was they'd only known him for three or four weeks. The incident was a month before. It was just as easy to reach the conclusion that he'd gone to the farm with the intention of being able to say that to the magistrate. A good friend of mine, a person who works with troubled youth, also takes the view that often people go onto welfare programs and church-based programs a couple of months before their court hearing as a way of getting a lighter sentence. So you've got to be careful but in the end, if there's a chance, you take it. It just might work and the system won't work if everyone's locked in prison. You've got to give people the chance.

It's the same with people who are released on parole. They get to serve out their sentence on parole so they can be monitored when they're back in the community. Now, every time the parole board releases somebody, they take a risk. These might be very dangerous people. They might do exactly the same thing again. All you can say is, "Well, perhaps the knowledge that there's someone there watching, who's going to send them to jail if they don't comply with their parole, is strong enough."

With kids who aren't in that deep, often the very fact that they've had to go to court is enough. It's a big issue in itself because they've had to reveal it to their parents and their friends and their employer. They have to say, "I've done an armed robbery on a shop," or something like that. So everyone knows about it. They've had long family discussions and they've had to ask people to come to court for them. If you've got someone who's not too far into it, often that's enough. You can say to them, "You know I can give you 25 years in jail for this, but I don't think I will today, as long as you're good for the next three years." In fact, someone like that appeared before me just a couple of months ago. He was from an otherwise good family but his girlfriend introduced him to heroin and he just wanted some extra money so he went down to the local shop and held up the owner in a really inexpert sort of way. No one in his local community could really understand it. "He's not the same guy."

With someone like that, you don't send them to jail unless you absolutely have to. Sometimes you have to because it's obvious that they're not really responding or they've done something that's so dreadful that you have no choice. But generally you take a chance when you can get it because our system depends on jail being for the few, not the majority. When you've got the prospect of doing something else, you take it. (Magistrate)

CHAPTER FIFTEEN

A rainbow out of reach

They know what they should be able to achieve but they can't seem to do it. Others accept knocks along the way because that's just part of life, but each time they get a knock back it's a much bigger blow to them. It's like a rainbow they can't reach. (Community worker)

In this conclusion to their conversation, the professionals in this chapter consider the imagined and actual futures for young people living on the edge of society. They note the dreams of a bright future typical of many living in adverse circumstances but also their unrealistic expectations and their lack of appreciation for the obstacles they find in their way. To some extent, the discussion rehearses those in previous chapters of the necessity for institutional change and the "comforts" of a life on the street that mitigate against a more prosperous future for these young people. The chapter concludes again with a case study, this time of one woman's hopes for the future in the face of significant addiction. This time, she predicts, things will be different.

Measured success

What are the aspirations of these young people for the future? How realistic are they?

The homeless are not absolute hopeless cases. We had one guy who at some stage did three quarters of a college course. Then he dropped that one and did half of another before he ended up on the streets. His explanation was that when the going got tough he dropped out. He was on the streets on and off for quite some time before he moved into an apartment. He's not in very good health now but he has really managed to change his life over the last couple of months. Hopefully something can be done with his health problems so that he can enjoy his change of lifestyle that he's been able to bring about. (Youth worker)

Surprisingly, quite a lot see going to prison as an opportunity for them to turn their lives around. Sometimes it's the first time in years that they've actually stopped using heroin or speed. It's freely available in prison and offered to them when they first come by other prisoners. It's also a lot cheaper in prison than it is outside. You can get heroin for the same price as a packet of cigarettes. It's not something that's difficult to get. Of course, it's not sanctioned by the prison. There are searches going on all the time to try to find it. But a lot of them have spent up to a week, sometimes two weeks in the cells where you can't get any drugs and before they actually get to the prison. A lot say that they've been able to get through the withdrawal period while they're in the cells, then they get to prison and don't accept the drugs when they're offered to them. They also seem to consider their sentence as an opportunity to do some work. I'm seeing a biased sample of the population, of course, because I'm seeing those who want to work on their problems. I assess everyone who comes in but they have the right to refuse that assessment. They don't have to turn up. The people I see on a long-term basis are those who are willing and motivated to address their issues. (Psychologist)

One young girl, who came to us a couple of years ago, has now been in employment for over 12 months. I still see her from time to time in the mall where she works. She serves in a take-away food outlet. She never went back to school after leaving in Grade 9. School was a major problem for her and she was a major problem for school. The teachers were throwing up their hands in despair, saying, "What can we do with Bek?" and she was on the point of being expelled. But since she's had this chance at a job, it's turned her life around. For a lot of people, getting an education, finishing secondary school, is a big thing. But for Bek, her life is probably better for working in the job she's in. Maybe she won't feel that way in a few years. Maybe she'll then think, "I need to go back to school. Now that I've got a bit of maturity about me, maybe I need to get Grade 12. Maybe I need to go to college." But when she was 14 or 15, that wasn't for her. To me, Bek getting that job and still being employed 12 months later is a big success. (Youth worker)

A good proportion of them aren't interested in gaining employment when they're released from prison. Of those that are, their expectations of themselves are quite high. Quite a lot will say that they have a desire to be a social worker or a psychologist or work in professions that require at least a three-year college degree. That doesn't necessarily translate into them actually starting those qualifications while they're in prison, even though those opportunities are available to them. (Psychologist)

I naturally thought to go to college after I finished school, but it's not something they naturally do. Sometimes they pluck up the courage to do something more than what was expected of them at school and by their parents. More often their family's expectations are the sum total of what they achieve. It's a self-fulfilling prophecy. What their parents tell them they'll attain is what they usually attain. (Community worker)

Some have aspirations to be social workers. They say, "I know what life's like to be a heroin addict." It's almost as if they are implying that to be a social worker you have to have gone through these life experiences yourself. It's as if that's the main criteria. That might explain why they don't engage in the courses that led to those occupations because they think that they have that knowledge already. In their eyes, they could almost walk out on the street now and be a social worker because they understand the problems. (Psychologist)

We had one young guy who went away for about 12 months so that he could get a bit more of an education. He started a college preparatory course but unfortunately didn't see it through. He is planning to go back again this year. He says he now has a little bit more of a handle on what's expected of him. He says as soon as the pressure grew too great last year he went back on the drugs and he's had to have some rehabilitation since. Now he's more aware of what will be expected of him in the course. He still has hopes of going on to become a social worker. Sometimes when somebody from that walk in life has tried something and, in other people's terms, failed, they still need our support to be able to pick themselves up and give it another try. Their desire is still there about what they want to do. You could say that he's failed but in a way he's succeeding because he hasn't given up. He wants to come back again. He wants to try again. And while he's still got that attitude I don't think he's a failure. A lot of people would, but I don't. (Youth worker)

When they get accepted into college, it's like they've broken through a barrier. It's a release. They don't feel like the system is up against them anymore. Once they see opportunities for themselves, and sometimes they see the extra benefits that aren't given to other people, they realize that they are able to do it. And, as difficult as it is, they develop new friends. They see that things are tough for their friends as well but they stick at it. It doesn't even enter the minds of some to pursue further education. They didn't like school in the first place so they don't even try to go to college. But those who did OK at school see it as a way of showing others what they can achieve. Some choose something to study because they've got a passion for it but most start just with the intention of showing others they can do it, to better themselves and to get a good job. (Community worker)

Paradise lost

What hinders them from realizing a better future? What are the obstacles to change?

Sometimes when you speak to them in hospital, when they're at their lowest, they'll talk about their need for change. But when you talk to them about the alternatives, what they could do to better themselves, that's not an option. It's not that they think they can't change; it's more that they don't acknowledge the problems in the first place, so they see no need to address them. (Community worker)

A lot of these kids have significant histories of abuse and trauma, which almost stunts their emotional and academic growth. Many have a block when it comes to dealing with any sort of official place. They have a fear of institutions. It's a fear that stops them from behaving normally and being able to answer questions and fill in forms. They've got so much happening in their lives that they expect that welfare payment to be in their bank account and when it's not, their whole world falls apart. They don't know how to rectify it because they never developed the skills to function in that context. (Welfare worker)

Drug addicts don't have any capacity to deal with their problems. Whereas it's such a relief when you come across people who aren't involved with drugs because you can say to them, "OK, you can do community work for 12 months. If you do that, that's it. I'll get you to do that instead of sending you to jail." But you'd be very silly to give those sorts of dispositions to people who are on drugs because they're so unreliable. They'll never do it. (Magistrate)

They also attempt to justify their behavior. One woman said to me recently that if she wakes up in the morning and she's suffering withdrawal symptoms and really hurting, she knows that all she has to do is take some heroin and it will stop. So it's quite easy for them to justify getting that money from anywhere they can, because they're hurting so much. I'm sure they see that as justification for committing drug-related crimes. (Psychologist)

One year I was in court hearing criminal cases the week before Christmas. I was doing appeals. I had about ten or twelve people in that one week. And, of course, you don't want to put people in jail for Christmas. So, I gave them bonds to all the people that came before me. I said, "Now, you won't do it again, will you? You're absolutely sure you won't do it again? If you come up on any other criminal charge, you will come back before me and I'll have to send you to jail. But I'll let you out if you promise you won't do it again." All of them were absolutely sure they'd never do it again but they all cropped up again through the next year. When they reoffend, you have to have another hearing and the only way to do that is to squeeze it in sometime in your schedule. So you have to sit early in the morning or late in the evening just to deal with the extra cases. For the whole of that year, I had all these people appearing before me because they had reoffended and the problem then is that they get a very heavy sentence. If they reoffend, you don't have much choice except to send them to jail. Almost everyone will tell you they will never, ever do it again. They're completely cured. They don't want to be involved in a life of crime. They've got a job. They get people to give them apprenticeships and things like that. And they'll never ever do it again. It's a real problem for magistrates because if you accepted their account, more than likely you would see all these repeat offenders reappearing. I think people genuinely believe that they won't reoffend but the problem is that they really haven't got the capacity to not reoffend. If you're living with your boyfriend and he's a drug user and he's used to making money out of petty crime and you're living with him, well, what are you going to do? Are you going to say to him, "No, I'm not going to be involved?" Or you go back to a family that may well be involved in the same things. You may not have a family that will allow you to be different. Many don't really have the capacity to take themselves out of that environment. It's only when they do, that people manage to stay straight. (Magistrate)

We've had some regulars over time. They might be regular with us for quite some time and then move to a different town. Some get their life to the stage where they just drop in occasionally. Others have gone to jail. Shifting to another town or getting out of jail is often a time that they think, "I'll start afresh." Then, because they tend to go back to the same type of company again, they end up with the same problem just in a different town. (Youth worker)

I guess they think that they're invincible, that they're not going to get caught. One woman said to me recently that since she's been in prison she's realized how stupid she was. She now wonders how on earth she could think that her parents and her friends didn't notice that she was stoned all the time. Now she sees other people in prison who are using marijuana or some other drug and it's so obvious to her. I think they have the impression that they're somehow able to hide things, that people can't tell what they're doing, so they don't really expect to be caught. (Psychologist)

I know of one guy who was in his 40s and he'd had the same job since he was 15 when he left school. Now, in all those years he never thought that one day he would get a pink slip saying, "You've been made redundant. The job isn't there anymore." He was at an age when nobody wanted to retrain him in any sort of vocation and he said himself that he didn't think he could go back to school again. He hadn't done well when he'd been at school all those years before. So to change and do some sort of office job or something like that was beyond him. He'd only ever done a manual job and nobody wanted a 45 year old. Gradually, because of the way it affected him, he lost his family and all of his lifestyle. He was unable to go forward in his life and he couldn't go back. He just sort of stagnated. Losing his family meant dividing everything up—selling the family house and the family car. He went through that money in no time. He was on his own and he found comfort in drinking. So, of course, the money that he did have from the sale of things didn't last and eventually he ended up on the street. (Youth worker)

They might try for a job but if they get knocked back once that will be the end of it. They're very fearful of rejection. That's why they get put off quite easily from trying to do something for themselves. (Community worker)

One reason for not seeking employment is that they're afraid of the stigmatism of having been in prison. They've been convicted of a crime and they feel that people won't employ them. That's the major issue. Others intend to go back to their criminal lifestyle, using drugs and so on, and that doesn't leave any room for employment. Some say that they're more interested in getting their life back on track. They don't feel that they can cope with employment as soon as they get out and that's more a longer-term goal for them. (Psychologist)

There's one guy who moved here with his family simply because they could afford to buy a house in this area and they couldn't afford to buy one where they came from. But things didn't go well and he ended up separated from his family. I hear a lot of that type of thing. People will say, "Well, I can afford to buy a house here but I can't afford to buy one there." They limit their ability to work so much more because there's less work in those areas. I know of one family that bought a very cheap house surrounded by a few acres in a remote part of the country but they couldn't do anything there. His idea was, "I can afford to buy this." But that's virtually the end of that guy's working life, even though he's only in his 30s. It's that narrow vision that limits them. They need to broaden their outlook. They don't think through the consequences of what that might mean, whereas I would sit and think about the pros and cons. I'd make a list and say, "Well, this would be an advantage but that would be a disadvantage." Another family in a similar situation has bought a property with a van on it. There's no electricity and no running water, only a gas bottle that runs a few appliances. And the land is useless. There's nothing you can do with it. It's just a dead weight around their necks. They have to drive into the nearest town to do their washing and buy their food. They got themselves into a situation where they couldn't rent anywhere because they had fallen behind in their rental payments and, because of their bad debt, they didn't have references that might have got them assistance from the government. Sometimes people put themselves into a position where their options are very limited. Or they'll come up with something they're going to do, which they see as the solution to everything and it's going to be perfect. In reality, they can't get themselves into that position and it's another disappointment for them. (Youth worker)

I don't think that a lot of them really have a full understanding of why things turned out for them the way they have. Part of that is them avoiding thinking about it themselves. It takes a lot of work for someone to fully understand how they came to be where they are in life. I often ask people, "Did you ever think that you might end up here?" Occasionally, I've had people say, "I did think about it once but I didn't really worry about it." But generally they say they never expected to end up in prison. It was a series of small steps that got them there rather than something really big. (Psychologist)

There are regulars that have a set place where they sleep under a bridge or in the park. And I can see the kids who constantly move around from house to house as being the future ones on park benches and under bridges if something isn't done to change their life now. I don't think you'd ever get the regulars who sleep rough back in a house full time again, not unless they really deal with some of the hurts and problems that they've had in their life. I think the lifestyle is known to them now and they're comfortable with what's known to them even though I wouldn't say they actually enjoy it. (Youth worker)

Making a difference

Where can we make a difference? What do we need to do?

Over the last few months, Sunday night has been a lot bigger night at the food van. We've had crowds of 50 and 60, mostly families. I see a lot of kids in the five and under age bracket who are probably the Matthews [see Chapters 12 and 13] of the future. It distresses me to see so many kids who I see having big problems in the future unless their lives change. (Youth worker)

If you don't make a difference in their lives somehow, they are going to become the criminals of tomorrow and the people who go in and out of prison, the people who abuse their own children, and so on. Because of the lack of understanding and caring and love that they've had, and their lack of knowledge and skills, it becomes a vicious cycle. There is some urgency to intervene now and make a change to break the cycle. (Welfare worker)

I think it would be much better and much less expensive if every time a young offender was sentenced to jail, the money was made available for proper drug rehabilitation and proper educational training, so they actually had a skill. The big problem for us is we can't really do anything much to solve the problem. We just keep sentencing them to jail until eventually, in their 40s, they realize this is a silly way to live their lives. But if the money was put in at that earlier stage, then you'd be able to break the cycle earlier. That's the frustration. Almost every magistrate that I know just shrugs their shoulders and says, "What can we do?" In sending people back to jail, they get drugs as easily as not in jail. There's no real way that we can change the system. We just deal with the problems. If there are any life-changing experiences, they'll have them before they come to us. We're not going to do it, really. There are some situations where we can do it by imposing a sentence, shaking people out of their lifestyle, but I don't actually think it happens often. (Magistrate)

My hope is that schools can be a sanctuary for kids like this. I hope that they can be a place where kids feel safe, where they can find relief from their home situations for a few hours a day, where they can see how other people live, have good role models, and develop healthy relationships. So, in the future, they might have something to base their life on, to inform changes in their lives if they desire to. (Youth worker)

We had a young guy that suicided at the end of last year. Putting it simply, he wanted to be back at school but the school wouldn't have him back. That was the trigger for him to take his own life. School was the only thing he felt connected to. He saw school as his only avenue of support and when that was denied him, he committed suicide. The students, his friends, were just overwhelmed by it. But there was just no capacity within the school to adjust to accommodate him. (Social worker)

It's so important to have a teacher that believes in you and cares about you, not just in what they are teaching you. But they also need to be aware that when these kids are finally able to deal with life properly and with enthusiasm, they'll need a love for learning. Good teachers pass on an enthusiasm for learning even if the reality is their students aren't in a position to be able to learn much most of the time. Some of these kids are emotionally and intellectually stunted because of abuse and trauma in their lives. Their school years are often a write-off because of drugs and family relationships and conflict. We need to realize that that's often the reality for them but that doesn't have to be the end of their education. They might be able to pick it up again. When they hit 19 or 20 they might realize, "Oh, I'm feeling better about myself. I've got a house. I've got a boyfriend. Life isn't so bad any more. Mom and I can have a coffee together sometimes. Things are looking up. Maybe I'll pick up a course to better myself." (Welfare worker)

I don't feel sorry for the teachers, that's not the right word, but I think they need a lot more support and encouragement. It can't be easy for them walking into a class full of problems. There needs to be some sort of community support for schools, particularly where teachers are facing these problems. And it's not just a problem for teachers. It's also a problem for the community. If these kids can be helped, hopefully they won't be the ones who are breaking into houses and stealing. (Youth worker)

If we keep looking at things from an individual perspective, at who's right and who's wrong, then we're never going to change anything. We really need to look at the system we're working in; the funding arrangements, what the environment is like for people making policies but who aren't working at the coal face and so on. If anything is going to change for professionals working with these young people, it has to be addressed on a broader level. We need to address what's going on broadly and who can contribute to making things different. We need to go beyond, "Well, this is what the teacher's doing, this is what they do in that school." That's just about keeping people busy down on the ground and about fighting with each other for resources instead of demanding that we all have a right to resources. (Social worker)

Back on the street

Why do some see their future on the street? What is the comfort that they derive?

I think on the street they have a sense of family because they meet other young people in similar circumstances. They have a sense of freedom away from institutions and people telling them what to do, people making their life difficult, like department workers, the police, and so on. A lot of young people I work with spent time on the streets because that's where their pseudo-family was, and that's legitimate, totally legitimate for them. (Welfare worker)

We've seen a few people who have come onto the streets after being in prison. Often they don't have the means to set themselves up in accommodation again. It's a time when a person really needs support to change their ways or they will go further down the wrong track. (Youth worker)

You need a strength of character to survive and survive well on the street. You need a real determination. Sometimes you actually need to be angry to survive. Some kids just don't do it well because they're not angry enough and they're not determined enough to get what they want. But when a kid has put up with enough injustice, they're generally very angry and I think that serves them well on the street. The last thing you want is for people to know that you're a pushover because you'll just be victimized. You'll be abused and used for other people's purposes. You need to be smart about when to be where and when not to be there. You need a sixth sense almost. Most kids would have a good idea about where police patrols are and go, so they would avoid those areas really carefully. Most can also tell you where the perpetrators hang out; people who are wanting to use or abuse street kids. They have to be fairly bright and quick and they often have very good memories. (Welfare worker)

Often they feel like nobody really cares about them. "Out of sight, out of mind," is how they have described it to me. Life is on hold while they're in prison. Everything else is still going on outside, but time has just stopped for them. (Prison psychologist)

These kids know that residential staff are paid. They know they're not there because they're family. Most of the staff are there because they're passionate about what they're doing. You don't do that work for the money. Believe me, you just don't. But the kids know that they're paid to be there. It's not even a pseudofamily for them. The other dynamic is you've got other high-risk adolescents in the house and in a really close environment, all with different issues. Then when kids have to move from family to family, it's really traumatic for them. (Welfare worker)

Some blame other people—their parents or partners—who they say have introduced them to heroin or have abused them. But there is also a tendency for them to blame themselves and I think that might partly be a kind of protective mechanism for them. (Prison psychologist)

Life is so hard for them. My heart breaks for them, really. The big thing for an adolescent is, "Who am I?" So when you don't have people around you that let you know who you are and that you're loved for that reason, you're in danger of growing up without a sense of self. (Welfare worker)

I was talking to the guy in charge of the assessment prison a couple of years ago. He thinks that the only thing that changes for these kids is when they get into their 40s and they finally work out that they don't have a life and everyone else does. So in their early or mid-40s they'll suddenly start to change. But there was almost nothing else that he could see that would change young men once they got into doing burglaries and armed robberies because there really is no other alternative. You can't go out and earn that sort of money. With girls it's a bit different because they can be prostitutes. They can actually have quite a long history of addiction and not come to court. One woman, who appeared before me on armed robbery, had been a heroin addict for 15 years and supported her habit by prostitution. But there came a time when she wasn't able to earn that as a prostitute because of her age and so she turned to armed robbery. That's not all that unusual with women. Virtually everyone at the women's prison is an addict. There'd be one or two people at any one time that depart from that but the rest of them are just addicts. That's why they're there. They commit crimes to support their addiction. (Magistrate)

Great expectations: A case study

The point of this case study is not to belittle the goals that people on the margins of society set for themselves or to suggest that they are too lofty for them to achieve. Rather, the case illustrates the potential for failure in not fully recognizing what it takes to reach those goals and not being prepared for occasional setbacks as part of the normal course of events in achieving anything worthwhile. Of course, it is easy to make such observations about others. It is much harder to follow through one's self, particularly if difficulty and adversity have been the norm in one's life. In this case, by pointing out their failures, we fall into the trap of blaming the victim and ignoring what it takes to even muster the courage to set out on a course of change. We also individualize their failure, dismissing the influence of institutions and systems in their demise. The woman in this account is in the beginning stages of her life-changing project, determined to rid her body of heroin. That, in itself, presents some measure of achievement.

I've got a client at the moment who has been using heroin for about 17 years. She is quite convinced that she has stopped using heroin completely and won't take it up again once she leaves prison. However, I think there's a certain amount of denial on her part about how easy that's going to be. She's quite motivated and that's great, but when I'm working with her she finds it really difficult to admit that there's any risk of her ever using it again despite her 17-year history of heroin abuse, which she's never actually attempted to stop before she came to prison. Her partner, who she intends to return to when she leaves prison, also has been using heroin for 17 years. So while I've put to her that people don't just stop all of a sudden because they come to prison and it's going to be a big issue for her when she gets out, she doesn't see it that way. It's quite clear and simple to her that she's stopped and that's it.

Her story is quite different from most women I speak to in that she really enjoyed school, although I don't think she actually completed it. She was very popular and stayed at school until she was 17. During that time she had two social circles. One was her weekend group in which she was a follower. She would join in with their activities and that was where she started to use marijuana, when she was 13 or 14. I wouldn't say they were antisocial but they'd get up to mischief, although nothing really criminal. Then during the week she would join in with her school group in which she was a leader. She would pass on those knowledges and behaviors she had learned from her weekend group. So, for example, she was the one who introduced her school friends to marijuana and to those kinds of activities. She says that she really enjoyed that part of her life, particularly when she was 14, 15, and 16. She lived near the beach and had a fantastic time. In her mind, there was nothing bad about that period. But then her whole life changed when she turned 17 and she got pregnant.

She's in her 40s now, but when she was 17 it was the norm for girls in her circumstances to get married straight away. Even before she got married she had doubts about the relationship. She knew it wasn't really good but she was hoping that she could change that later on. Getting married and having a baby meant that her whole focus in life changed. She wasn't interested in her weekend friends anymore. She completely stopped using marijuana and didn't drink at all during her pregnancy. She describes being a mom as the most important thing in her life. She had four children altogether with her husband and had a complete shift in her life. There was also a downside to that time, which she has now come to admit. At first she described that period as being absolutely fantastic, everything about it was good. Now she says she really missed those years when she was very popular with her friends and into a lot of activities.

Over the years her husband developed some quite strong religious beliefs that she didn't share. He also became quite dominant toward her and toward other people as well. She describes how she would be at home with some friends—by this time her friendship group had changed to be other mothers with children—but when he came home, everybody would leave. The whole house would clear out and her husband would ask her, "Why does everyone leave when I come home?" Eventually she told him, "It's fairly obvious. They don't like you." She stayed with him for about nine years. She didn't like the relationship but she really enjoyed her children. She wasn't totally miserable. She was enjoying being a mom but she got to a stage where she felt that her children were going to grow up to be embarrassed or ashamed of their father. Also, he had been violent on a couple of occasions although only toward the end of their relationship. Eventually, she left with the kids, when her youngest was only a couple of months old.

Up until that time, she hadn't used any heroin at all and she had stopped using marijuana when she was 17. But shortly after she moved in with her current partner of 20 years, they started using heroin. I really haven't been able to explore very much of what was going on when she started to use heroin. She says that she just liked it and so did her partner. At first it was a case of enjoying heroin, liking the effects of it, and then later she felt that she had to use it to ward off the withdrawal symptoms. It takes around two weeks to get over the physical addiction to heroin although to get over it completely takes a lot longer because of the psychological addiction. I think it's years before they actually don't crave it but it's less physiological after a few weeks. I'm told, though, that the first two weeks are the most physically painful and awful.

Now, there's a contradiction there between her identification with being a mother, really finding that to be very rewarding and enjoying that experience, and having her children watch her use heroin and seeing the effects that that has on her. She has described to me her children's distress at her using heroin and what it was doing to her, even when they were quite young. They would draw quite distressing paintings about their mother's heroin use. So there's that contradiction of her responsibility and enjoyment as a mother and then ignoring her children's distress with her behavior. She obviously sees that because she now says she's going to give the heroin away. She's very confident now, after being in prison for a couple of months, that that's it. It's all finished now. She's going to give up heroin after having used it for 17 years. But I'm just not sure that her expectations of herself are realistic. It's a fantastic aim and she is very enthusiastic about the prospect of a new life and I support her in those decisions. It's just that she's setting herself up to fail because she isn't prepared to acknowledge the difficulty in achieving what she is setting out to do and, because of that, she hasn't worked out a plan to achieve that over time. It's like buying a lottery ticket. "One day I'm poor, the next day I'm rich." They want instant results, whereas the issues we're dealing with require setting reachable targets and considerable perseverance over time. (Psychologist)

# PART THREE

In my shoes

People have no idea where the hell you're coming from until they've actually spent a night on the streets…It's honestly too hard to put into words…that's the only way I can say it. You have no idea where somebody's coming from until you've actually walked a mile in their shoes. (Jordan)

CHAPTER SIXTEEN

Jordan

Jordan is a member of Generation Y and one of a growing number of young people who live on the streets of western nations, in a time of considerable economic prosperity (see the Introduction). At face value, his middle-class background provides little explanation; even his two-parent and extended family is surprised (and initially repulsed) by his deference for street life. However, within Jordan's account is evidence of deep-seated feelings of rejection by significant individuals and the institutions they represent (to which he responds angrily with threats of violence and dismissively with substance abuse), and a related search for acceptance (evident in the spin he places on his abilities and experiences). On the streets, happiness is derived from food, clothes, body adornments, and drug use, typically in forms that test his acceptability within mainstream society. If Jordan were to name this chapter, it might read something like, "I live on the streets but that's not who I am." Indeed, he is very conscious of appearances and what others take these to mean. While pointing out the errors of a school system that he feels misunderstood him, he does not reject its legitimacy in bestowing qualifications as passports (for some) into a better life (see Bourdieu and Passeron 1977). Beneath the bravado of Jordan's story is considerable hurt. There is much still to be worked through. In this sense, Jordan's is a story still in the making; a work in progress.

Father–son stuff

I get on well enough with my parents now, but when I was a kid they were constantly arguing with each other. It wasn't until recently that I sat down and had a chat with them and they said it was just a big joke, that they were acting. They say they weren't really angry at all, which is still a bit hard to believe. To me, as a kid growing up, it seemed that my father was just an animal and I honestly never wanted to grow up like him. It caused me a hell of a lot of emotional problems, mental problems, just the fact that I'd been brought up with this father who was an absolute pig. It was a real big kick in the teeth, I suppose you could say, having a father I hated and I thought hated me.

When I was in Grade 8 the school sent me to a psychologist because I didn't really have too many friends and they thought I was really depressed. This psychologist put it down to the fact that my father wasn't really a father figure. He was never there for me as a kid. He was always working, trying to do what he thought was best for the family, trying to earn money, and he didn't really have much time for me. All I really wanted was for him to take me camping and fishing and general father–son stuff. But even when he was around we never got along well. My father believed that kids should be seen and not heard. He was brought up like that himself. He had a father who was very straightforward, straight down the line. "You do this. You do nothing but this. If you step out of line, I'll kick your arse." I think that's probably one of the main things that led me to have so many problems. All the problems I've got now, they probably relate back to that.

The simple fact is my father was never really interested in me. When I was 14 or 15 he was still asking when my birthday was. That's about the time I thought, "Look, if you don't pick up your act, I'm either going to punch you in the head or I'm going to leave." I eventually left home when I was 16. In the beginning, my mother and I played the part of me being the good son, pretending I was living at home so the rest of the family didn't realize what a bad child I'd become. Then I was interviewed on a television program about homeless kids, while I was smoking a joint. My family ended up seeing it and didn't want to have anything to do with me after that. My father's side of the family especially doesn't want to know me, basically because they think I'm a bad person. I'm the black sheep of the family. Even now they don't want me at their Christmas parties.

My grandmother wouldn't talk to me whatsoever when I first rocked up to see her because I had a nose ring. I mean it was just a small ring, nothing vicious or anything. And it was the only thing I had; no earrings, no eyebrow rings, no nothing, just a simple little nose ring and she wouldn't talk to me unless I took it out. She'd never done that before. I had always meant the world to her because I was her first grandchild. She used to live with us when I was a kid so we were very close. Anyway, I said, "Fine, if you don't want to accept me for the person I am, I'll see you later." So she finally said, "Well, OK. Come in." I think it was a hell of a shock to her, just the fact that I was living on the streets.

Hanging out

When I first left home I moved in with my girlfriend from school and some other guys. I was with her for a couple of months. That pretty much ended when she started cheating on me and I basically said, "Well look, I don't really care. You're just a stupid harlot anyway. Just f-off." Sorry about the language, but that's just me.

I wasn't getting much from welfare at that stage. I don't think I actually got the dole until nine months later. I think it was about that. Four months of that I spent camping out, sleeping rough. I can't remember the name of the place where we camped. You go down the main street to the end, past a small shop, left a bit, past a couple of houses along a sort of alleyway, then you come out onto a dead end street and that brings you out to a children's play area, a playground. You walk across there to the other side and that was where I was living, in the bushes on the edge of the playground. After that I lived in a squat, an old abandoned house. I was there for about five months when one of the guys accidentally burnt it down one night. He went to sleep with a cigarette in his hand and set the house on fire and the whole place went up. Thank God some of the walls stayed up. I kept living there for a couple of months after that. It was quite funny, actually. You'd wake up in the morning and see the neighborhood passing by where there used to be walls. (I could go into so much more detail. I could describe the walls. I could even draw you a floor plan of every house I've ever lived in.)

I moved into Matt's place on New Year's Eve a couple of years ago and he said, "Hey, let's get stoned." It was sometime in February before we woke up to ourselves and I said, "Look, we're absolutely blowing out our brains. What the hell are we going to do?" We made the decision that we were tired of hiding from people we'd borrowed money from to buy drugs. So we agreed, "Let's get away from this place."

We moved to another city but there was nothing to do there. There was absolutely nothing for anybody our age to do. Kids would just sit around inhaling. When you walked down to the park there'd be all these black kids sitting there inhaling their glue and shit. We'd buy ourselves a "carton of doom," you know, really crap wine in a box, and sit down underneath the bridge and get drunk. In the end we were having mass parties, to the extent that there were 130 people coming around. The police were actually driving people home because they just couldn't find their own way.

Eventually we got on to the paint something fierce because we didn't want to smoke pot and we were getting too bored drinking beer all day. We used to spray paint or hairspray into a plastic bag and inhale the gas out of it. I could inhale a full bag, then blow and light a flame from my mouth for a good 30 seconds.

Most of the time we were absolutely off our heads, rolling around on the ground laughing at pretty stupid things really. Then I thought, "Hey, this'll get me f-ed up in the end." It was absolutely horrid. I mean it does weird shit to your mind. Matt was getting that f-ed off on it, he'd sit there and blank out for five minutes. Then he'd come to five minutes later and inhale and pass out again for another five minutes. Eventually I told him, "Matt, wake up to your f-ing self before I actually have to break some of your limbs."

We decided we'd stick to the pot, so one of the guys we'd met said, "I can score you a pound," which is like $3500 worth. He said he had some contacts. A couple of days later, his dealer was sitting in intensive care in hospital after getting the shit absolutely flogged out of him with a baseball bat and $3600 stolen from him. The deal went wrong. He'd gone through the wrong people and the deal went bad. We ended up with guns pointing at our heads and big guys leaning on us who said, "Look, you've got till tomorrow to get the f-k out of town." And we said, "Hey, look man, we had nothing to do with it." They thought that we'd put them in, but it turned out it was one of their own guys. The police were paying him bulk money for information, which shows that people will do just about anything including putting in their own friends for money or drugs.

I've been smoking pot since I was 13. I'm 20 now, so for seven years. I've been into stronger stuff but I haven't yet gone anywhere near heroin. It's something I never want to touch. Same with cocaine. Pot's more natural and does the job for me; it gets me happy. It's definitely not a good thing to be in though because it can lead to stronger stuff unless you've got some self-control. I haven't had any for ages so I'm actually really craving it at the moment, but I don't want my life being controlled by it. Most people around here use pot. Just about everyone is willing to trade something for it. I know so many people who use their dole to buy drugs and then sell them at a profit. A lot of people do really good deals. Others go out and steal some and then sell it to friends. I could go out and steal a car stereo or something, go around to a friend's place, sell it for about $150 worth of pot, about half an ounce, which I could probably then divide up and sell for about $210 so I'm banking $60 profit.

A matter of survival

Toward the end I was spending that much f-ing money on drugs it was ridiculous, so I didn't have much for food. That was when I could get the dole. I actually spent 26 weeks of last year without any money at all, absolutely f-ing nothing. So, of course, I turned back to my criminal ways, like going out and stealing shit and doing stuff I know I shouldn't. One time we stole a box of cereal from a house we broke into, as well as some other stuff. It was a pretty bad thing to do but I mean it was a big house and they probably had enough to buy more. We went home with two containers of milk and just broke the box apart. We poured the milk into this one bag of Cornflakes and everybody got spoons and we just sat there munching on them.

I also used to scrounge around in the trash at the back of food outlets, in the big skips in the alleys behind the shops. I got a full family-size pizza one time. I actually dug three of them out at once, still in the boxes, still absolutely fresh apart from a use-by date that was one day old. And cereal bars, that sort of thing. I found boxes of them thrown out because they were a couple of days out of date. Why can't there be a law that stuff like that has to be put in a separate container and all the f-ing scraps, the vegetables and stuff that aren't actually any good, put in another? We used to leave quite a mess because they put all the best stuff that we could actually eat right on the bottom, deliberately, so we would actually have to dig through the whole damn thing just to f-ing get a feed.

Another time I came home to the squat and the guys had been shopping and put their name on every item of food in the house and wouldn't let me eat for four days. It got to the stage where I was just about to stab someone in the throat before Matt said, "No, let me handle it. I'll talk to them." They finally agreed to let me eat something.

Sometimes I got a packet of two-minute noodles from someone. They're not exactly cooked but they've sort of been half cooked so you can eat them without too many worries of f-ing up your stomach. Eating one packet of those a day and then a meal from the food van at night, I actually got down to the lowest weight I've ever been, under a hundred pounds. And that's just simply because I could not buy food. But then, I suppose, when I did have money I was eating stuff like McDonald's and that sort of crap.

I've actually smartened up a bit these days, sort of got a bit more intelligence. Now if I need a feed I'll go into a bakery and buy myself a bagel or something, maybe grab some ham or some chicken or something and just do up a couple of sandwiches for myself. I mean it's a lot cheaper that way. You save a hell of a lot of money. You actually get a pretty good feed too. It's what keeps me healthy, apart from the fact that I haven't gone out and bought fruit for a while, which is something I'm probably lacking. I need Vitamin E and Vitamin C for sure.

Sometimes I've had to ask for money. I walk up to someone and politely ask, "Excuse me sir. Would you happen to have a dollar or something so I could buy a bagel to eat?" Some have actually given me money, thank God, but others just turn up their nose at me. "No, f-off. I don't want to know you," and they just kept walking. "As if I'd give you money," kind of attitude and actually saying that to me. Then they wonder why people like me run after them and punch them in the head and bob them for their wallet. I mean, honestly, it's just a dollar. Compared to the money some people are making these days, it's nothing.

The way I see it, what goes around comes around. Lots of people have been generous enough to give me money, but there are lots that haven't and they can be really fierce about it. At one stage I wanted to get every nuclear warhead on the face of this planet and just blow them up so I'd completely wipe out all human life altogether, because I think rejection is the most f-ing destructive thing on earth. We're the only creatures that go out of our way to destroy our own kind rather than look out for each other.

About the only ones I've actually found that helped on the streets are the people who run the food van in the park. They're the only people I've been able to sit down, have a chat with, express all my problems. They actually listen to me. I don't even care if the food is bad, if they really listen to what I'm saying. I'm not really complaining about the food because when you're really desperate for a feed it's pretty good. If you can get something that you're really happy about, it just makes the world of difference. It's just the fact that they actually look interested. It's somewhere I can get a lot of problems off my chest. If it weren't for their help providing meals and being interested in me, I probably wouldn't have survived. That has helped me enormously to actually get my life on track a bit.

No visible means of support

At the moment, I'm just looking for general work, not laboring, but things like fruit picking every couple of months. That's honestly about the only work I can actually find, looking the way I do. People aren't going to hire me because they take one look and say, "No, f-k you. I'm not going to give you a job. F-off. Next." I can't actually get a job working too many places unless I become a hairdresser or a tattooist or a body-piercer or something. I could always change but I dress and look the way I do for the simple fact that I don't think it's right that society in general should degrade people because of the way they look. I'm not trying to make a statement as such, but I just like to dress like this. It gives me something to do. It makes me feel good.

I used to look a lot worse. At one stage I had two earrings, an eyebrow ring, nose rings, lip ring, and one through my nipple. I also wore a chain from my nose ring to my left earring. A friend of mine, Matt, who stands up to about my eyes and is a good six inches either side of my shoulders, said to me one day, "Look man, you take all that shit out of your nose or someone's going to beat the crap out of you." Done. He's like a big brother to me; he just wants the best for me. He wants me to get on with my life and settle down and do something decent with it rather than hang out on the streets, even though he does it himself. I guess he doesn't actually have the will-power to be able to do it himself so he's trying to help me by making me do it, which is pretty cool.

But it isn't all that easy. I actually know one guy who got himself all cleaned up and got a job down at the brewery. He'd been clean for about two years when they shut it down and he's back living on the streets again. I mean it's shit like that that annoys me. It's those company CEOs and politicians that I'd really love to kill, simply because they say, "Oh, we're doing good for the f-ing country." If you want to do f-ing good for the country, take a flat $250,000 a year. If they want a f-ing holiday, take it out of the $250,000; if they want a car, take it out of the $250 grand. That way at least you'll have somebody who's actually running the country for the f-ing country, not for goddamn money. To me, all their trade agreements are to help themselves, not the ordinary person. I suppose that's why I think places like the local employment agency are absolutely pathetic at helping me get a job, basically because everybody these days is looking for 16 or 17 year olds with at least two years' experience. Employment in this country is a joke. All the jobs I could have got have been moved to some third world country.

Working the angles

You don't even want me to start on what I think about employment agencies. I'd put my form in every week. I'd fill it out to the letter. And I actually went and looked for jobs, not like some people who just sat on their bums writing up some made-up f-ing thing they got out of the telephone book. But they would cut me off after every payday. After about three months I just walked in, pushed the computer screen off the desk, and said, "Keep your f-ing money." Well, they weren't too happy but it did get them moving! It actually took that much anger from me before they did something about it. I don't know. Ever since they've become privatized, it's like they love to screw people around for some reason. It's ridiculous. I got out of that one by telling them I had an epileptic fit and couldn't control my hand when it knocked over the screen. I've got quite a silver tongue so I can talk my way out of most situations that seem to happen.

Generally, I'm pretty smart when it comes to doing stuff like that. I consider every variable before I actually go out and do something. If I was going to do a place over, I'd actually give it two days' thought and sit down and think of every variable like, "Who might happen to be walking past? Is there likely to be a police presence? Is there somebody who's going to set off an alarm?" Just general stuff like that: video cameras, security systems, how to bypass them. If you don't actually sit down and think about it and you do something off the top of your head, then you're going to get caught. But if you actually sit down and fully work something out, then there's not a hope in hell that the police will catch you.

I've been lucky enough not to end up in jail, thank God. I've been so close, though. I've got about $2300 worth of warrants at the moment for break and entering, theft, drug charges, vandalism, vagrancy, that sort of stuff. If I appeared in court the magistrate would probably say, "Oh, Jordan. I see you owe us some money. Bang. You're off to spend six months in jail. See you later." I need to walk in there with about $2500 and say, "Look, I'm paying off all my fines at once." Otherwise, they'll lock me up. If I produce the money, I'll be cool, but where the hell am I going to get $2500 from unless somebody gives it to me or I steal it? So I have to stay low till I can get the money together.

I'm pretty smart at staying out of the way. Other people use street names to avoid being identified. They're very wary about trusting people, just about anyone really, even people who live on the streets. I'm a very trusting person but they're really wary about trusting people basically because they trusted people in the past and they've been screwed around. So they're very wary about giving out their real names because it makes it too easy for the police to track them. There are a lot of people living on the streets with long criminal histories for the simple fact that they need the money. They don't want to give out their real names because it just makes it too easy for them to be tracked by the police.

Problems at school

I sat an IQ test a couple of months ago and I got 121—130 is considered genius; 100 is average—imagine if I actually sat down and applied myself to something. I could probably get really far in life. Even just sitting here talking to you, I notice myself using some quite big words. But realistically, even with a high IQ, I haven't got very far. It's just one of life's little idiosyncrasies, isn't it? Being smart doesn't guarantee success and being successful doesn't happen just because you're smart. It helps though to be smart when you live on the streets. I actually spend a lot of time sitting back and fully taking in a lot of my surroundings. It's stuff like that that I think has made me a bit smarter than others because I can actually take a lot of notice of what's going on around the place. I think the main reason why I manage to stay out of too much trouble is the fact that I am pretty bright. I actually have a brain that I can work out what I have to do. I know what I want and how to get it.

I had a real lot of problems at school though. I started hanging around with a really bad crowd. The second day of Grade 8, actually, I started smoking pot, which wasn't a real good move. I was only 13. Then I got caught up with a group of guys who were living in a squat. I mean this place was the kind of place you could rock up to at four in the morning and there'd still be nine people sitting down smoking pot. I started going around there about halfway through the year. I'd go there after school, smoke some pot, and just spend the whole night. Some of the girls I used to go to school with would come around in the morning, wake me up, take me back to my mom's place so I could get changed, and I'd go back to school again the next day. That was just absolutely screwing me because I wasn't getting any sleep whatsoever, so I was falling asleep in class, which probably didn't help in the end. It's probably why I was such a bad kid.

I also became really slack with my schoolwork. I wasn't bothering to do assignments because everything was just too easy. Or I'd get all the homework done in class, in the normal lesson. I could do all the work; everything just came absolutely naturally to me. I didn't consider it work, actually. Take French for instance. I did French in Grades 6, 7, and 8. I didn't even bother studying and I was getting 99 out of a 100 for some of the exams. Half the kids were flat out getting Cs and there I was getting As for absolutely every exam possible. It was just stuff like that that bored me. It was probably the fact that I could do all the work. I'm really good at doing a lot of stuff in my head, like numbers, words, whatever. I guess it was pretty natural.

The other problem I had was with the teachers. There was this one teacher especially, my Grade 8 mathematics teacher, that I had real problems with. She would say, "Do this and this and this on the blackboard." One day I said, "Miss, I already know how to do it that way. Can I try it this other way?" But she just said, "No. You can do it this way first and then you can go onto that." I just wanted to go and punch her in the head. She was always putting me down. She'd say things like, "You're never going to make anything of yourself. You'll just be a worthless blight on humanity your whole life." It's probably because I used to use the outer casing of BIC pens for blowing darts and spitballs around the room, but it still was a pretty vicious thing to say to a 13 year old. Why do they do it? What's going on in their head that makes them say those things? I have no idea. They must know that it doesn't achieve anything.

I think a lot of teachers don't actually see the point—what teaching is all about. There are different ways of teaching people and you do get different teaching methods from different teachers. There are some teachers who basically teach in a monotone voice all day. "Rah rah rah. Blah blah blah." On and on and on. I guess they get bored with what they're doing, teaching the same lessons over and over, especially in high school because they've got class after class after class of basically teaching the one subject, maybe two or three if they're lucky, depending on what they actually teach. But if they stopped treating their students like little three year olds and actually make the lessons half-interesting, they might get students a bit more involved as well as teaching them at the same time.

The best advice I could give teachers is, don't think all bad students are bad people because some of them are like me, trying to get on with their lives and trying to make the most of it. You do get a lot of smartarse students who just sit there and cause trouble mainly because they're dumb. They don't actually know how to do the work. But you also get people like me who don't do any work in class simply for the fact that it's too easy for them. Teachers should take it case by case. They should sit down and actually listen to what students have to say because most of the time they are just people who need to have someone there to talk to.

Moving on

At one stage I wanted to become a psychologist so I could actually help kids who are going through similar things. I wanted to be someone they could talk to; someone they could tell their problems to; someone who actually had a bit of a background of living on the streets and knew where they were coming from rather than all these psychologists and psychiatrists who think they know f-ing everything. I then decided I wanted to become a social worker because the social worker course is about four years whereas psychology is about ten or some weird amount. I haven't looked into it too greatly. There was a social worker that I started talking to when I first left school. She was actually pretty good. She helped me through a lot of my problems. I used to have a really bad anger problem but I didn't want to go to anger management classes because I thought if I actually needed help, there was something wrong with me and I didn't want to admit it. Whereas if I could sit down by myself and try to get myself through it, then I felt like I would have achieved a bit more because I actually did it by myself and I'd be a better person for it.

Then I met this social worker. She was actually the reason why I decided to do social work because she helped me out when I was living on the streets and I thought that's what I want to do for someone else. I knew how much it actually helped me. The psychologist I saw when I was in Grade 8 assumed a hell of a lot, whereas the social worker sat down and listened to what I had to say about living on the streets. She had a better understanding of what someone was actually talking about when they come with all their problems. I just hate psychologists now for the simple fact that the majority of them you see around here are trying to talk to you as if they've actually got some idea of what the f__ they're talking about. Whereas, realistically, they're just brainless fools rattling on with just absolute crap. They act as if it can't be that hard living on the streets, which makes me feel like jumping on them, smashing them in the face and saying, "F-ing wake up to yourself. The world is not as pretty as it bloody well seems." But I think they'd probably lock me up and throw away the key if I did something like that.

Last year, I finally gave myself a real kick up the arse and said, "Look, you're going to have to do something otherwise you're just going to end up like all the other stupid druggies and not get anywhere." Looking at everyone else on the street actually scared the shit out of me because I actually do want to get somewhere in life. That's when I saw an advertisement in the paper for a college prep course and thought, "Yes, it's probably my one way of getting into a university." So I gave it a try but unfortunately I ran into a couple of friends I went to school with who were doing exactly the same sort of thing. I got messed up with drugs again and getting drunk and I couldn't be bothered doing the study. I ended up leaving about halfway through the first year. That's where it's at. I'd like to have another go at it if they'll let me come back. If not, I'll probably end up going to a business college.

I wouldn't mind doing a business degree because I've always had this idea of setting up a 24-hour café somewhere where people can come, sit down, and have a quiet chat, somewhere where they can get off the street and just have a cup of coffee or something. I'd like to set up a place for people who want to get away from the clubs, where they can meet with whomever they've picked up that night and just sit down and have a nice quiet coffee before they go home and do whatever they do. It also could be somewhere that street kids come and hang out for a bit. Maybe it could have a pool table or something where they can just come and have a couple of games—even if I start running it at a loss. That probably wouldn't be good to start off with but after a while it wouldn't worry me because I'd feel like I was doing some good for other people.

On reflection

It's hard to give meaning to living on the streets. I think I've had it pretty easy compared to some but there were times when I was cut off from the dole and I had no money so I had to dig through the trash to find food to eat.

What gets me is how other humans can look at a person who's trying to survive by digging through the trash and yet still call out and harass them about it and give them grief. They don't understand what it's actually like, to be absolutely starving and not be able to get any food because you're not getting any money from anywhere. People have no idea where the hell you're coming from until they've actually spent a night on the streets.

I've been living with Matt for the last couple of years and we've kept in touch. I've actually moved into my parents place now for a couple of weeks but I still like spending nights on the streets with him, just for the simple fact that it was actually something that I enjoyed by the end of it. That was just my normal life. That was what I did from when I was 16, the years of my life I should have been having a bit of fun. I like catching up with him at night, just sitting there, having a chat, crashing, waking up at seven in the morning and going back home to have breakfast with mom. Living on the streets wasn't what I wanted to do but it became just that normal that it felt weird not doing it. It's honestly too hard to put into words. You never know what it's like to be a different person until you've walked a mile in their shoes, as the saying goes. I've never really been much for philosophy but that's basically the only way I can say it. You have no idea where somebody's coming from until you've actually walked a mile in their shoes.

It's about trying to survive as much as humanly possible and not die or get your head beaten in. It actually takes a hell of a lot of intelligence to be able to get around on the streets without getting yourself into too much trouble. If you make one wrong move, if you head down one wrong route, it could get you shot or in trouble with drugs. If you steal something off the wrong person it could turn out that they've got a knife. It's about trying to find somewhere safe to live where you haven't got people coming through your house with baseball bats at night smashing up absolutely everything; where you haven't got people coming around and stealing stuff; where you haven't got police coming around at ten every morning to do a head count to make sure nobody's died from an overdose or something. It's about making do with what you've got.

CHAPTER SEVENTEEN

Jenni

At the time of telling her story, Jenni is in her middle age. For her, it is a time of reflection but also of new horizons. She is one of the baby boomers who grew up in the 1960s; in western nations at least, a period of considerable social experimentation and, for many, economic prosperity. Jenni's story traverses issues typically associated with the marginalized in our communities: racism, illiteracy, teenage pregnancy, single parenting, youth unemployment, mental illness, difficulties at school, and so on. Throughout her account there is a sense in which she draws on her past to explain her present. In this, she is particularly focused on power relations (for example, parent–child, teacher–student, school–home relations) connected with schooling, no doubt influenced by her current studies preparing her to become a teacher but also by her own experiences (as student and parent) with the education system. "Dumb-smart" dichotomies are singled out for special attention. It is apparent that Jenni has experienced something of an epiphany, having recently crossed this divide herself and recognized its largely social construction rather than the natural outworking of one's intellect. In her analysis she attributes much of this positioning of students to differences between rich and poor but not in a simply material way. While there are echoes of Bob Connell's clever summation of the well-documented connections between wealth and success at school—that is, "the best advice we can give to a poor child keen to get ahead through education is to choose richer parents" (Connell 1993, 22)—it is relationships that provide the primary forum for her discussions of social justice issues. Jenni's is a remarkable and somewhat contradictory story. Schooling, the very thing that initially failed her, now serves her well and provides the avenue through which she seeks to serve others.

Beginnings

My father was brought up as an illegitimate child, to put it nicely. His father was black and his mother was white with red hair and blue eyes. That's about all we know about his background because in those days it wasn't spoken about. I *do* know that he had a really bad childhood. The only meat they ate was when his father caught rabbits. They lived in tents, there were no welfare payments and his mother was pushed out of her community because she had a baby to a black man. Even though my father was a fair child he never had any schooling because they were excluded from the white community. His poor upbringing, being shunned, came into our lives later as well.

When he was 11 or 12, dad went to work full time on a farm where he lived in the barn. He'd have to get up at five o'clock in the morning to start his chores and it was freezing. One of his jobs was to rake all the stones in the same direction because they didn't have grass in front of the house. And he worked in bare feet because he didn't have any shoes. The woman who owned the place—they were wealthy property owners—used to watch him from the window. She took pity on him and sent him to school in the local mining town. She also had a son of her own, a year or two younger. That was the first time dad went to school, but he still worked on the property and lived in the barn. He was very academic. He went to the top of the class and he only went for a year. From what I can remember as a small child, I recall my father was always reading.

Later, he married my mother who came from a better part of society. It was a horrible marriage. Both my parents are dead now and in our family not a lot was really said, so we only really know bits. As a child, I didn't hear or know about what was happening in the family. I was too young. I can just remember glimpses, like being shut in rooms and things like that. My mother did tell me once that when I was born, I had to stay at the hospital until I was five before I was allowed to come home. She said that I was sick, that I had a hole in my heart and I was going to die. But guess what? I didn't die! And the hole healed. Well, that's the story anyway. What really happened was I was put in an orphanage not a hospital. I only found that out when I had my own child and told my doctor about what I thought was my heart condition. He said there was no evidence of a heart problem and that the hospital I told him about actually had been an orphanage!

I can remember different parts of the orphanage. I can remember statues and I recall walking around the gardens. It obviously left an impression on me. To this day I have to sleep with hospital pillowcases, the white cotton ones. I just don't feel secure if I don't have one. I've even got pillowcases I've stolen from hospitals along the way, on my visits. Whenever I go to a hospital, I feel right at home. I love it. I love the smells and those white sheets, which we don't seem to have now, the really old-fashioned starchy white sheets. I came out of the hospital when I was about five. I say "hospital" but as we know now, it was an orphanage.

I had an older sister who really brought me up. I had another older sister as well and two older brothers. There were five of us and I was the youngest. One of my brothers was old enough to be my father. I don't mean that he was, I mean he was older. I don't remember him very much and I've had no association with him since. He was into a lot of criminal activity and left home by the time I came along. My oldest sister left school in her first year of high school to look after the family because my mother worked at a local hotel at night. We rarely saw her. And my father worked shift work on the buses at night. We very rarely saw him either. That was normal for us. We were horrors. We did the sort of things that people would complain about. Nothing criminal, we just never went to bed. We roamed the streets, dressed ourselves, and made our own lunches. My sister cooked our food. We were totally independent of our parents.

I would go off to school with my second oldest sister. My mother didn't even take me to school on my first day. I remember that explicitly. On my first day at school, I can remember seeing all these crayons. I thought they were lovely, all the different colors. I was envious of the other kids with all their crayons and little packet pencils and wooden boxes and things like that. I don't remember their names but I loved those thick old-fashioned crayons especially, so I took some. I didn't have any of my own. I don't know why, perhaps because we didn't have much money. They're more freely available now. I took about three or four crayons but was immediately gripped by fear. In those days, the nuns ran the school and they were absolutely vicious, and that's all I'll say. They were very strict. To this day I remember the nuns and I can feel the fear. Like, when kids wet their pants, they would get belted. I expect my experience is no different than a lot of people my age who went to Catholic schools. I didn't own up to stealing the crayons, by the way. I was too scared thinking about what they might do to me.

I can also remember in first grade having no idea what the teacher was talking about, absolutely nothing. I remember trembling because I had no idea how to tell the time. We had to tell the time on a tree clock before we left each day. I remember lots of other incidents when I was scared, so that school became something to fear. But I had lovely handwriting; I was very neat and tidy. I was also a great cheat, the best cheat you've ever seen. I actually got good marks but not because I could do anything. I remember in fourth and fifth grades when I used to have to write stories, I would copy them from *Golden Books* and the teachers never knew. It used to amaze me. I used to steal whole sentences. So I sort of got by. I was slow at reading but they never knew; my marks never reflected any of that. Just before high school, though, we did a final exam. I don't know if they still do that. And, of course, I failed that miserably because then I couldn't cheat. We all sat in different seats. After that I used to have the answers written on the back of my hand. I was bright enough to know what was going to be in the exam and I used to have the whole thing written out on the back of my hand.

In the end, it was because of my parents that I left school. As I said, my parents had a really bad relationship. They fought constantly. Because I was the youngest, my mother would say, "As soon as you're educated, I'm out of here." I became her reason for staying and I took that on board. I'm not blaming her, that's just what I thought. So I left in the second year of high school. Now, in those days—and I'm not that old—you could do a Public Service Exam. You didn't have to have a birth certificate. So I did this exam, which was mainly typing and I passed it. It was copy typing, so they didn't pick up that I couldn't read. And I played the piano at school so I was very good with my hands. I also did really well on their mathematics exam. I was always quite good at math. So, at 14, I went into the public service and my first job was down at the new technical college. I was on the reception desk. I didn't really have to read anything. I did lots and lots of typing but as a copy typist. I couldn't read the sentences but I did quite well. Then, after that, I worked for an insurance company. Same thing; I got on really quite well.

Becoming a "screaming mother"

Then, at 16, I had my first child, which I shouldn't have but I did. I got married because of my father's background. He just could not handle me having a baby without being married because of the ridicule he felt his whole life. So I got married and had three children, two more after my first one. Not long after the third child arrived, my marriage broke up. At that stage, I had two or three jobs. I was a waitress working in a pizzeria and in a Chinese restaurant. I always had multiple jobs but they were always at night because I had to be at home in the daytime with my kids. I had just bought a house but because I worked at night I could keep paying it off. We lived in a very small town, right on the coast, a beautiful area. It was a carefree life. Money was not an issue because I had all these part-time jobs.

Then my children became teenagers but there was no work for them where we lived, no full-time work. There was always part-time work like waitressing, but they usually wanted older waitresses like me. My oldest son managed to get a job at the local supermarket but they would only offer him two hours at a time and they'd ring when they wanted him. Their attitude was: "We'll ring you when we want you but when we don't want you, we don't want to see you." We lived half an hour away from the store and there was no bus route there or anything like that. So he'd have to sit around for three or four more hours before his next shift started or he'd have to hitch-hike out there and we had big fights about that. I don't class that as work, not work that does you any good anyway. He was paid $3.50 an hour and, to me, there was no opportunity to go anywhere.

I also had lots of fights with their teachers, over different things where I thought my kids were being punished when it wasn't really their fault—for things like not being dressed properly. I rang up the school board a few times, especially once when my oldest son had been sick with measles, mumps or chicken pox, I can't remember which now. He was off for about eight weeks. He did some schoolwork at home so he was academically OK, but when he went back to school they had changed the school sports' day. Now, for some reason, my oldest son was a stickler for wearing good clothes to school, he was just that type of person. On that day they were trying to make everyone wear sports uniforms and, of course, he wasn't in one. So they made him be a goalpost during football. For a start, he didn't have a permission note from me to allow him to go. Secondly, the teacher should have known why he wasn't in a sports uniform. So, I called the school board. In the end we had a big meeting with about five people, at which the teacher said they didn't want his clothes to be spoiled; which I just thought was a woeful excuse. That was a minor thing really but there were a lot of things like that.

On other occasions I just used to lose my cool. I used to scream at the teachers, which wasn't very good but I just couldn't believe what they would do. When I worked at the school cafeteria, for example, I would see them shaking students and I used to just lose my temper. I can remember thinking at the time that I'd become a "screaming mother" but that's because I *was* a mother; I wasn't a paid professional. I hadn't had the education to be a professional. I always expected a lot more out of them than what I received.

My brightest child

My second son was 17 when he died. He had lots of friends, was very athletic, and a really good footballer. He was an outgoing child, lively, talkative, a sporting hero. When we went on holidays he'd have all the kids in the pool coming around saying, "Jake, come play with me." He was an extrovert and he always seemed to have people around him. I think he was my brightest child and his teachers found him very challenging. He could read before he ever started school. He also made bombs and did lots of things he shouldn't have done, very creative things but not always what you would call normal. He was usually the class leader—he would make jokes in class and things like that—and usually teachers don't like class leaders. I remember he was doing French once—and this is typical—the teacher said something like, "Can anyone speak French?" So he put his hand up and said, "Yoplait." The whole class broke out laughing. He didn't get on well with his teachers, I think because it was a power play. I was always being told, "He is very noisy in class. He never seems to be doing what everyone else is doing." From what I know now, I think it was because he was bored. I used to say, "Jake, why don't you just be quiet in class." He didn't have an attention deficit disorder or anything because he could concentrate. He could do puzzles at three years of age that I couldn't even begin to do.

But if he didn't like the teacher, he'd give that teacher hell. He would just pick on what the teacher hated most. There was one in particular, Mr. Robb, who really disliked him intensely, intensely. This is the same teacher who made my oldest son stand all day as a goalpost as punishment for not being in his sports uniform. The school administration was very clothes conscious. So, Jake would do things that he knew would send this teacher crazy. I'd describe his tactics as "passive aggressive." Once he wore a different kind of shoe on each foot. Another time he wore different colored socks. He'd say things like, "My mother's a single parent. She can't afford to buy me new socks." Of course I could, but he knew that would drive this teacher crazy because he couldn't do anything about it. Then I would have to back him up. I don't know if I did the right or wrong thing in that respect but I wasn't going to say, "No." I'd already had problems with this teacher and I wasn't going to do anything to get my other son in trouble with him.

In the year before Jake died, we discovered that he was schizophrenic. At first I thought he'd taken some tablets, after seeing some friends of mine who had taken acid and, to me, that's what he was like. It was like he was on an acid trip. It was just horrible. He went from this extrovert child, really intelligent, to crying in his bedroom because he thought he was having sex with the devil in his sleep. It was just absolutely horrific. He'd be fine some days and you would think he was OK, but then you'd be having a conversation with him and he'd say something like, "Joshua is going to be the new Messiah," about his younger brother. It also started to affect his schoolwork but he didn't want the school to know and I can understand that. To this day I don't know if I should have told the school. But remember, it wasn't diagnosed as schizophrenia then. We hadn't gone to a psychiatrist. I thought he was doing drugs and we were just trying to keep it quiet.

A year later, when he was getting psychiatric help—which I found absolutely no help at all—he left school and went to trade school to do carpentry. He always wanted to be a carpenter but he couldn't get a job, not because of his schizophrenia because they didn't know about it. He did really well at trade school, just as he did in school. He got really high grades but that did nothing to get him a job. A lot of people don't realize, especially the well-off, that when you do carpentry or sheet metal work or one of those, if you don't get taken up as an apprentice, those skills get you nowhere. Do you think we could get him a job anywhere, in carpentry, in a trade? I must have sent out four or five hundred letters just in our little area looking for one. So he did another six months of sheet metal work but you can only do so much at trade school and then you've got to find an apprenticeship. Jake was very depressed that he couldn't get a job, very, very depressed. By then I began to realize—I mean, we'd been everywhere—that the chances of him getting an apprenticeship without knowing someone was very, very slim. But he didn't want to go to university and he wasn't the type anyway. He'd always wanted to be a carpenter but we couldn't find him a job.

During all of this time, he was going in and out of psychiatric hospitals, having big troubles with his schizophrenia. They gave him Risperdal, a hallucinative drug, which I would still argue to this day made him absolutely off his face, but they believed it brought him back. He used to lie to the psychiatrists so he could get out of there. I would tell them, "He's lying to you," and they'd say, "But this is what he's telling us." He was telling them that so he wouldn't be committed to a psychiatric ward and he'd get out of there. He knew enough to know what to say to them and he would tell me things that he wouldn't tell them. Then, one time when he was in hospital, he called me. They'd dosed him up with drugs, drugs, and more drugs, which put him in a stupor. I remember he said to me over the phone, "Mom, what's wrong with me?" And I just said, "Oh, Jake. Stay there and I'll come and get you." But by the time I got there they'd discharged him and he was gone. I don't know exactly what happened except that he got involved in a fight and was run over by a train or he killed himself; I don't know which. It was inconclusive. Either way, he ended up dying a tragic, horrible death. I can remember him saying to me, "What's my life now?" because he had a great childhood. He even said, "I'm so glad that I had a great childhood," but he didn't see any future for himself. I know that because he asked me, "Am I going to be crazy like this all my life?" Besides their hallucinative side effects, the drugs used to make him wet the bed, which was absolutely horrific for a 17-year-old boy. He also used to get outrageous headaches and I think he just thought life was not worth living. Maybe if he had a different personality things might have been different, I don't know. That was the saddest part of my life really.

Returning to study

That's when I thought, "What can I do with my life?" So I turned to education again. By then, I used to love reading books. I could read and understand what I read quite well, even though I was an atrocious speller and my sentences were not grammatically correct. But my attempts to re-enter the education system failed miserably. I thought, I'm just not an academic at all. Eventually I got married a second time, moved, and had two more children. But when my second marriage was on the rocks, I decided to try education one more time. I thought I would try nursing because I'm a practical person, so I enrolled in a special program for mature-age students wanting to get into university. I went into it knowing nothing. I had never done high school mathematics or high school English or researched the library or used a computer for that matter. But I did really, really well and my mathematics teacher at the time said to me, "Why don't you be a math teacher?" And I said, "You've got to be kidding." And he said, "No. You're brilliant at math. You should be a math teacher."

My English teacher was just fabulous too, absolutely fabulous. She showed me how to write an academic essay and that's how I write everything now because I never learned to write any other way. This English teacher believed that you could do anything you wanted if you put your mind to it. When I handed in the first thing I ever wrote for her, I said, "Don't look at the grammar, punctuation, or the spelling because I haven't got any of those skills." But she said, "That can all be taught. What's in your mind cannot be taught and that's what I'm looking for." That would be the advice I'd give anyone coming in to teaching. I've been taught to write an academic essay and get As, from not being able to write a proper sentence. Those skills can be taught. Factorizing can be taught. I think a lot of teachers think, "If a child isn't writing a really nice sentence or doing their algebra properly, well, they're dumb." But they're not necessarily dumb. It might be that they haven't been taught properly or at all. And it certainly doesn't mean they can't be taught. So, learning these new skills, my confidence and expectations were raised and I ended up getting top marks and was offered a place at university to study teaching.

I decided to major in mathematics but I wasn't sure of anything else so I took geography and English as well. I just thought I'd see how it went. Well, for my first essay I got an A and there was no looking back. I started to think, "Oh, I am smart!" I had never felt that before. It wasn't that I felt better than everyone else, just that for the first time I was doing well at academic things. It wasn't the attitude of some of the girls in my class though. They thought they were so good, that they were wonderful because they got into university because of their great marks at school. They were all about 18 or 19 years old.

I remember one day our tutor asked the class what social justice has to do with mathematics. "What would you do if one of your high school students couldn't read a word problem? Should you read it out for them?" One of the girls in my group said, "Well, if they've been to school all this time and they can't read, what's the point?" This is the same girl I overheard in another class refer to "problem" students as "filth." I was horrified. This is someone who is going to be a teacher! So I said, "I believe you should read out the questions because the students might be able to do math really, really well but they mightn't be able to read." Then another girl argued that it would be unfair to everyone else if you read it out, especially in an exam, because the words are part of working out the question. So I said, "If the student was blind, you would read it out because that would be equitable, wouldn't it? So what's the difference?"

Introductions

I was so excited the first time I went to a school as a student teacher. I bought new clothes and I pulled off the biggest hoax you have ever seen. I was really so thrilled for myself, personally, given where I'd come from. As a student in school myself, I was just the dunce of the class. I couldn't spell, couldn't put a sentence together. As I said, I used to steal sentences out of *Golden Books* and that was as good as it got. I suppose at the time if I had to do a test, they would have said I was illiterate. I used to produce essays like babies. To this day I can't believe myself how badly I used to write. But that all changed when I got to university.

So, I'm out at school as a student teacher and I just had such great expectations, until I got into the teachers' staff room. I was very naive. I thought that educated people wouldn't be as judgmental, that because they're educated they would be really concerned about their students. I didn't expect to hear comments that had been said to me as a student. I expected a lot more. I mean these were educated people. I looked at people with degrees as above all that. Well, I learned very quickly that it was a horrible place to be. As a student teacher you couldn't escape and I just had to sit there with "tape" over my mouth, otherwise I would have said something I shouldn't have. So I was sitting there and a group of them came into the staff room laughing, "Oh, ho ho, he's only a C student and he wants to be an airline pilot." These were the preconceived ideas of the staff. They'd told him, "You haven't got the ability. You can't do that." But they didn't know what his mind could produce. He might not have had the academic skills then but maybe he might want to go back one day and study really hard and become an airline pilot.

Then I overheard a teacher on the phone talking to someone about one of her math students: "Well, what do you expect? His father doesn't work." I couldn't believe it. Then, when she got off the phone she introduced herself to me: "Hello. I'm Sandra, your supervising teacher!"

In that school they divide the kids into different classes for mathematics and the bottom class was called the core group (because they concentrate on the "core" or basic skills), which is then divided up into two groups: one group of students with learning difficulties and another group with all kinds of disabilities. Sue, a lovely teacher, took the very severe cases of learning disability students and taught them special mathematics in one corner of the room. Most of them were badly handicapped with intellectual and physical disabilities. One little boy wet his pants all the time but I think that was because of his medication. He also used to call out, "Aah aah," and they'd just say, "Be quiet or you'll have to sit outside." He would be OK then. He needed constant attention. Another one had Asperger's syndrome. There were about six of them. Sometimes they put on a little show for you; they would play up just to get attention. At least in that regard, they were fairly normal kids really.

Sandra, who I was with, took the rest of the core group. The students in the other math classes called them 'veggies.' I was a bit horrified that that wasn't picked up by the teachers. Anyway, Sandra was actually very, very good at math but she thought these kids were in the bottom class because their parents didn't care. Maybe that was true, I don't know, but what I was really angry about was no one seemed to think these kids might have potential and that they didn't have people who were willing to sit with them and help them to realize it. The boy Sandra was talking about on the phone—let's call him Robert. She virtually said, "Don't bother with Robert. He can't factorize." That was the attitude. Now, Robert didn't have any learning difficulties at all. He just came to school when he felt like it. He wasn't dressed properly. He didn't have a pen or paper. And he just played up like merry hell, along with his three friends in class. Sometimes they weren't even allowed in the classroom they were so bad. Robert's father might have been unemployed and that might have influenced how he behaved but as far as I was concerned Robert wasn't his father and he had his own capabilities.

Attitude

Anyway, Sandra said, "You take this little group," which included Robert. "Just do what you can with them but don't bother with factorizing with Robert because he can't possibly factorize." Surprise, surprise, these kids told me they didn't like math. So I said, "Well, if you want to be a builder, or something like that, you'll need mathematics." My heart went out to them because they reminded me of myself when I was their age. So, I decided then that when Robert got out of my class, I was going to make sure he could factorize. I used to tell him, "You can do this Robert." I spent a lot of time working with him and his friends and after four weeks, at the end of my time there, they could all factorize. So I said to them, "You're going to at least pass that part of the exam." The way I see it, when they see they can do that, they might go on to try to do something else.

There was another little girl in my social studies class who hadn't once brought a workbook to school or done any work in the whole time I was there. One day I said to the teacher I was with, "I'm going to work with this girl today. She's going to do some work." So I gave her a pencil and some paper. I used to give my pens out all the time. We were studying some community issue and she did a great letter. She was so proud of it, she showed the teacher when she'd finished and the teacher praised her so she felt really good. But where did it go? It didn't have a book to go into. All the work I saw her do in class was on photocopied worksheets. And where did they go after class? Well, most of them were left on the table or went into the trash. So when she came back the next day, where are all the things she's done? How are you supposed to build on that?

One time the kids in my math class had been playing up and Sandra had had a bad day. Some of the boys had called her a bitch, which was just dreadful but after seven weeks I could sympathize. Her writing on the board was hard to understand, there was no discussion in class, and it was all about control. A typical lesson was, "Walk into class, put your bags down, open your books to page 42, do exercises three to eleven, copy this from the board, complete this worksheet..." the whole time. This particular day she said to me, "Wait till their parents get their results." I was appalled. Admittedly, the kids weren't very nice to her but, to me, that's no excuse to take out your revenge on them. That's just a power trip. It was like, "You wait. I'm going to get you back." I don't know what you'd call it but to me it's not a teaching attitude.

Another time, Sandra asked me to do some marking. I said to her, "Well, if I mark them, you mightn't like my marking because I'll always find one good thing to say about them," because that's what I really believe. If a child comes out of your class with no knowledge—whether it's because they don't want to learn or they're playing up or because of their home background—they should at least leave with their self-esteem raised and knowing that one day their circumstances might change and they can do things. I hate it when teachers say, "Oh, he's only a C student," which I've heard many a time. "That's all you can expect from him. He's only a C student. He can't do better than that." That attitude locks kids into categories. I've told myself there is no way that I will make a child feel dumb. It doesn't matter how much they play up in my class or what they're like, I'll always tell them, "You mightn't have shown much knowledge on this test, but I know that you have got the ability. When your circumstances change or if you want to change, things could be different."

Professional assessment

I also hear comments like, "Oh, he's a level three, don't bother." The schools ascertain the learning disabilities of kids who are not doing well. In my Grade 8 geography class, there were about seven boys—it always seems to be boys—who were ascertained. I could see them saying to themselves, "I don't have to do that. I'm level three. I'm level whatever." It's just the old intelligence test again. That's the way I look at it. It seems to me we're just giving them excuses for why they don't have to work, and we're also giving ourselves excuses for why they can't be taught. Once when I worked with one of these boys, I was telling him the answers to the questions and he was writing them down with no mistakes in them. It made me think, "He's a lot more clever than I ever was because I couldn't have done that at that age. So, how can he be ascertained?" I'd been told, "Oh, Ben's ascertained at level two. He can't concentrate." But when I realized he could do the work, I said, "Ben, if you do this work with me, you can go early." And he said, "Well, let's do it then." So we went through all the questions and he did the work perfectly. We'd discuss the questions, I'd make comments and so would he and then I'd say, "Write that down," and so he would. Now I could not have written that down when I was his age. So, I can't help thinking, where's the value in telling kids what they can't do?

Einstein never spoke until he was four. What would he be ascertained as? How many people ended up being geniuses and yet failed those intelligence tests? At the other end of the scale, I often hear teachers in class say, "Oh, he's a gifted student." And I think, "No, he's not. He just had parents who gave him all the resources." In the state where I grew up there are special schools for the gifted. If you reach a certain standard you can go to the number one school. Now, are those kids gifted? Of course not, not in my opinion. They come from backgrounds where education has been a priority. They've had books read to them. They've had the equipment. They've all been tutored, even unconsciously by their parents. That's not being gifted. The real gifted child is probably there in the classroom, probably coming last in something, the one who's leading everyone off doing something they're not supposed to do. That's my personal view, anyway. I believe they are gifted in that they've got the right parents and they've been coached and they've been sent to the right school. That's where I think their giftedness comes in. Until four years ago when I went to university, my whole life I believed that my lack of academic skills was because I was not intelligent. Because I didn't have those skills, I believed I was never going to be academic. Never would I have thought that I could ever go to university.

Before I went to university I went through primary school with my children. It was like I was doing it all over again. I was really good up to about the sixth class but it got to the point where I would get a note from their teacher saying, "Stop helping the kids do their assignments." I took it so seriously and I won quite a few awards! I wanted my children to do well at school but I really did a bad thing because then they didn't have to do it. I was doing the work for them. That was when I was only a mother. Whereas now, I think children need to learn to be independent and to learn to do those things for themselves. I won't touch my daughter's schoolwork now. I've got a little daughter, seven years old, and I won't touch her work now. Still, why is it that some kids have those skills and others don't? Why do you think some people live highly successful lives? For the most part, it's because of their families. It starts when they're young. I read a lot with my daughter when she was growing up. By third grade, when she brought home her folder with her eight words to learn, she already knew them and could read all the books because mom sat there every night listening to her read and going through the words with her. Whereas, as a small child, why do you think I couldn't read? Why do you think my family, my sisters, have struggled? There's obviously nothing wrong with my brain. I wonder how many kids are out there, labeled like I was, but there's nothing wrong with them. When I say to a kid, "What do you do for a hobby?" and he tells me he makes ships, how could anything be wrong with his brain? The whole thing just frustrates me.

On reflection

We need to think seriously about what we want to do with our children. Do we want to educate them and give them equal access to education, because I don't really see much equal access to education going on. For a start, if your basic needs aren't being met, how can you be educated? It's not just access to material things like a computer, pens, pencils, books, or even food to keep their minds alert. It's the person to help them. It's access to the knowledge that mom has or dad has, which can be quite different depending on who they are. And it's not even just that. It's the home environment where they have a bedroom to go to do their homework, where there's time to do it, and a home environment where that kind of thing is seen as important. Kids also need equipment in schools but they especially need teachers who will personally sit with them, who will do what their mom and dad never did with them. If kids have got to high school and they can't read, for example, teachers have to go back to the books, to teaching them how to read. It's not much use learning about the Greeks and Indians or Shakespeare when they can't access that knowledge for themselves because they lack the skills. I think we've got to give them skills and stop labeling them. What does an exam show? That they can't do those things. It doesn't show that they're dumb—that's what they thought about me when I was a kid—it only shows that you can't do that exam.

But you can't just say to a teacher, "You've got 25 children. Everyone has to be treated equally and educated the same." To treat everyone the same is not treating everyone the same. If Robert can't factorize, then I've got to show him how to factorize whereas another student who can factorize, for that child to get an equal education I've got to take them up to the next level. So equal education can be a totally different education in the same classroom. It's not everyone doing the same work. Everyone could be doing a different level of work but our classes and schools aren't geared for that, are they? For one teacher, that's impossible.

The current education policies say that teachers have to treat students fairly but what does it actually mean, "fair and equitable practice"? As I said before, I think it's fair that if someone can't read, you read out the question, but that's not what everyone thinks. I'm not even sure that that's what most teachers think. They think social justice in school has to do with just respecting and celebrating different cultures, and some of them don't even do that. But if you want to change the patterns of injustice, you have to change what happens in schools. These are the teachers of the future and yet they go from school to college and back to school thinking that if students can't read then they're dumb. Sometimes I see it as an insurmountable problem. I get really angry about it because I see me and I see these other kids in schools who are like me, who teachers just dismiss as dumb. They're not dumb. They just need people to believe in them and to provide them with support and opportunities. I think I'm a living example of that.

CHAPTER EIGHTEEN

Joan

Joan's story is told from the comfort of her old age. It covers primarily the years of her pre-adolescence and adolescence, during and after the Great Depression. Many people throughout western countries experienced hardship in these years, although the severity of Joan's personal circumstances appears qualitatively different from most. But even if we were to regard them as typical of the times, it is sobering to recognize their strong similarities with growing numbers of young people today who again face lives of fear, ridicule and effacement associated with their poverty (see Community Affairs References Committee 2004). Our social institutions (our families, schools, hospitals, et cetera) are probably less overt now in their contributions to such a miserable lifestyle; their interactions with individuals are probably more "politically correct" yet their contributions to our formation are no less significant. It seems we still like to mark out people as "different," in a derogative sense. We still like to exploit their weaknesses and we still like to explain their positioning as a function of their own doing. Certainly, there is a degree of agency in Joan's story, of her choices—good and bad—accounting for her immediate situation. But there is also clear evidence of a structuring of her life, largely outside of her control, which dictated her course. This is a story of the search for acceptance in the face of adversity; a search that was not without reward, albeit accompanied en route by considerable heartache and sorrow. It is also a story of great courage, to believe that there must be something better and to struggle to attain it.

The early years

The first thing I ever remember in my life was being in hospital. I had diphtheria. I can remember being there and my mother coming out with my sister to take me home. I really didn't want to go because I must have been so young that I'd forgotten who they were. So I hid behind the nurses' skirts and peeked out at them. Eventually they coaxed me into going. I remember that on the way home my mother bought us a balloon and I was sitting in the train making faces at my older sister because I didn't like the look of her. But when we got home everything was OK. The second thing that I can remember is being sick again. I had shingles and they were right around my stomach. They were so itchy that I couldn't stop scratching them and I made them bleed. The doctor said my hands had to be tied to the top of the bed to stop me scratching. So, the only way I could scratch was to move my body around on the sheets to get some relief.

But probably the most vivid memory I have of my early childhood is when my mother died. My grandparents—Dad's parents—lived near a coal-mine. We were visiting them and there was some sort of upset with my sister and grandpa. He was a bad-tempered man, my grandfather. So we left— mom, my sister, and I—and we went to stay with my mom's cousin who lived just behind them. Or maybe that was planned. In any case, we'd gone there. While we were there, the night before mom died, my sister went out to the picture theatre. It must have been with someone from the house or with some friends. She'd asked mom if she could go. She'd never been to the pictures before. Mom had said she could and, of course, "yours truly" wanted to go too. I sent up a big wail. I can remember kicking up a big fuss. "I want to go to the pictures." "You can't go. You're too young."

That day was also my 8th birthday and there was a birthday cake. Even mom had a slice and I was really amazed because she never ate cake. She'd been a diabetic for a long time and was often very ill. Sometimes she would fall unconscious. Her blood sugar would get too low and she'd fall down on the floor and my sister would look after her. It put her in hospital quite a bit. Anyway, I can remember she used to test her urine with a tube. They didn't have the testing equipment we have today. So, I said I wanted mine tested and I think she agreed just to keep my mind off going the pictures. Well, what I did was, I pinched some of hers. You had to use a chamber pot to get enough urine to test. I got some of mom's from her chamber pot and put it in whatever container I had and said, "There you are. That's mine. Test that." Well, she tested it and there was sugar in it. She was terribly worried. Then I had to admit to what I had done.

That night I slept with mom in her bed. We were sharing because we were on holidays and I suppose they didn't have any spare beds. The next morning I woke up and felt all wet and I was a bit worried at first because I thought, "Oh, I've wet the bed." I found out later what had happened. Mom had edema in her legs. They were all swollen up and she had fluid in them. When she died, that all came away, that fluid in her legs, and that was why I was wet. Anyway, I remember turning over and saying, "Mom, wake up, wake up." She had her eyes closed and wouldn't wake up. I did that a few times. Then it just seemed a bit strange to me so I put my hand on her head and it felt cold. I'd learned at school that when people died, they were cold. I don't know why they taught me that at school or how I knew it but I did. That would have been about eight o'clock in the morning. At six o'clock, my mom's cousin had brought mom a drink and apparently mom had said to her, "I feel better than I've felt for ages. I feel really good." After that she must have gone to sleep again. A couple of hours later I woke up and she was gone. So she really just died peacefully in her sleep. Later, I can remember going to the funeral parlor to see mom in her coffin. The coffin was lying on the floor.

After mom died

Up until then, I had a very happy time. I was in a very good situation. It was after that, that things went downhill. In fact, the rest of my childhood was dreadful. You've no idea how awful it was. Mom dying was just the start of it. Life was dreadful for my sister, too. There was no fun, no happiness, no pleasure, and no caring. After mom died and dad started to go out with Stella, we were taken from our home—the only place I ever thought of as home—and we went over to this other place and, you know, I just felt insecure. Stella's mother used to live there but she died not long after we moved in. She was a really nice lady. She was in bed all the time as I recall. She spoke to me very nicely and I used to sit and talk with her. Anyway, mom died in March, the day after I turned 8, and I really don't know whether it was the June of that year or the next—I can't really remember—when my dad married Stella.

Before they met, Stella had had a nervous breakdown and had been put in an asylum. I remember her saying once that when she'd "come to" she was in this asylum. In those days, it must have been pretty awful. She said she was standing in a long line of people with no clothes on, holding a towel and waiting to go into the showers. That's sort of when she came back to herself. So in a way, things weren't all that good for her. She had the breakdown while she was living with my dad's sister and from then on Stella hated her. She also hated grandma and grandpa, my dad's parents. She used to say, "All those damned..." Oh, I forget the word she used about them. So they never came to our place, although grandma did come to visit once. She needed some money to get home but dad wouldn't give it to her. And at that stage I was saving up. I had some money because I was going to visit my sister in the country so I gave it to grandma. I said, "Oh, grandma, I've got my fare for the train. I'll give you that. Will you send it back to me?" She said yes but she forgot all about it. I remember I had trouble trying to get it back. But grandma was nice. I loved her. She was really lovely.

I suppose dad found life very difficult as a widower, trying to care for two young girls while working long hours. He was a blacksmith's striker. He was a very strong man with strong arms. He worked for a company that made tractors and he used to pull the big hammer up and down. He worked hard, I think. But outside of work I think he just wanted a quiet life. He didn't want all the worry but it didn't quite work out that way, marrying Stella. As soon as you walked into the house there'd be trouble. She'd say you've done something wrong and they'd be simple things. She would go on and on about it. She'd even go for dad. Stella would be sitting there and she'd have an argument with him. She'd do things like pick up the salt-and-pepper shakers and heave them over the other side of the room. She'd throw them and he'd dodge and then she'd say they just slipped out of her hand. And she used to froth at the mouth. When she got angry, the froth would flow from her mouth down her chin. Her eyes were the palest blue I've ever seen in my life. Icy eyes. She even came in one day with an axe and chopped up her wedding photos. My boyfriend—he's now my husband—was with me that day and he pulled me out the back door and said, "You can't go back and live there." So we sat in the park till midnight arguing about him wanting to take me home to his mother and me saying I couldn't go because I knew his older sister was there and I wasn't welcome. This was later when I was about 16.

But Stella would do those sort of things all the time, from the time she moved in. She even sold mom's furniture. Mom had this nice sofa she had bought not long before she died and, of course, she was paying it off. Stella would go on and on about how wasteful she was and that she was cross-eyed and that she was a thief and so on. You had to try to block it out and I did do that. When I went to church, I was all bright and sparkly and everything because it was somewhere to escape. I was quite popular at church. Quite a number of boys asked me out. But it was all so scary because Stella was always saying to me we had to move. "You've got to find a place for us to live." How could I find a place for us to live? I was just a kid. I used to have to go with her while she looked at houses but all the time I felt on edge. She'd say, "If you don't find us somewhere to live, we'll all be out on the street." How can a kid find a place to live? That went on for years, at least till

I was 11. It must have been longer than that because she even asked my boyfriend if he knew someone who would buy the furniture. But, of course, he said, "I've never sold any furniture in my life!"

The house itself was horrible, too. It was dismal and dark and horrible and cheerless. Even the bedroom we slept in looked out on a brick wall. And it smelled. Stella would leave the chamber pots under the bed all day so that they would stink. There were no nice curtains, a couple of old cushions, and papers would litter the place, piled up on every available surface. The kitchen was barren and we never got decent food. Everything was burnt or uneatable. Stella couldn't cook. I don't know why. She never ever cooked a cake, only sago, and bread and butter puddings. There was no boiled pudding or anything really nice. And she hid the fruit; it would get doled out occasionally but you wouldn't have a piece of fruit every day. You wouldn't even have a piece of fruit every week. So my sister and I were both run down. We were both skin and bones. My sister, especially, was so thin. If she stood sideways you'd hardly see her.

Dad just buried himself in his books—that was his way of dealing with it—and Stella would tell him we'd done this or that. He would then come out and give us a belting. One day, dad came into our bedroom and kicked my sister. Stella had told him something about her, I can't remember what. Anyway, she fell down on the floor and he kicked her in the doorway of the bedroom. Another day he gave me a black eye. When they got rid of mom's furniture they brought these big old-fashioned chairs with wooden backs, which came around the side. Either side of the chair you'd have wings of wood that went around the back. Well, he slapped my face and I caught my eye on a bit of wood at the side of the chair and it gave me a black eye.

It must have been a Saturday because my boyfriend came around later that night and he saw what had happened. We had another night session in the park with him saying that I've got to get out of there and me saying there was nowhere else to go. We used to have these huge arguments along with gallons of tears from "yours truly." Anyway, when I got home that night, dad was waiting for me with some raw steak. He said, "Put this on your eye and it will take the black out." He didn't want anyone else to see what had happened. But I didn't want him to touch me or put anything on it. The next day, I went to church wearing dark glasses and he came too. He didn't go much, then, but he came that day and he got up and spoke. I walked out. I couldn't stand it.

I think the tension was probably the worst thing. There was always tension. All the time we were living in this tense atmosphere thinking, "What's going to happen next?" The whole thing was absolutely horrible. You'd be scared to go home, but you knew you had to go home. You had nowhere else to go so you'd go home and the atmosphere would be so tense, you could cut it with a knife. One day, when I was 11 or 12, I was so miserable that I decided to take a swig from a bottle marked "poison" I found in the laundry. At the time I didn't know what phenol was or even what it was used for or what effect it would have on me, only that life didn't seem to be worth living and this bottle with the word "poison" on it seemed to be the way out. But just as I put the bottle to my mouth to take a dose of it, my sister came into the laundry, saw me with the bottle at my mouth, grabbed it off me, and called for my father. They both then proceeded to pour what seemed like gallons of salty water down my throat to make me sick and bring up the poison, which hadn't gone down in the first place!

School life

Life at school wasn't much better. I used to love playing basketball and I was good at it too. I was on the school team. I loved it because we used to go to other schools and play. But you had to wear a white shirt under your tunic and mine was all torn under the arms. Stella wouldn't mend it. I tried to do it myself with a needle and cotton because she wouldn't let us use mom's machine, but it all came apart when I played. So, the teacher who was coaching the team told me I couldn't play until I got decent clothes. I never played anymore. I suppose the teacher thought, "We can't have someone representing the school and looking like that." To be fair, she did say, "You'll have to get another shirt if you want to play on the school team." She did say that but I knew there was no hope of getting another shirt. So she just got someone else. I was a bit grubby, it's true, but the teachers didn't seem to be interested in helping me do anything about it. One time, I was asked with another girl to go down to the teachers' staffroom to be a sort of monitor, you know, to get the morning coffee, put the water on, and get the cups and things out. But then I was stopped from doing that job because of the way I looked.

Another day my sister put my hair up in rags. My mother used to put my hair in rags because I had straight hair whereas my sister had curls and I loved curly hair. So, this day my sister put my hair up in rags like mom used to do but she left them in too long. Anyway I started to do a bit of a whinge when she put the comb in my hair but couldn't get it to run through. It was all frizzed up and I didn't want to go to school looking like that. Then Stella said, "Alright, I'll fix it." She got the scissors and cut my hair off below my ears right around. I had to go to school like that and you can imagine what a laughing stock I was at school, can't you?

No teacher ever offered to help me, but what could I have said, anyway? "I just hate my stepmother. She's nasty to me." What can you say? You can't say any more. My clothes weren't torn—well, only the shirt underneath my basketball tunic—but none of them fitted. Stella bought me two dresses once and when I put them on they came down to my ankles. I said, "They're a bit long. Can we take them up?" "No. You touch them and I'll take them back." But, you know, no kid of that age wants to look different to anyone else, do they? I knew that I'd be a laughing stock if I went out in these dresses, so I just tacked up the hem myself. I never saw the dresses again. She took them back. Can you imagine? Oh, and my shoes were worn and my socks had holes in them. Stella would tell me to mend them myself. I didn't know how to do that. I also remember that the hem would come down on my school dress.

The whole experience of school was just terrible. I never had the proper books because Stella would buy cheap books. You know how sometimes you can get secondhand books from other kids in the year ahead of you, but they wouldn't be the current issue. The teacher would say, "Turn to page 20," and on page 20 there'd be something different altogether to what was in the book that I had. So I was never in sync.

I hated school. I hated it when it rained and all the mothers came up and took their kids home with umbrellas. I hated it because my shoes were always worn. And I hated school because I never had any money. The school used to have a day selling toffees to raise money. I used to pinch some money from Stella's purse now and again, when I could, so I could buy toffees. So even the good parts about school were hurtful. I had a very nice friend. She took me home one lunchtime. Her house was double-fronted, what you would probably call today "old-fashioned." It was really nice inside. It was nice outside, too, with a nice garden. And her mother was so nice. I cried all the way home that day. You know, her house and life were bright and colorful and I went back to hell, really. It seems awful just thinking about it now.

I also hated school because I was always terrified Stella was going to come up and see the head teacher about me. One day she found out that I'd skipped a few pages in my workbook at school. You know how you've used half of the page and it's a bit untidy and you decide to make a new start. I'd do that. I'd write beautifully for a while till it sort of dwindled off and I'd make a new start on the next page. Stella found my book in my school bag one day and went up to the head teacher and complained—about the waste! So next day he came down to the schoolroom and gave us all a lecture about it and I knew it was my book. He said, "If this person does this again she'll be up before me." At the time I was about 9 years old. Isn't that awful?

Another time we had to knit a white singlet for a baby. It was part of a school project we had to do, but I couldn't knit very well. Besides, the wool Stella gave me was all dirty; it was dirty white wool. She wouldn't go and buy any, you know, and I didn't have the money to buy it myself. We only had a few weeks to get it done and I was petrified so I told my sister—she was five years older than me—and she said, "Don't worry. I'll fix it." She bought some wool and knitted it for me. In the meantime, the kids were really cruel. They were all saying to me, "You're going to get into trouble," and I knew I couldn't knit this wretched singlet. I was terrified I was going to be in dreadful trouble because it wasn't done. Anyway, my sister gave it to me the day before it was due and I was absolutely overjoyed. I took it to school but I didn't let on straight away that I'd got it done. The kids were saying, "Nah, nah. You're getting into trouble." And then I presented this beautifully knitted singlet and they were speechless. That's one of my better memories of school. I'm sorry I don't have many.

Then there were the school papers; they were a penny each. You had to get one every month and you kept them in a folder. Well, Stella ordered the school paper from the shop near where we lived. Because I suppose he only got one school newspaper, it would always be late. And so when the teacher would say, "Right, get out your school paper," I never had it. I had to wait two or three days until it arrived. Well, this particular day, the teacher said, "Alright, all those who haven't got the latest school paper by this afternoon will be in trouble. They'll be going up to the head teacher." I was terrified of the head teacher by this time and so I ran all the way from school to our place to tell Stella that I needed the school paper and to get a penny to buy it. She wasn't home so I went down to the local shop and asked if they had arrived. They hadn't and because I knew the school shop over the road had them I asked, "Well, can you give me a penny to go and buy it and put it on the bill?" So he did. He gave me a penny and I ran all the way back, got the school paper and got into class just in time. But the teacher never asked us. He never even mentioned those school papers that afternoon. Of course, everything was all right till Stella got the bill and she saw the penny on it. So she asked the local shopkeeper, "What's this for?" So he told her and I got into dreadful trouble. I got a thrashing for that. And she accused me of being a deceitful liar and a thief.

Growing up

One day I went on a Sunday school picnic on a train. I had a hat on but it blew off out the train window. I was terrified about going home to tell Stella. When I did go home and tell her, she confronted the man in charge—he was really kind to me—and she made such a scene and went on and on about it and took me away from there. We never went there anymore and I was sent to a different Sunday school. At another picnic, I had a blue dress on and I slipped in the mud. Other people did too because it was very muddy and, of course, I got mud on my dress. I was terrified of Stella and what she'd say. So when I got home, I sneaked in without her seeing me—it was fairly late in the evening—and I put it in the trough in some water. I thought, "I'll get up early and wash it out and hang it on the line. She won't be able to say any-thing." But I slept in and she saw it. She told my father that there was blood on it—that I'd been with boys and that's why I'd tried to wash it out. Well, my father went to the minister at the church and asked him why he was al-lowing this to happen. The minister was absolutely furious about it because he knew there was nothing like that happening at all. He knew that the teach-ers were with us all the time. But that was like Stella. She would make innu-endos. She seemed to say and do things to make you feel dirty, to make you feel that you were somehow inferior.

Once I got a secondhand bike for Christmas, which is OK because lots of kids had secondhand bikes. It was V-shaped and every now and then my feet would slip off the pedals and I'd fall and crash my legs either side of the bike frame and it would hurt like crazy. When I got my first menstrual period I'd just fallen that day again and I thought that I'd hurt myself badly. I didn't know what was happening to me. Nobody had told me a thing, not even my sister. I remember once she had this packet of things. She was with a friend of hers and I was there and I said, "What's in there?" They said, "Snowballs." And I said, "Well, I want one," and they started to laugh but she still didn't tell me and no one else told me either. I don't really know how I found out. Stella must have said something. Anyway, she gave me these old rags; pieces of torn old sheet. That's what I had to use. I was always afraid that I'd lose them or the blood would show through because they weren't very absorbent. And then what I had to do—and you know, blood, it's very difficult to get out—I had to soak them in a bucket. So I did this and periodically I'd go and wash them out. At the time I was still at school, I was only a kid. But Stella would complain to dad about them being in the bucket and he would tell me to go and wash out my filthy rags. That's the way I was spoken to, you know. I didn't expect Stella to wash those sorts of things. I understood that it was my responsibility, but everything was like that. Nothing was nice or pleasant.

It was so bad you couldn't bring any friends home. I remember once some boys from church came around on their bikes one Saturday afternoon to see me but they weren't game to knock on the door. They were back-peddling their bikes to let me know they were outside and she heard them. She saw them through the window so she shut the door in the passage and wouldn't allow me even to go to speak to them. She was horrid. And then things would go missing at home. I remember my sister lost her glasses. She thought she'd left them on the train and she went to the station to inquire about them because she was doing work at the time where she needed her glasses. It was some sort of spinning work. She was terribly upset about it because she didn't have the money for a new pair. Years later she got them back. Stella gave them back to her. She'd also take dresses. By the time you got them back they'd be about five years out of fashion.

Leaving home and school

One time, Stella's cousin came to live with us but soon after he got tuberculosis (TB) and went off to a sanatorium. He was a very, very nice man; a real lovely gentleman, he was. He would have been about 45. Because we were so run down, my sister caught it too. She'd gone to our aunt's place for a holiday and while she was there she coughed up what she said was about a cupful of blood. So when she came back she went to the doctor and he sent her for tests and they found she had TB. Immediately, they took her out to the sanatorium on the outskirts of the city. Well, I got to see her once after that. I went out there by myself and she was in this long ward—a huge ward—and she said to me, "People are dying around me all the time." In those days they didn't have the same drugs that we've got today. She was really scared, really upset. The hospital staff believed the fresh air was part of the cure so they put wire netting in place of the glass for windows. I think I might have gone there twice but it was such a long way and I didn't have any money. I would have been about 12, then. Dad never went to see her. Stella never went to see her. She was there for 12 months and they never went to see her. She told me later that the nurses used to say to her, "Aren't your parents interested? They never come to ask us how you're getting on or anything."

After 12 months, they sent her to another hospital in the city to have her lung collapsed. They put a needle through the side of her chest into her lung and filled it full of air so that it couldn't work and it would rest it. From there, they sent her home. With no money, the only home she had to come to was ours, but she was met on the front porch by Stella screaming at dad, "Get that thing out of here with her germs." That's when dad said, "Well, you had better find somewhere else to live." So my sister, pointing at me, said, "What about Joan?" "Take her with you." In that one moment, we were homeless, with no place to live. We knew a lady at church who ran a boarding house, at least my sister did. I didn't know much about her only that she was the Sunday school superintendent and I never had much to do with her really. My sister got in touch with her. I don't know whether she went to the minister's place or what she did. Anyway, she came to us and she said, "Well, we've got a room in the boarding house. Get your things together and we'll go." So we did. Fancy a father allowing a 13-year-old girl to go to live in a boarding house. What was he thinking about? And a sick girl—his daughter—who was just 18.

That's when I started work, when we left home. I had to earn some money to help pay for our room. I went to work and my sister had her pension. She got social security; she couldn't work because of her health, she had to rest. She paid part of the rent for the room out of her pension and I paid the other part. I started out working at a clothing factory, making men's trousers. It was piecework, really. That's pretty hard stuff, piecework. But I was OK there. I had friends. You'd start work about seven in the morning and you might go till eight or nine o'clock in the evening. There was a lot of compulsory overtime, then. I had to get an exemption from going to school so I could work. You had to go along to some place—I forget the name—and say why you had to leave school. I had to get the head teacher's signature as well. They just let me go. They were probably glad to see the back of me. I was glad to be rid of them too, at the time.

As well as working through the week, I had to help on Saturdays to clean this Sunday school teacher's two boarding houses, to pay for our food. I don't know if you know these boarding houses. They have huge passageways and huge stairs that go up and down, and bathrooms and sitting rooms and then other passages down the back. And the two houses had to be cleaned. You had to sweep them, vacuum the carpet on the stairs, dust the stair railings, wash the entrance hall, clean the baths, and clean the sitting rooms. There was another girl—Paula—who was about my age, who also lived and worked in the boarding house. She used to work in the kitchen with the cook. But the lady who owned the houses was so critical. It was awful. Paula didn't seem to get the criticism, I don't know why. I hated her, too. I was pretty good at hating people by that time. It wore me down after a while and my sister left to get married so I was there on my own. I was so tired of it all, working all the week and then cleaning up both boarding houses. I mean, the owner helped, but chopping the wood, doing the ironing, and then being told she knew who did this and that because Paula did it better than me, it became too much. I thought, anything is better than this. And after you've been away for a while from something that's terrible, you think, "Oh, maybe it wasn't as bad as what I thought. Now I'm older it will be alright."

A proposal

When I went back, it was just the same. I tried to get into a hostel. It was for girls, a homeless girls' hostel. They closed it down later, after the fire in the men's hostel. The fire brigade said to the owners, "This place is dangerous too and you've either got to fix it up or close it down." So they closed it down. I went before that to try to get a place there and they just told me there was no room. I didn't know where else to go, so I went back home. I also tried to get a job in an office in a factory but they turned me down. I thought no one wanted me so I didn't try anywhere else. I couldn't type or do anything in an office anyway.

By then I must have been getting a bit independent, as you do, although kids get independent earlier these days. I began to think there's got to be something better. I can't stand this for the rest of my life. I didn't know where else to go. I tried to get in at the girls' hostel and failed. I had tried to get an office job and failed at that, too. Then a new girl arrived at church and she befriended me. She said she was going to train to be a nurse. She was always talking about it, you know, how you live in and you get your meals, get paid and get days off, and so on. I thought, gee, that would be a great place to live and get food and get a bit of money and work as well. I didn't really know what nurses had to do. So, I said, "Good, I'll go too." She encouraged me. She said, "We'll go together," which we did. My boyfriend's sister-in-law made the uniforms for me. I bought the material and she made all the uniforms. She did a good job on them, too. So, I got into the hospital to train as a nurse. You really had to be 18 to get in but they took me when I was 17. I started in September and I turned 18 the next March. They started me in the children's ward and I was in theatre on my 18th birthday. We had a nice night sister. Once, when we were in theatre, she said to me, jokingly, "If I could catch you, Wilkins, I'd ring your neck." She was a big woman and she was really good fun and nice. But the sister who was the dietician, she was really strict, straight as a rod and bad tempered.

It was hard work in those days, being a nurse. They don't do today what we had to do then. We had to do all the cleaning as well as the nursing. We had to sterilize the beds and wash the skirting boards and the rails. The charge sister would come to look over you, to see whether it was done correctly. When you were on night duty you had to clean the kitchen stove as well. We had to clean this stove with steel wool and then we had to polish it with some black stuff.

Well, one particular night I hadn't had a lot of time in the kitchen to do it because we were so busy. I don't know why we were so busy, but we were. In the middle of cleaning they called me upstairs again to help in the ward. Anyway, all of the night girls came down to breakfast at the end of the shift and we were tired. We were all sitting down to breakfast when in stalks this woman, the dietician. She says, "Who was the junior on duty in the kitchen last night?" You had to stand up with your hands behind your back. I stood to my feet and she said, "You haven't cleaned the stove properly. You can come and do it now."

But before I could move the night sister stood to her feet and said, "Sit down nurse." She was the night sister but this dietician was senior to her. "Nurse Wilkins will not be coming back to clean the stove. She's done all the work she's going to do for tonight. You can go back and clean it yourself." Oh, boy, was that a fireworks display. I was wishing she hadn't said anything. I would have been happy to go back to clean it because I've always been a weepy individual. I was hanging my head to make myself as inconspicuous as possible because she'd have it in for me, then. But the night sister wouldn't allow me to go. "You've done your share for tonight. Sit there and eat your breakfast."

I realized fairly quickly that I didn't want to be a nurse. In fact, I hated it. I liked the children's ward though. That was really good because I loved the kids and they were great. I was making bottles to feed little babies and giving them washes and so on. They were so tiny. But you couldn't stay there for a great length of time. They would move you around the hospital. It wasn't long after I left the children's ward that I was put in a ward where a man was dying. They put him in a wing that was closed. It was the first time I'd ever seen someone dying, apart from my mother. He was calling out, "Oh, I never knew it would be like this. I never knew it would be like this." All his family were standing by the bed and they were crying. It haunted me for weeks. I just hated it.

But I had food to eat, a place to live, and I had friends. And I still had my boyfriend. Even before I went nursing, from the moment I started to go out with him things seemed to get better. There was someone who loved me and he used to take me home to his mother's place for dinner on Sundays. His home was so different. I'm sure they had their arguments at times but his mother was just so welcoming. And his father, well, he didn't go overboard but he was pleasant to me and it was just an absolutely different atmosphere. I wanted to stay there all the time. His mother was a good plain cook. She'd make beautiful boiled puddings and there was always a roast for Sunday dinner, which was something I'd never had. They just seemed to like me and nobody criticized me. I was very, very happy being there until his older sister came home from interstate. I'd never met her before, so when my boyfriend talked about his sister I just imagined she'd be like the rest of the family or like my own sister. I was so excited about her coming home, but she disliked me from the moment she saw me. I could see it. She genuinely loved her brother, she really did. It was very obvious. She was about 15 years older than him and I think she had visions of them doing things together, which is natural if you really care about your family. But when she discovered that he had a girlfriend and he wasn't going to be spending much time with her, from that moment she looked on me with disdain.

One night my boyfriend asked me if I would marry him so I quickly said yes, before he changed his mind! We fell in love and have been in love ever since. We got engaged in the middle of the month of May. We planned that. There used to be a song about the middle of the month of May and getting engaged. I can't remember the exact one. I said to him once, that would be a good time, the middle of the month of May. Boy, was his sister angry about that. About a year later I left nursing to marry him. I didn't finishing my training. I was happy to leave. I only had a year to go but getting married was the chance to start a new life.

When Stella died

When Stella died I was in my early 30s. She'd had an operation to remove some bowel cancer and after the operation she'd gone home to recuperate. I found out later that she was very ill so I went over to dad and Stella's house. The walls were made of sacking and the bathroom was absolutely full with old papers. It was in the middle of the day and she was in the front bedroom and dad was out the back, asleep. He would fill himself with drugs he got from the return servicemen's hospital. As a return serviceman he used to get his drugs free, no questions asked. Then he'd just lie in bed. I think that he had had such a terrible life, he really wanted to sleep the rest away. He didn't want to be awake.

Anyway, Stella smelled to high heaven. She really stunk. I had a look at her stomach where the colostomy was. It was red raw. It was dreadful. So I went out and shook dad and said, "You should be ashamed of yourself leaving this woman in this condition. She's had nothing to eat or drink. She's in a terrible state in here." His own room stunk of stale urine as well. I said, "She's got to come home to my place. I've got to take her home." There was nobody else. She'd made no friends so it just had to be me. I can't say I was perfect. This is the same person who had told me to wash out my own dirty rags, but you couldn't leave a dog in the condition she was in. I took her home and got in touch with the doctor and he said he wanted to see me. He explained that she was full of cancer and that she was dying. It was just a matter of time. She was in such a lot of pain. It was terrible. The cancer was giving her tremendous pain and all the doctors could provide was a morphine mixture to give her.

Well, shortly after that, my husband got this dreadful pain with a hernia and he had to go to hospital. I was really beside myself with worry because dad kept taking these drugs and he wouldn't do anything to help. I had three young children at the time to look after as well and I was finding it hard to cope. And Stella was incontinent, which I didn't mind but it made for a lot of work. I used to get some help from a nurse who came in every day to give Stella a bath and fix up her wounds. I told my problems to one nurse who came and she said, "Look, you've got to get some help here. You've got to get your stepmother into respite care or get her into a place where they'll look after her until your husband is back on his feet again. Then she can come back." Well, she never did come back. She went to a terrible place. I went to visit her one day. They hadn't changed the sheets and, of course, she was filthy. She died not long after that.

On reflection

I think the reason I've been crying while telling you all this is because I've been crying for the child that I was. I'm sure that had my mom lived, dad would have been a better father because he was different when she was alive. He sort of went with the flow. You see, he had been a prisoner of war for two and a half years and though he told a lot of funny tales about it, it couldn't have been easy. I've also heard some of the not-so-funny stories, too. They were badly treated. Yet, he said that the few times they received Red Cross parcels, they'd give some of the chocolates out of their parcels to the local children who used to come to the wire fence. So he obviously cared for other people. I think he just had a hard time, really. He was the one grandma worried the most about because he had to leave school early to go to work in the mines with grandpa to help feed the family. There were 14 of them. I think she felt bad about that. He was sort of her white-haired boy and he was very fond of her.

He was a stubborn man and his father before him was a stubborn man. I think I'm a bit stubborn, too. I'm just not prepared to give up. Now I am. I'm old now. I don't want to fight any battles. I've lived with my husband for 56 years. Never once has he ridiculed me and he very rarely criticizes me. The lady who owned the boarding house always used to say that my hair looked awful, that it was lifeless. But my husband thinks I'm stupid to believe that. He says to me, "Your hair's beautiful. You've got lovely hair." He really restored my self-confidence in many ways. I think, too, if I had been a stronger personality I would have come out of it better than what I did. I've always let people walk over me. I should never have let all those people—my stepmother, the boarding house lady, my sister-in-law—walk over me.

I could never have imagined the life I live now when I was a teenager and probably never would have believed it possible when I got married. But I was just so absolutely determined, especially after I had my children, that they were going to have a better life than I'd had. And I knew that if they were going to have a better life, then I had to work. I know that along the way I made mistakes. For example, I didn't save my money. I should have done that. When I first got married I bought a bedroom suite for $400. Now, I should never have done that. Knowing what I know today, I would have bought a secondhand bed and a cupboard to put some clothes in and put the extra money toward a house. Things might have been a lot easier and I mightn't have had to work so hard. I couldn't do anything to change those early years, those circumstances. All those things that happened to me were out of my control. Nevertheless, I should have sat down and used my intellect and said, "Right, the way I'm going to get out of this is to save my money and have a house before I have a family, to get somewhere to put them." Then I might have been able to stay home with my children.

Instead, I worked hard to buy them an education. I saw education as the pinnacle. Now I think about it, that was probably a misconception. I looked around me and saw the people who were successful or had good jobs. They had an education and they had money and they could buy nice houses and provide nice things for their children. I think that was the driving force, the fact that I would have loved to have had those things as a child. I couldn't go back and have those things again myself, but I could give them to my children by giving them an education. But what I couldn't give them was my time, as much time as I would have liked to anyway, and I regret that greatly. Still, I don't think I would have done anything differently, if I went back again and had the same options. The only thing I would do is be a lot wiser with money.

From the time I had children it was very difficult. There was always money going out. There were shoes and clothes and school fees and food and all those sort of things. It was very difficult to save. Anyone with a family today—or any day—will tell you that; unless they have a really good job. My oldest daughter said to me a couple of years ago, "Mom, how ever did you afford to pay for our music lessons," because at that stage she was paying for music lessons for her children and she was finding it expensive. That's part of bringing up a family, providing them with opportunities. All good parents do that. Plus, my children are spread over so many years. Most of my friends would have been on their own in their mid-40s or early-50s. They had 15 years then to provide for themselves, for their retirement. We didn't have that period, but I don't regret that. I do regret my own lack of forethought in trying to save some money. Maybe if someone had said to me, "Now, look, sit down. If you save so much here and put that away, you can have an easier life later on." Instead, I was thinking only for the moment. Yes, I wish I'd done that, but I can't go back.

The only time I have ever seen idle money was when I cleaned out Stella's wardrobe after she died. It was full of it. I couldn't believe that she had so much money. All that time she was getting the pension for dad's war service, which included—and I didn't know this at that time—an allowance for me and my sister up until we were 16 or 18—even after we had moved out! She didn't trust banks or anyone else. She was mad with dad one day and put a stop on their bank account, so he put a stop on it as well. So neither of them could get any money out of the bank. Stupid! Whereas, my mother-in-law never had any money. She had lots of friends but she never had any money. She used to spend it. She'd buy presents for the grandchildren. Her husband and her daughter used to be angry with her for spending all her money but she was just that sort of person, generous. She wasn't a spendthrift. If you came to her place, during the war years and said, "Oh, we haven't got any sugar," she'd give you half a pound. She'd do that with anything; butter, whatever. People would tell her a sad story and she'd be there giving them something. She'd even knit socks for the woman up the street who had half a dozen kids. I didn't have anyone to do that for me but still, I should have used my own commonsense a bit better.

It might sound like I'm complaining but really I'm not. I'm just telling you how it was. I'm not unhappy with how it turned out. My childhood and adolescent years were very difficult times but when I think about where I am now, I can't complain. In some ways, I feel as if I have made up for what I didn't have by providing for my own children, as much as I've been able to. I even got a university degree along the way, when I was in my 40s. My six children all have university degrees, too, and good jobs and stable homes. But I do feel for young people today. Some of them aren't having a very good time of it and I know what that's like. It's like history repeating itself.

CONCLUSION

by Kathleen Densmore

In times past, coal miners in the United States of America would take a canary into the mines to alert them when the air was dangerously toxic. If the canary died, it was a sign for the men to leave the mine. Metaphorically speaking, *Rough Justice* is about the experience of the canary. It is about what the lives of the poor and the marginalized, especially youth, can teach us about our communities, our society, and about how contemporary times are experienced by others. In short, it is about the atmosphere in the mines. In that environment, the miners knew that the atmosphere, not the canary, was the problem. Similarly, many young people today are struggling to find meaning and value in "advanced" marketized societies. Many are struggling simply to survive. Yet, human beings need not be canaries in a poisonous atmosphere. Our young people need not be sacrificed to the toxins in their sociopolitical and economic environment. Together and individually, we can confront and change pernicious public policies and other forms of injustices and create opportunities to work toward the empowerment of the poor and marginalized.

In this Conclusion, I take up a number of these themes and others raised in this book, addressing them in a more global way particularly, but not exclusively, featuring the US context. I begin by briefly revisiting the widening gulf between rich and poor (see the Introduction to this book for a fuller account) and then move to an exploration of the ideologies of market economies and associated assaults on social services that are responsible for its production. Current forms of globalization are also implicated in this championing of neoliberalism. The intent in these accounts is to provide an explanation for "the way things are," in particular, to debunk existing socioeconomic arrangements as "natural" or simply as the outworking of individual choices. Finally, I conclude with an account of resistance to current "development" trends, arguing that the marginalization of the poor is political as much as it is economic and making this explicit where it was earlier implied. Cutting across these themes are different explanations of poverty, the reality of interlocking public and private spaces, and analyses of social and economic justice. Like the book generally, this Conclusion suggests that there is no simple way to understand the problems facing many adults and youth today, especially poor people of color. Still, we unquestionably have an obligation to try to do so, to endeavor to understand these as complex issues and to face up to them ourselves.

The gulf widens

Over the last three decades of the twentieth century, the gulf between rich and poor widened to an unprecedented scale worldwide. In the United States alone, the number of homeless, many of whom are employed, grew at unprecedented levels, as did the number of people with incomes at or below the federally defined poverty level (Center on Budget and Policy Priorities 1994, 11; US Bureau of the Census 1996). In 1998, the United States had the highest gap in income between rich and poor since the Census Bureau began publishing annual figures in 1947 (Henwood 2000). Henwood's more recent analysis also shows that people of color have greater unequal distribution of income than whites. The most fortunate one percent of households in the United States holds more wealth than the bottom 95 percent of the population (Hartman 2002). Also true for the by far richest country in the world, one fifth (20 percent) of adult men and women can neither read nor write and 13 percent have a life expectancy shorter than 60 years (Bauman 2001).

These are not figures particular to the United States, but have parallels with other western nations such as the United Kingdom and Australia. They are also conditions that have been deteriorating over decades; they did not suddenly appear in the twenty-first century but neither have they always existed. The ratio of poor men of color in prison, for example, compared with their numbers in school, has not always been as high as it is today. And, challenging the belief that "the poor always have, and always will, be with us," the degree of homelessness we are currently witnessing in our metropolitan areas in "developed" countries has not always existed. Why then, and how, have we permitted so many people in our own communities and across the globe to suffer and die in such dehumanizing conditions? Is it that most of us really do not care about people who desperately need medical or psychiatric attention? Do we really feel it is "natural" that millions of people turn to trash dumps for food and materials? Do most of us really believe that quality health care and education should only belong to those who can afford them? Are we really convinced that the poor and the rich come to market economies on an equal footing? Are we simply unaware of the fact that so many people live in drastically worse conditions than we do? Are urban decline, rising crime in the suburbs, rising university and school fees, child poverty, and prison expansion inevitable features of postindustrial society? Is it that those who manage or work in welfare organizations are simply frustrated and disillusioned with government bureaucracy and see no real possibilities for making a difference?

Since the early 1970s, the world has experienced an offensive led by US corporate interests, aimed at further transferring the world's resources from the public to the private sector. While the United States is taking a leadership role in this, other capitalist powers in an emerging transnational elite are also playing their part in advancing procorporate, anti-"big government" policies and strategies. In brief, the recipe for a "free" market embodies the notion that the individual should be free to make their own choices (whether or not to have a pension or health insurance, for example) and in making these self-interested choices, all of society will benefit. Margaret Thatcher, Prime Minister of the United Kingdom from 1979 to 1990, expressed this belief in her now famous claim that: "There is no such thing as society. There are [only] individual men and women and families" (in Ball 2003, 38). In this account, promarket, probusiness, free-trade policies appeal to "personal responsibility" to provide social safety nets, if they are needed at all.

Such policies have resulted in an even greater concentration of wealth among fewer corporations and individuals. A changing combination of players (and, as Bourdieu [1997] would say, the relative value of their stakes in the game) have joined in this offensive, including multinational corporations, military contractors, right-wing ideologues, religious fundamentalists, and both centrist and liberal policy makers. Since Keynesianism occupied the hearts and minds of government, we have witnessed the rising dominance of a new orthodoxy in social policy. Part of this dominance has involved its claims to universality. The almost simultaneous emergence of similar policies across different countries is clearly evident, contextual specificities notwithstanding. Operating at different speeds, to different degrees and via changing relationships among the various elements, economies are being "opened" so that the "logic of the market" can operate. It is this agenda that has been driving much of US foreign and domestic policy. Its central objective appears to be global control or power to privatize and deregulate economies throughout the world, to impose free markets and to ensure its rule. International organizations such as the World Bank, the World Trade Organization (WTO), the International Monetary Fund (IMF), and the OECD are its instruments. By restructuring how goods and services are produced, by conducting a relentless assault against unions or any organization that potentially advances the interests of working people or the poor, by creating new trade agreements, and by preventing the rise of alternative models of socioeconomic development, especially popular democracies, capitalist globalization has deeply impacted the daily lives of individuals in almost all countries of the world.

For example, millions of lives have been affected by: jobs that require increasing work for lower pay, dramatic job losses in both the manufacturing and services sectors, pressure for low wages, rising medical costs, declining environmental standards, an ongoing shift of the tax burden from the rich to the general public, heightened military spending, greater corporate control of the media, and corporate influence in public education. Although the incidence and intensity of these vary across western nations, most are evident at least in the United States. They are also matters interrelated with other countries around the world, particularly those within Asia. For example, an increasing number of jobs in western nations are now sent offshore, even professional work. On average, an engineer in India costs companies 10 percent of the cost of employing one in the United States. In the context of maximizing financial returns at all costs, it is difficult to imagine why companies would not avail themselves of such economies. Counting on this market logic, India is attempting to position itself as the world's major service provider—the outsourcing of "call centers" to India is a case in point—while China is seeking to become the world's leading manufacturer. Quite apart from what this means for western workers, when manufacturing jobs are transferred overseas, they frequently transform into part-time, temporary work, in sweatshops, located in "free-trade zones" (Klein 1999). Klein also explains that in many nations, migrants are typically preferred instead of locals because they are more ignorant about or fearful of claiming their rights as workers. For example, a construction worker in China, typically sourced from outlying regions, currently earns just US$50 per month. In addition, younger workers are preferred because employers can pay them less and avoid paying benefits (Klein 1999, 195–229). The impact of such practices these young people is enormous. For example, Klein reports on meeting a

17-year-old girl on the outskirts of Manila, assembling CD-ROM drives for IBM: "I told her I was impressed that someone so young could do such high-tech work. 'We make computers,' she told me, 'but we don't know how to operate computers'" (1999, xvii). In brief, euphoric reports about how the "global village" is equalizing the planet beckon our critical attention.

International financial policies also preserve extreme poles of wealth and poverty instead of closing the gap. And a unilateral foreign policy imposed by the world's only superpower, the United States, has heightened armed conflicts and terrorism while exacerbating and encouraging ethnic tensions. Youth growing up in many parts of the world today witness death, maiming, and violence on a scale previously unimaginable. US economic and foreign policies often create the conditions that force people to flee their own countries for economic survival or physical security. For example, in the mid-twentieth century, US and allied military campaigns in Southeast Asia led to large waves of immigration from that region. With the immense difficulties in becoming "legal," undocumented youth typically faced multiple barriers in pursuing education and work. Residential segregation and the exponential growth of the minority prison population, especially in so-called western democracies, have further fueled racial tensions.

Despite the fact that many in western nations enjoy relatively high living standards, the results of free-market globalization for most of the world's peoples, have been catastrophic. Nominally independent nation-states are being pressured into reducing, eliminating, or privatizing vital social services and key industries. For example, intense struggles have been undertaken in Bolivia over the privatization of water while India is privatizing its electricity. In many of these locations the diversion of money away from human welfare has drastically increased overall economic inequality. For example, at the end of the twentieth century, 1.3 billion people in the world lived on less than US$1 a day and 3 billion lived on under US$2 a day; 1.3 billion had no access to clean water, and 3 billion had no access to sanitation (Wolfensohn 1998). Child poverty worldwide has also worsened as incomes in western nations have risen over the past half-century (Williams 2000). By way of illustration, manufacturing a pair of Nike shoes, with a retail price of US$120.00, is estimated to cost 70–80 cents to produce in Indonesian sweatshops (McLaren and Farahmandpur 2003, 318). Even in the United States, the wealthiest nation on earth, one out of every six children lives in poverty (McLaren and Farahmandpur 2003, 319). In Australia, the figures are similar (see the Introduction). Still, it is difficult to compare this western poverty with how it is experienced in developing nations. According to Kevin Bales:

> The 11-year-old boy I met in India six weeks ago had been placed in bondage by his parents in exchange for about US$35. He now works 14 hours a day, seven days a week making *beedi* cigarettes. This lad is held in 'debt bondage,' one of the most common variations on the theme of slavery. Debt bondage is slavery with a twist. Instead of being property, the slave is collateral. The boy and all his work belong to the slaveholder as long as the debt is unpaid, but not a penny is applied to the debt. Until his parents find the money, this boy is a cigarette-rolling machine, fed just enough to keep him at his task. (2000)

Regardless of our personal comfort with, or views about, rising inequalities, for us to reject cynicism and more skillfully engage with diverse individuals and institutions, it is important that we understand both the economic realignments that have taken place, creating and maintaining conditions of human degradation, as well as the ideological grounding that underpins them, encouraging us to believe in or accept the current dismal state of affairs.

Neoliberalism: The market shreds safety nets

"Neoliberalism" is the term most commonly used to refer to the specific combination of economic, political, and cultural polices and values that have dominated societies in recent decades, and that are responsible for the dire circumstances that so many people find themselves in today. Importantly, neoliberalism, or "economic rationalism" as it is sometimes called, is not only about economics even though it sees all in terms of economics. In fact, it constitutes a specific kind of broad cultural project, changing institutional procedures, goals, values, and social relationships. Global neoliberalism is based in, but not limited to, US corporate dominance (see Duggan 2003). As an ideology, it draws on the classic liberal faith in unregulated economic markets (which have not existed since the eighteenth century), privatization and, consequently, the "proper" withdrawal of government from the welfare of the public. This faith justifies a climate in which it "makes sense" that business should strive, above all, to continually increase profits. Such endeavors frequently come at the expense of public welfare; a stance which also has to *make sense* to the citizenry. According to this now dominant ideology, increasing corporate profits is in our best interests because they make our economy strong. Somehow, these profits are said to "trickle down" to the general public (see the Introduction). And, a sure way to subsidize corporate profits is to lessen its tax burden, which in turn diverts money away from social uses. Increasing public ownership of corporate stock may also work at the expense of public resources. In 2004, for example, Australia had the world's highest level of "mom and dad" share ownership with 51 percent of all citizens owning shares, just in front of the United States. If most of the general public own shares, it is much easier to argue for worker layoffs and redundancies to increase company profits and, therefore, higher dividends and share prices, which reduces the number of wage earners that pay into social services funds.

Critically, to make this diversion go smoothly (that is, without social protest), most people must take for granted that "public" is inferior to "private"; that competition for a good education (that is, there will be winners and losers) is positive, and that "handouts" destroy initiative. Arguments for "small" government, whose primary role is to enable free exchange between individuals, fit nicely with an individualistic stance toward the world. The belief that acting in one's own self-interest, in competitive environments, is best for oneself as well as for others, lies at the heart of neoliberalism's faith in the rationality of markets. Instead of state-sponsored assistance for those in need, new welfare programs typically require the poor to work for the lowest wages, in dead-end jobs, to demonstrate that they are worthy of assistance. In Australia, for example, there are "work for the dole" schemes justified by notions of "mutual obligation" but the enforced obligations often appear one-sided. Such programs claim to "empower" the poor, liberating them from their "dependency" on the state (Brin Hyatt 2001; Kingfisher 2001). No more welfare cheats. Calls for increased responsibility, independence, even entrepreneurship, align the goals of "free" individuals with the strategic withdrawal of public resources from all communities. Ironically, neoliberals are silent when it comes to the billions of tax revenue dollars that are given to corporations (including, or especially, when they fail)—such as banks, private universities, research and development (R&D) centers, and so on—in the form of subsidies. In this sense, neoliberals approve of private welfare but condemn public welfare. Further, public welfare is frequently reduced to "bidding wars" between nations and states (prompting propositions such as, "We'll charge you less tax if you set up your business in our state and not theirs or if you don't go offshore") in an effort to get corporations to stay/move to their locality and secure flow-on financial benefits.[1]

Whereas previously many people believed that low-income individuals were entitled to state or community assistance—if they were in need—neoliberal ideology maintains that "entitlement" only creates dependency and apathy. Even trying to challenge this way of thinking by arguing that individuals have a right to the basic necessities of life, can be difficult when the kind of welfare systems we are familiar with really do encourage dependency and when systems and corporations benefit from that. The point is that such programs could be organized differently. Furthermore, there are different levels and forms of "dependency." For instance, young women typically have sole responsibility for the care of dependent children. On this point, Skinner and Hickey (2003) note the findings of a recent report by UNICEF (2001), which indicates that Australia has the sixth highest teen pregnancy rate among all OECD countries. Other accounts suggest that teenage mothers in Australia are "more likely to be single" and "living in an area of socio-economic disadvantage" (van der Klis et al. 1999). Single mothers especially, often the target of new welfare programs, are treated as though the major problem is for them to assume increased responsibility and independence in general, and particularly if they are going to receive financial assistance. Raising children is not considered a job or as work. Social policy is thus directed at reforming negative personality traits rather than structures. This is one way in which neoliberal discourses of individualism are inimical to women's interests (Kingfisher 2001, 278).

Clearly, personal choice plays a role in the circumstances within which individuals find themselves. Disagreeable personal appearance, low self-confidence, drug use, absenteeism or tardiness for appointments, are all traits you can find among the poor. It is also clear that all of us benefit when individuals take appropriate responsibility for their actions. However, the point is: (1) the poor have less control over their decisions than do others and less ability to negotiate difficult circumstances, and (2) personal and public (institutions) are intricately intertwined. Job training, for example, has different effects on people depending upon whether they have repeatedly failed (in school, in work, and so on) or are more accustomed to success (see, for example, Shipler 2004). Our task is to recognize both society's (government's) obligation to those in need and the individual's obligation to be a responsible member of their community.

The notion that the free market is the most efficient means to provide for the general welfare of citizens and, as some argue, to realize equal opportunity, is simply not supported by mounting evidence from different parts of the world. The neoliberal valorization of the market is based on ideology, not empirical evidence. The claim that private hospitals or private schools, for example, produce better results than public institutions, *because they are private*, is a contrived argument, not a data-driven one. The only exception is when the anticipated or implied results in question are exclusively narrowly financial. Looking at education, for instance, we find increasing empirical evidence from around the world indicating that markets in education, or quasimarkets as they are usually referred to (see, for example, Whitty et al. 1998), neither improve academic performance nor even out inequalities.[2] A similar example in the social services arena can be found in the recent decision by the Salvation Army in Australia to put its retirement villages up for sale, proclaiming that it wants to focus its energies and resources more directly on helping the poor. Retirement villages, it suggests, are, by and large, not the places where the poor locate. Nevertheless, their inhabitants are fearful that a private company will take them over and run them like businesses. Intuitively, the residents are aware that the marketization of old age care does not lead naturally to increased services.

In addition to lacking empirical evidence and placing private gain before people's needs, neoliberal discourse makes government (for example, their social programs) the problem. Rather than identifying poverty as the problem, the former safety net itself is blamed for stripping individuals and communities of their capacities for self-sufficiency (see, for example, Brin Hyatt 2001). A direct government role in job creation, human service provision, and community development is now blamed for urban decline! Rather than rational analyses (both theoretical and empirical) of the causes of poverty, neoliberalism asserts a moral entreaty for greater personal responsibility. Importantly, however, the appeal to personal agency is not connected to the actual processes of economic development; that is, the actions that individuals are exhorted to take are not those that can revitalize communities for the long term. This is because eliminating poverty, challenging the unfair structure of the labor market, and reversing current patterns of economic polarization and social inequality are not the goals. Geographic concentrations of poverty, patterns of disinvestment, racial discrimination, tax laws that favor the rich, and a lack of material resources—often due to the withdrawal of public (that is, government) resources from low-income communities—are simply not concerns of neoliberal policies. Yet, as has been demonstrated over a long period of time, real equality cannot be achieved by ignoring structural, systematic, institutionalized political and economic relations, based on race, gender, and social class.

Perhaps one reason for the strength of neoliberal discourse is that it is emotionally or psychologically optimistic, at least for the relatively privileged. It is dispiriting to view the poor as passive victims in situations over which they have no control. Furthermore, the poor are now viewed as an affront and a danger to the middle class, in part because this middle class in many ways stands on its hard work and corresponding belief that "you can make it if you try." Such belief has been somewhat more true in periods other than the current one. In the United States, for example, during the years from post–WWII to the early 1970s, socioeconomic mobility was objectively much more possible that it is today. Joan's story (see Chapter 18) is illustrative of this potential mobility of an earlier time, particularly for her children. Maggie holds a similar view, evidenced in the "counsel" she offers young people on the streets (see Part 1). Believing that the marginalized can and should rise to the challenge of taking responsibility for their own lives, seems: (1) in tune with the obligations of good citizenship (Brin Hyatt 2001, 206), (hence the notion of "mutual obligation"); (2) apparently less ideological ("there's no one to blame but yourself"); and (3) more respectful of personal agency ("if everyone, namely government bureaucracy, gets out of your way, you can make it"). Pragmatic policies appealing to such beliefs and advocated by too many policy makers, scholars, and the media, typically consist of programs such as those that claim to build self-confidence, self-esteem, and "soft skills" (being on time for work, for example). The imperative is to eliminate "dependency" and anything that encourages it, rather than eliminating the basis for inequality and poverty.

Defining the individual's role in her/his own poverty is difficult. In part, this is because each ingredient of poverty is magnified by and interlocked with the others (Shipler 2004). Yet poor people do not choose poor schools (Ball 2003; Lauder et al. 1999; Thrupp 1999). Rather, they do not have the assets to purchase homes in neighborhoods known for their good schools. Just for a moment, try to imagine the effects, the cumulative effects, of being born into a poor family, growing up in a poor community, going to poor schools and then finding that if jobs are available, they are those with the lowest wages and that they lack benefits, stability and long-term guarantees of continued employment (Piven 1998). Add to this situation other likely possibilities, such as a long commute to work, unpredictable shifts, no real promotions, no affordable child care, little support for learning English, no cushion of money, health problems compounded by a lack of health insurance, and the fact that in many urban areas black men are more likely to spend time in prison than in school. Precisely because this scenario is real for many people today (as the stories in this book illustrate), we find the very opposite claim of promarket ideology to be most plausible; that is, privatization has a *disempowering* effect on the poor.

Another market-driven precept is the injunction to volunteer. Volunteerism is on the rise in Australia, for example, although welfare organizations are finding it taxing on their resources to train them for the short-term contributions this new brand of volunteers make. The point is, by emphasizing volunteerism (primarily among the middle class), individual responsibility, self-help and market "discipline" for the poor, neoliberal discourse obscures the fundamental class inequalities created by capitalist development (Ruben 2001, 463). Masking the importance of the social class structure in neoliberal development leaves us susceptible to those discourses that vilify, pathologize, or romanticize the poor (Goode and Maskovsky 2001). If, however, we entertain the possibility that the primary explanation for poverty is neither individual nor cultural deficits, and if we do not succumb to the fallacy that the poor are really not suffering after all because they are used to it, then how do we explain it? A place to begin is by examining how the necessities of life are produced, distributed, and consumed, the racial/ethnic, gendered relationships among us, and what we actually experience in this process. With this kind of analysis, we can begin to understand how we come to hold certain ideas about ourselves, money, social relations, and the nature of society. These ideas include our beliefs about individualism, choice, competition, and worth. Importantly, this kind of analysis can also help us understand how poverty is created and maintained and what it might take to significantly reduce if not eliminate it.

Globalization: Disparate potentials

As I have pointed out, economic restructuring in recent years has reflected a withdrawal by the state from its responsibilities to provide and administer public resources. Drastic cutbacks in social spending, increased privatization of social services, education, health, housing, and a widening gap between rich and poor have heightened social injustices. These elements of economic restructuring have been concomitant with the trend toward globalization. Different views of globalization notwithstanding, patterns of global economic restructuring have emerged, along with the implementation of neoliberal policies in many nations.

To be clear, globalization refers to a process within which information technology, energy technology, telecommunications, biotechnology, an international division of labor, media, shopping, work, finances, to name just some elements of economic life, are more tightly connected on a global scale than ever before. Globalization is an essential trend of development in *our* times. It is neither temporary nor spontaneous. Nor is it neutral. Significant cultural, political, and economic changes are affecting public and private life in new and profound ways. In today's world, globalization is capitalist in nature where social classes confront one another over the exploitation of human and natural resources. Enthusiasts view globalization as an inexorable trajectory of progress that should not be reversed, even if this were possible. They point to new technologies in diverse fields, enabling a global flow of culture and communications previously unwitnessed, enriching the lives of people everywhere. Others oppose globalization, pointing to such realities as the accompanying environmental destruction (for example, global warming), the destruction of local traditions, the homogenization of culture, and the ongoing subordination of poor nations and regions by wealthier ones.

A third, more insightful perspective on globalization is that it has both progressive and regressive features (Kellner 2000). A feminist analysis makes this readily apparent. Although globalization has created more opportunities for women to work and develop their talents outside of the home, in many contexts this has meant working in sweatshop-type conditions. Historically, as women increasingly found work outside the home, feminists in some countries demanded, and won, more social services (for example, child daycare). In the present climate these services are being sharply cut or eliminated, placing the burden back on women (and elders) to be solely responsible for the young and for domestic work. Jill Blackmore (2000) similarly explains how globalization is used to justify both markets and social conservatism, tapping into social prejudices about gender (and race and class). Paradoxically, while women benefit, for example, from the exercise of "choice" (in specific contexts), they also bear most of society's responsibility as the state withdraws from its social welfare obligations and reprivatizes women's productive labor. Globalization thus has positive effects as well as potentials for greater domination and subordination within nations and by the developed nations.

Resisting marginalization: Down but not out

Neoliberal ideology maintains that public-sector austerity is necessary to make way for market-based models, which in turn will solve both our private and public problems. With private business taking over public systems, profit—not the well-being of people, especially not those in need—is the explicit, even laudatory purpose. Previously I outlined the many ways in which this especially affects the poor economically; however, the poor are also affected politically. While poor people in many wealthy western countries have historically fought for and won needed resources, benefits and safeguards from state-based institutions, over time these social movements have been seriously undermined. With the role of the state supposedly brushed out of the picture, in a neoliberal system it is more difficult for individuals to organize and make demands upon government.[3] Under neoliberalism, the institutional and ideological aspects of social welfare, and in politics generally, the poor have become invisible or marginalized (Goode and Maskovsky 2001).

Key to understanding the marginalization of the poor is the fact that global ruling classes act as though everything belongs to them, as though they are entitled to the resources and labor of society. They undermine any movement, nation, or popular group that tries an alternative way of development, using the resources, the markets, the labor of their society for social or public needs, rather than for the benefit of corporate and global investors. Nevertheless, ever since the early 1990s, marked by the Zapatista uprising in Mexico, we have been witnessing, if not participating in, opposition and resistance to neoliberal globalization. Demonstrations at meetings of the World Economic Forum, the G8, and the IMF (International Monetary Fund) have drawn thousands of concerned citizens in cities throughout the world. And these are only the most publicized of the ongoing challenges to the corporate state's utter neglect of and contempt for public life in general and the most disenfranchised in particular.

This resistance reflects growing demands for systems of governance (locally, regionally, internationally) that treat all people with equal worth.

Viewing and treating all people as inherently equal to one another would mean that everyone would have access to resources to adequately and safely shelter, feed, and educate themselves, their partners, and their children. Under the current reign of the market, it is very difficult to argue that the state should ensure that these needs are met. Yet democratic government, with a strong civic commitment accountable to ordinary citizens, is an ideal to hold and a goal to work toward.

Rather than being governed by an ostensibly weak state (for example, one that provides minimum funding for social services), a stronger democratic state (for example, one that is accountable to various representative bodies) could not only maintain past benefits but also provide new ones. For instance, government could directly fund public schools and health care plans, and it could provide full employment and meet basic housing and nutritional needs. Public policies could be directed at lessening the gap between rich and poor, within and across nations. On an international level, people in different nations could be brought closer together in ways that do not depend upon winners and losers, dominant and subordinate. Instead of becoming poorer and poorer, more countries could become richer. International bodies that are trying to promote global democracy and justice could be supported, as we create new types of international bodies. All the while we could continue to create, maintain, and expand networks of activism and popular governance.

Social and economic justice can and must also be sought on an individual level. Teaching, mentoring, apprenticing, or counseling the poor, especially youth, provides opportunities to help individuals access resources for themselves and their loved ones, to stay in or return to school, and otherwise take steps toward creating a positive future. We need to recognize and understand the fact that young people are facing a more complex world when they leave school. Further, the demands of an increasingly sophisticated economy and a more complex and rapidly changing society require all of us to do what we can to improve educational outcomes for all. We can help young people understand their everyday lives, including everyday inequities, in this larger social context, with the goal of seriously questioning the present system, assuming both self and collective responsibility, and exploring means of optimistic social action.

Finally, while it is true that many adolescents are living in an intimately woven web of poverty, danger, discrimination, and limited opportunities, it is neither correct nor helpful to perceive them as passive victims. The importance of developing a political–economic analysis of poverty is not to imply that there is nothing we can do because, for example, economic forces are bigger than we are. On the contrary, such an understanding properly focuses our attention on the material realities of people's lives, making it more difficult for us to romanticize the lives of others and helping us understand why poverty persists, despite our efforts. Indeed, it seems to me that a central endeavor within *Rough Justice* is to do just this—to raise our awareness of the lived experiences of many young people in poverty and to help us recognize the need to critique middle-class analyses that impose deficit explanations of their behavior from peripheral distant locations.

Instead, we need to create new ways to think about and work toward social justice. There is, even as you read this book, much activity going on around the world from which we can draw inspiration and learn. The Kensington Welfare Rights Union in Philadelphia (Ruben 2001), the struggle against the Acme Boot Company in Appalachian Tennessee (Weinbaum 2001), the Lavalas movement in Haiti (Glick et al. 2001), and such forums as international popular education networks, workers' assistance centers, and activists' summits (see, for example, Klein 1999) offer insights into the importance of and ways to involve the poor in alliances that are working to reduce poverty, strengthen communities, and foster international solidarity. As Lisa Duggan argues, in this way we can learn to respectfully affiliate with, rather than be paternally pedagogical toward, others as we experiment with new ways of collective caretaking (Duggan 2003, 88).

NOTES

[1] As discussed in the Introduction, this is a suspect equation.

[2] See Ball (2003), especially pp. 25–52, for a review of relevant literature; also Lauder et al. (1999); Thrupp (1999).

[3] For analyses of how the state remains in the picture, not foregrounded but backgrounded or "steering at a distance," see Kickert (1991) and Marceau (1993). Also, see Gale and Densmore (2003, 36–53) for how teachers can engage productively with these steering mechanisms.

BIBLIOGRAPHY

Australian Institute of Health and Welfare. "Homeless People in Supported Accommodation Assistance Program." Sydney, Australia, 2003.

Bales, K. "Throwaway People." *Index on Censorship*, January 2000.

Ball, Stephen. *Class Strategies and the Education Market: The Middle Classes and Social Advantage*. London: Routledge Falmer, 2003.

Bauman, Zygmunt. *The Individualized Society*. Cambridge, UK: Polity Press, 2001.

Bell, S. *Ungoverning the Economy, the Political Economy of Australian Economic Policy*. Melbourne: Oxford University Press, 1997.

Bernstein, B. *Class, Codes and Control*. Vol. 1. London: Paladin, 1971.

Blackmore, J. "Globalization: A Useful Concept for Feminists?" In *Globalization and Education: Critical Perspectives*, edited by Nicholas Burbules and Carlos Alberto Torres, 133–55, 2000.

Bourdieu, P. "The Forms of Capital." In *Education: Culture, Economy and Society*, edited by A. Hasley, H. Lauder, P. Brown, and A.S. Wells, 46–58. Oxford: Oxford University, 1997.

Bourdieu, P., and J. Passeron. *Reproduction in Education, Society and Culture*. London: Sage, 1977.

Bourdieu, P., and L. Wacquant. *An Invitation to Reflexive Sociology*. Cambridge, UK: Polity Press, 1992.

Brin Hyatt, S. "From Citizen to Volunteer." In *The New Poverty Studies: The Ethnography of Power, Politics and Impoverished People in the United States*, edited by Judith Goode and Jeff Maskovsky, 201–35. New York: New York University Press, 2001.

Burgess, S. "Sorting Matters: Choice and Selection in English Schools." *Market and public organisation*, no. 12, Winter (2005): 7–10.

Center on Budget and Policy Priorities. "1993 Poverty and Income Trends." Washington, DC, 1994.

Chamberlain, C., and D. MacKenzie. "Counting the Homeless 2001." Canberra, Australia: Australian Bureau of Statistics, 2003.

Clark, Andrew. "CEOs Doing Well from Doing Good." *The Weekend Australian Financial Review*, 23–28 December 2004, 18.

Community Affairs References Committee. "A Hand Up Not a Hand Out: Renewing the Fight Against Poverty." 511. Canberra, Australia: Report on Poverty and Financial Hardship by the Australian Senate, Parliament House, 2004, March.

Connell, R.W. *Schools and Social Justice*. Leichhardt, NSW: Pluto, 1993.

Danaher, Patrick, ed. *Beyond the Ferris Wheel: Educating Queensland Show Children, Studies in Open and Distance Learning*. Rockhampton, Qld, Australia: Central Queensland University Press, 1998.

Development Cooperation Directorate (DAC). "The DAC Journal Development Cooperation Report 2003 (Volume 5)." Paris, France: OECD, 2004.

"Down and out on the Streets of Melbourne." *The Age*, 27 December 2004, 14.

Duggan, L. *The Twilight of Equality? Neoliberalism, Cultural Politics and the Attack on Democracy*. Boston: Beacon Press, 2003.

Forster, M., and M. Pearson. "Income Distribution and Poverty in the OECD Area: Trends and Driving Forces." *OECD Economic Studies,* Winter (2002): 7–34.

Foucault, M. *Discipline and Punish: The Birth of the Prison*. Harmondsworth: Penguin Books, 1979.

Fraser, Nancy. "Clintonism, Welfare and the Antisocial Wage: The Emergence of a Neoliberal Political Imaginary." *Rethinking Marxism* 6, no. 1 (1993): 9–23.

Freire, P. *Pedagogy of the Oppressed*. London, UK: Penguin Books, 1972.

Gale, T., and K. Densmore. *Engaging Teachers: Towards a Radical Democratic Agenda for Schooling*. Maidenhead, UK: Open University Press, 2003.

———. *Just Schooling: Explorations in the Cultural Politics of Teaching*. Buckingham, UK: Open University Press, 2000.

Gewirtz, S., S. Ball, and R. Bowe. *Markets, Choice and Equity in Education*. Buckingham, UK: Open University Press, 1995.

Giddens, A. *Outline of the Theory of Structuration*. Cambridge, UK: Polity Press, 1984.

Glick-Schiller, N., and G. Fouron. " 'I Am Not a Problem without a Solution': Poverty and Transnational Migration." In *The New Poverty Studies: The Ethnography of Power, Politics, and Impoverished People in the United States*, edited by Judith Goode and Jeff Maskovsky, 321–63. New York: New York University Press, 2001.

Goode, Judith, and Jeff Maskovsky. "Introduction." In *The New Poverty Studies: The Ethnography of Power, Politics, and Impoverished People in the United States*, edited by Judith Goode and Jeff Maskovsky, 1–34. New York: New York University Press, 2001.

Hartman, C. "Shifting Fortunes." *Facts and Figures* (last updated 8 October 2002). Accessed 01/03/05. Available from http://www.inequality.org//factsfr.html

Henwood, Doug. "Boom for Whom?" *Left Business Observer. No. 93* (February 2000). Accessed 01/03/05. Available from http://www.leftbusinessobserver.com/IncPov98.html

"Income Gap a Reflection of Culture." *The Weekend Australian Financial Review*, 21–22 February 2004, 29.

Kellner, D. "Globalization and New Social Movements: Lessons for Critical Theory and Pedagogy." In *Globalization and Education: Critical Perspectives*, edited by Nicholas C. Burbules and Carlos Alberto Torres, 299–321, 2000.

Kickert, W. "Steering at a Distance: A New Paradigm of Public Governance in Dutch Higher Education." Paper presented at the European Consortium for Political Research Conference, University of Essex, March 1991.

Kingfisher, C. "Producing Disunity: The Constraints and Incitements of Welfare Work." In *The New Poverty Studies: The Ethnography of Power, Politics, and Impoverished People in the United States*, edited by Judith Goode and Jeff Maskovsky, 273–92. New York: New York University Press, 2001.

Kirk, A. "Centrelink Staff under Pressure to Get People into Work." In *A M*, presented by Tony Eastley: Australian Broadcasting Corporation (ABC) Radio, 2004, December 10.

Klein, N. *No Logo: Taking Aim at the Brand Bullies*. New York: Picador, 1999.

Lacharite, J. "Sustained and Growing Underemployment in Australia and Canada: The Truth Behind Government Employment Figures." *Journal of Australian Studies* 14 (2002): 243.

Lauder, H., D. Hughes, S. Watson, S. Waslander, M. Thrupp, R. Strathdee, I. Simiyu, A. Dupuis, J. McGlinn, and J. Hamlin. *Trading in Futures: Why Markets in Education Don't Work*. Buckingham, UK: Open University Press, 1999.

Mackay, Hugh. *Reinventing Australia: The Mind and Mood of Australia in the 90s*. Sydney, Australia: Angus & Robertson, 1993.

MacKenzie, D., and C. Chamberlain. "The Second National Census of Homeless School Students." *Youth Studies Australia* 21, no. 4 (2002): 24–31.

Mandela, Nelson. *'Make Poverty History' Speech*, 2005, February 3.

Marceau, J. *Steering from a Distance: International Trends in the Financing and Governance of Higher Education*. Canberra: AGPS, 1993.

McLaren, P., and R. Farahmandpur. "Critical Revolutionary Pedagogy at Ground Zero: Renewing the Educational Left after September 11." In *Education as Enforcement: The Militarization and Corporatization of Schools*, edited by Kenneth J. Saltman and David A. Gabbard, 311–26. New York: RoutledgeFalmer, 2003.

Mills, C.W. *The Sociological Imagination*. Oxford, UK: Oxford University Press, 1959.

Peel, M. *The Lowest Rung: Voices of Australian Poverty*. Cambridge, UK: Cambridge University Press, 2003.

Piven, F.F. "Welfare Reform and the Economic and Cultural Reconstruction of Low Wage Labor Markets." *City and Society: 1998 Annual Review* (1998): 21–36.

Ruben, M. "Suburbanization and Urban Poverty under Neoliberalism." In *The New Poverty Studies: The Ethnography of Power, Politics, and Impoverished People in the United States*, edited by Judith Goode and Jeff Maskovsky, 435–69. New York: New York University Press, 2001.

Shields, J., M. O'Donnell, and J. O'Brien. "The Bucks Stop Here: Private Sector Executive Remuneration in Australia." 75. Sydney, Australia: A report prepared for the Labor Council of New South Wales, 2003.

Shipler, D. *The Working Poor, Invisible in America*. New York: Alfred A. Knopf, 2004.

Skinner, S.R., and M. Hickey. "Current Priorities for Adolescent and Sexual Reproductive Health in Australia." *Medical Journal of Australia* (November 2003).

Thrupp, M. *Schools Making a Difference—Let's Be Realistic! School Mix, School Effectiveness and the Social Limits of Reform*. Buckingham: Open University Press, 1999.

Tripp, D. *Critical Incidents in Teaching: Developing Professional Judgement*. London, UK: Routledge, 1993.

UNICEF. "A League Table of Teenage Births in Rich Nations: Innocenti Report Card No. 3." Florence, Italy: Innocenti Research Centre, 2001, July.

US Bureau of the Census. "Poverty in the United States: 1995." Washington, DC: US Bureau of the Census, 1996.

van der Klis, K., K. Westernberg, A. Chan, G. Dekker, and R. Keane. "Teenage Pregnancy: Trends, Characteristics and Outomes in South Australia and Australia." *Australian and New Zealand Journal of Public Health* 24 (1999): 316–19.

Weinbaum, E. "From Plant Closing to Political Movement: Challenging the Logic of Economic Destruction in Tennessee." In *The New Poverty Studies: The Ethnography of Power, Politics and Impoverished People in the United States*, edited by Judith Goode and Jeff Maskovsky, 399–431. New York: New York University Press, 2001.

"What's This? Melbourne's Best." *Sydney Morning Herald*, February 6, 2004.

Whitty, G., S. Power, and D. Halpin. *Devolution and Choice in Education: The School, the State and the Market*. Buckingham: Open University Press, 1998.

Williams, J. "Look, Child Poverty in the Wealthy Countries Isn't Necessary." *International Herald Tribune*, July 24, 2000.

Wolfensohn, James D. "The Other Crisis, October 6th." World Bank's Board of Governors, 1998.

World Bank. "World Development Indicators (WDI), 2004." Washington, DC, USA: Author, 2004.

Young, I. *Justice and the Politics of Difference*. Princeton, NJ: Princeton University Press, 1990.

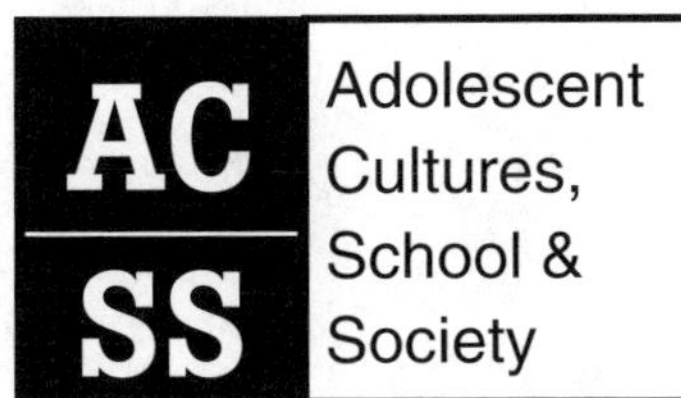

Joseph L. DeVitis & Linda Irwin-DeVitis
GENERAL EDITORS

As schools struggle to redefine and restructure themselves, they need to be cognizant of the new realities of adolescents. Thus, this series of monographs and textbooks is committed to depicting the variety of adolescent cultures that exist in today's post-industrial societies. It is intended to be a primarily qualitative research, practice, and policy series devoted to contextual interpretation and analysis that encompasses a broad range of interdisciplinary critique. In addition, this series will seek to provide a pragmatic, pro-active response to the current backlash of conservatism that continues to dominate political discourse, practice, and policy. This series seeks to address issues of curriculum theory and practice; multicultural education; aggression and violence; the media and arts; school dropouts; homeless and runaway youth; alienated youth; at-risk adolescent populations; family structures and parental involvement; and race, ethnicity, class, and gender studies.

Send proposals and manuscripts to the general editors at:
> Joseph L. DeVitis & Linda Irwin-DeVitis
> College of Education and Human Development
> University of Louisville
> Louisville, KY 40292-0001

To order other books in this series, please contact our Customer Service Department at:
> (800) 770-LANG (within the U.S.)
> (212) 647-7706 (outside the U.S.)
> (212) 647-7707 FAX

or browse online by series at:
> WWW.PETERLANGUSA.COM